Beverly Hills, 90210

Feminist Cultural Studies, the Media, and Political Culture

Series Editors
Mary Ellen Brown
Andrea Press

A complete list of books in the series is available from the publisher.

Beverly Hills, 90210

Television, Gender, and Identity

E. Graham McKinley

PENN

University of Pennsylvania Press

Philadelphia

10 9 8 7 6 5 4 3 2 1

Published by
University of Pennsylvania Press
Philadelphia, Pennsylvania 19104-6097

Library of Congress Cataloging-in-Publication Data
McKinley, E. Graham.
    Beverly Hills, 90210 : television, gender, and identity / E. Graham McKinley.
        p.   cm. — (Feminist cultural studies, the media, and political culture)
    Includes bibliographical references and index.
    ISBN 0-8122-3409-X (cloth : alk. paper). — ISBN 0-8122-1623-7 (pbk. : alk. paper)
    1. Beverly Hills, 90210 (Television program)   2. Television viewers—United States—
Psychology.   3. Television programs—Social aspects—United States.   I. Title.
II. Series.
PN1992.77.B47M35   1997
791.45′72—dc21   97-13120
                                                                                    CIP

Contents

Acknowledgments

This book would never have been written without the support of many whom I would humbly and appreciatively like to recognize:

My Rider University colleague Dr. Thomas Simonet, who copy-edited the manuscript, offered insightful suggestions, and supplied constant encouragement;

The members of the First Presbyterian Church of Matawan and the Rev. Charles Cureton, who listened endlessly to my woes and unfailingly offered words of support and love, and especially Jane Price, who doggedly plowed through a difficult draft version;

My dissertation committee at Rutgers University, adroitly led by co-chairs Dr. Stanley Deetz and Dr. Linda Steiner, who read and revised version after version after version of my doctoral dissertation, on which this book is based, and who spent indefatigable hours shaping it; Dr. Robert Kubey and Dr. Nancy Roth, who encouraged and guided me; and especially my outside member, Dr. Andrea Press of the University of Illinois at Urbana-Champaign, who encouraged me to submit the study for publication;

My Communications Department colleagues at Rider, especially my chairman, Dr. Howard Schwartz, who supportively arranged my schedule, and Dr. Jonathan Millen, who carefully and perceptively read the manuscript;

My family, especially my mother, the Rev. Dr. Ellen McKinley, and my brother and sister-in-law, T and Gracia McKinley, who were always willing to open the floodgates and endure my rush of commentary and complaint that inevitably spilled out whenever we were together;

My students, who generously tolerated my distraction, especially Michael Blank, who still doesn't have the information I owe him for our Web site;

My fellow "rim rats" and bosses at The Times of Trenton, who put up with my sporadic late arrivals and occasionally divided attention;

And my generous interviewees, who cheerfully and unstintingly opened themselves to me, whose voices I have striven to reproduce faithfully and sympathetically, and who I hope will find the analysis meaningful and thought-provoking;

Thank you all. I couldn't have done it without you.

Chapter 1
The Enthusiastic Voices

Across the United States for most of the 1990s, millions of girls and young women gave special importance to Wednesday evening, when *Beverly Hills, 90210* aired. This prime-time soap opera chronicled the lives of a group of upscale students who attended two fictitious schools in glamorous southern California: posh West Beverly Hills High School (the numbers in the title refer to its envied ZIP code), then enticing California University. Dedicated viewers arranged their weekly schedules—homework, shower time, night classes, work schedules—to free themselves to watch *90210* and its spin-off in the following time-slot, *Melrose Place.* Whether they watched alone in their bedrooms or with boisterous friends in crowded dormitory lounges, their devotion bordered on the religious. Almost from the time the Fox network program debuted in the fall of 1990 (on Thursday nights the first season), to well beyond the spring of 1994, when the interviews for this study were conducted, the show commanded the airwaves for American girls and young women. At this writing, during the summer of 1996, it still draws a hefty following.

Experience of *90210* transcended the hour from 8 to 9 p.m., spilling into a world of orchestrated fandom and promoted merchandise—magazines, books, bubble gum cards, T-shirts, and cosmetics. The controversial central character, Brenda the "bitch," became the focus of a national "I Hate Brenda" fan club. A World Wide Web site offered extended analyses and running commentary on the latest episodes. The show became part of the lives of millions of young viewers—perhaps most importantly in their conversations about it.

It was these enthusiastic discussions that first attracted my attention. In the fall of 1992, I heard intense conferences, even arguments, about *90210* among a number of junior-high-school girls with whom I worked. I learned that they often videotaped and rewatched episodes, read about the performers, purchased promotional materials—and exhaustively discussed the show with friends. In some cases, they said, they even dreamed about the characters. To me—an infrequent television watcher—the show seemed a largely empty portrayal of an ensemble of wealthy, unsupervised young characters with improbable cheekbones. Though its dramas highlighted salient social issues, to my eye it represented a typical Hollywood effort: superficially liberal in its treatment of individual rights, but ultimately perpetuating conservative values. However, the charisma of the cast, allurement of the settings and fast pace of the plots were captivating, and it was obvious that the show resonated with teenage girls and young women.

My observation of their excited conversations led me to believe that talking about the show was an important part of their viewing experience, and I wanted to explore that intuition. Obviously, talk about television shows is a ubiquitous phenomenon in our culture, and numerous other researchers have explored various ramifications of this behavior. In no way do I mean to suggest that there was anything particularly unique in the talk about *90210*. Indeed, it is my hope that readers will use my ideas as suggestive for analyzing talk about other shows, even other media experiences. Here, I simply want to make the point that, in this study, I confined myself to talk about *90210*, and I cannot make claims about talk about other shows.

I wondered what this talk accomplished. As the girls' choir and drama director, I had discussed with them their goals and aspirations. They talked about their thoughts, fears, and hopes with considerable intensity and, it seemed to me, some vulnerability. I suspected that the similarly intense discussion of *Beverly Hills, 90210* might be playing a role in their thinking about their own lives and world. As they talked about the show, they seemed to be wrestling with important issues concerning their own identities.

This study is the outgrowth of my desire to understand whether and how such talk accomplished identity work. The voices you will hear in the succeeding pages belong to 36 girls and young women, ranging from sixth grade (age 11) through college age (22). As I drew on various personal and professional connections to find fans who would agree to be interviewed, I looked for people who described themselves as fans of *Beverly Hills, 90210* and who had watched the show for at least a year, preferably since the first season. In some cases I knew the viewers fairly well; in others we were strangers. I mustered representatives from a range of socioeconomic classes, though racially my panel was primarily white, with three Asian exceptions (for a more detailed description of methods and of each set of viewers, see Appendix).

I gathered my data using qualitative methods familiar to cultural studies and other ethnographic researchers, who were among the first to study media users in the real contexts of their lives (for an overview of this research method, cf., for example, McGuigan, 1992, or Moores,

1993). I visited the viewers' homes or dormitories and tape-recorded their talk, loosely following a set of prepared questions (see Appendix). I also recorded their spontaneous talk during viewing, a procedure I have not seen elsewhere but one that proved exceptionally generative. My data comprised transcripts of these tapes; in the excerpts provided in this book I have, of course, changed the names. Sometimes we watched an episode in real time, or watched the most recent episode on tape if the viewers hadn't seen it (I occasionally asked them to postpone their viewing until we could get together; in that way, I could watch the same episode with more than one group). Sometimes, the eagerly awaited show turned out to be a rerun, a situation viewers cheerfully accepted. In all cases, we watched three short clips that I thought would be provocative (for a more detailed description of them, see Appendix).

A few interviews were one-on-one, but most were in small, pre-existing groups of friends. We usually met in a dorm room, bedroom, or living room—wherever the viewers felt comfortable watching their show. I feel deep gratitude to the families, sororities, and roommates who welcomed me into these private spaces, and I cannot thank enough the girls and young women who opened their personal worlds to me.

The study proved an odyssey in many ways, as the particularly bitter February and March of 1994 dumped snow on New Jersey and Bucks County, Pennsylvania, almost every Wednesday night and forced a number of frustrating cancellations. One of my most salient memories is of trudging uncertainly through the drifts of the Princeton University campus one such Wednesday after the weather had caused my scheduled interview to be postponed. In one residence hall, I followed the familiar opening music of *90210* and found a television room with a group of students gathered around the set. I will never forget the burst of laughter that greeted my announcement that I was doing my dissertation on the show, and would anyone be willing to be interviewed?

Through this and other improvisatory techniques, I managed to assemble my panel, who generously made time for me in busy schedules, postponing homework or recreation and surrendering earnestly to what must have seemed an arcane if not nonsensical process. Sometimes they exhibited a touching, even awe-inspiring, faith in me. One father whom I had never met confidingly dropped his ninth-grade daughter off at her friend's house, where the interview was to take place, and gratefully accepted my offer to take her to the county library to do her homework after the interview. I had a long talk with her during this drive, beginning with a discussion of the psychology major of one of the *90210* characters. The girl asked me about the difference between psychology and psychiatry (I was getting my doctorate, so of course I should know everything), then touchingly revealed that a schoolmate had slit her stomach open and was in the hospital in psychiatric treatment. Her confidence that I could help her work through her distress made me feel honored, if inadequate. Frequently I was privileged to encounter this kind of trust and openness.

As much as possible, of course, I tried to remain subdued during the discussions, making every effort not to elicit responses or generate "right" answers that might be an artifact of my interventions. As I sat on dorm room floors or leaned against living room couches, I tried to enter into viewers' speech patterns, tempering my language to theirs. Some of this comes through on the tapes (COLLEEN: "The guy who was selling them. I don't think he should of took the bag of drugs anyway." G: "Oh! When he was in there and they were giving them, he took the bag into his apartment, yeah"). At other times, of course, I blundered in with my own "reads," but generally the community set me straight:

G: So, you think by doing this they really helped David?
JANE: Yeah.
G: (to Katey) You look doubtful.
KATEY: Not really, because now he's on drugs a whole lot more.

I can of course only speculate about the impact of my presence on viewer talk; however, as is explained in more detail in the Appendix, my theoretical base allows me to value as data all the talk generated.

I came to love the young viewers' candor, enthusiasm, and willingness to engage with my questions. Their voices have stayed in my head to this day—in no small part because I've spent two years with their tapes and some 500 resultant pages of transcripts! Some statements still make me smile, and a few break my heart. In a certain way, viewers bared their souls to me.

In poring over their words, I brought to bear an analytical technique that supports empirically some rather lofty theory that is explored in Chapters 3 and 4. Drawing on techniques of discourse analysis (cf., for example, Burman and Parker 1993), I scrutinized viewers' words for their identity implications—how the talk positioned the speaker, her friends, and the characters, and how these patterns shifted over the course of a conversation. I tried to examine not only what was said, but also where the silences were; to look at what identities were articulated, and what was so taken for granted it did not need to be mentioned.

Accomplishing this analysis was a journey of discovery for me, and has changed the way I look at myself and my world. I have tried to share some of that odyssey here. If my analysis occasionally sounds distant, even disapproving, it is not from any lack of appreciation for viewers' positions. Indeed, the playful escapism I witnessed was compellingly attractive, and to criticize it can seem pompous and carping. Yet I was disquieted by the processes that these buoyant young voices helped me uncover. The complex, contested interaction of television, gender, and identity in the end led me to confront the double-edged sword of enculturation: the contradictory joys of consumerism, the righteous tunnel vision of capitalism, the seductive security of patriarchy. Pinning these elusive concepts to strong empirical data was an exhilarating and sometimes frightening voyage into relatively uncharted waters; my hope is that this book can contribute to a growing body of empirical testing of poststructuralist theory.

The book is organized in a way I hope makes it as readable as possible. A glossary, which aims to provide guideposts for what may be unfamiliar terms, includes references for further reading; its entries re-express the concepts in ways I hope will increase reader understanding.

Chapter 2 situates *90210* as a significant event in its economic and cultural context. The characters are introduced and the show's content synopsized. *90210* has been touted in the popular press as raising topical issues, such as drug addiction, teen pregnancy, and date rape, which producers have said they hope would teach viewers important lessons; in part to prepare for an examination of this claim, I overview the issues treated in the episodes viewed during the course of the study. *90210* is then situated in the history of women's depiction on television, and my own take on the show, which admittedly is somewhat cynical, is summarized.

Because this is not a text-based study, Chapter 2 does not attempt to theorize about the potentially insidious relationship between dramatic content and advertiser requirements, nor about the role that political and economic pressures play in all of this; these themes have been ably explored elsewhere (e.g., Turow, 1992). Ways in which the show worked to perpetuate capitalist values are mentioned from time to time, particularly in places where the passive woman constructed in patriarchy gives way to an active shopper (re)constructing herself through consumerism. But this study does not focus on interrogating capitalism per se. Rather, I chose to concentrate on the role talk about the show plays in female identity formation. I was interested in whether the passion and engagement with which young fans talked about *90210*, and the amount of time they invested in such talk, connected with who they said they were and might become.

Indeed, this concern with the intersection of self and media has driven much mass communication research. One school of research that has consistently emphasized these issues, particularly with regard to women watching television, is cultural studies, whose work on females and media is overviewed in Chapter 3. The cultural studies approach to understanding television viewing developed out of a direct concern about mass culture and mass media as they affect those culturally perceived to be disadvantaged—young people, women, and the working class. Here, central questions revolve around agency, pleasure, and community, especially with regard to women and soap operas: whether and how television works to perpetuate dominant and oppressive ideologies; whether and how pleasurable communities of viewers resist and subvert these forces.

Chapter 3 examines ways cultural studies researchers are divided on these issues, posing a dilemma for those who would follow in their footsteps. Some emphasize the manipulative power of the television text, while others argue that viewers are active and in control of their viewing experiences. In the former category are those who subscribe to what has come to be called hegemony theory, who suggest that engagement with and involvement in certain types of fictional media, including soap operas and dramas, work ultimately to enmesh women more deeply in a patriarchal, consumerist society that disadvantages them. Indeed, hegemony theorists say, this very engagement and activity works seductively to beguile women's willing consent to the status quo, in part by "naturalizing" existing conditions, presenting them as taken for granted and thus immutable. However, other cultural studies researchers argue the opposite—that active female viewers, who often criticize and make fun of media content, build empowering communities that can serve as springboards for political action to resist and transform patriarchy. Such disagreements over what counts as resistance and agency, and whether resistance must be linked to political action, have left theorists calling for new ways to understand these concepts.

In seeking to reconcile these opposing viewpoints, I turned to the work of social constructionists, who offer a different way to conceptualize the notions of agency, pleasure, and community. Thus, in Chapter 4, I explore the American school of social construction, whose particular interest is identity and relation to others. These social constructionists have drawn on a long line of European philosophical thought to investigate community and agency in relation to issues of identity, which they conceptualize as discursive—as importantly constructed in talk. In this literature, attention is directed to the shifting patterns of "I"s, "me"s, "we"s, and "they"s that come into being, or remain unspoken, during conversations. However, these theorists point out, our culture works to conceal this process, suggesting to us that it is we as individuals, with unique traits and characteristics, who "author" our experiences, not the culture that shapes the things we value and the meanings we make. When a viewer says she would like to be pretty, like Kelly, she positions herself as the "author" of that desire—it is *she* who wishes to be pretty, not the culture that defines what is pretty and invites her to value it. From this perspective, social constructionists say, it is not solely the viewer speaking in the language of the culture; the culture also is "speaking" her.

It seemed to me that a study based on this literature could illuminate disagreements in the cultural studies field over the issue of television viewing and the active viewer. As outlined in Chapter 4, the social constructionist approach revives the poststructuralist ideas on which both hegemony theory and theories of activity and resistance are based, and I believe it reveals ways in which these theories are two sides of the same coin. Indeed, I argue throughout the analysis, that social constructionist tools make possible a discussion of the ways in which viewer activity propels the microworkings of hegemony, willing participation in a disadvantageous culture.

It is important to clarify the way I intend to use "identity." As Chapter 4 explains, I am not attempting to delve into the psychological structures of these girls, their traits, attributes, cognitive processes, or needs hierarchies. Instead, for this study, "discursive identity construction" refers to the process of verbally positioning the self (I, me, us, versus various theys) within an interaction, a situation, a culture, and highlights ways that process makes certain possibilities readily available, while curtailing or concealing others. Following the social constructionists, I define discursive identity construction as talk that presents the speaker as a particular kind of person, within a particular community, subject to certain constraints and alive to certain possibilities. Rather than hypothesizing a developmental "I" in the psychological research tradition, this approach analyzes identity on the level of its symbolic construction. And it addresses the nagging question of agency by moving it to a discursive level, where it can be empirically studied.

Females are in a particularly difficult position with regard to identity because of the ways certain patriarchal discourses impact our talk about ourselves. Most obvious is the construction of the male as the norm (doctor, lawyer, athlete) and the woman as other (female doctor, female lawyer, female athlete). Here, the work of feminist writers, particularly the literature of poststructuralist feminism, helped highlight specific patriarchal narratives that get stirred into female identity construction, and Chapter 4 also touches on this literature. The chapter concludes with a brief description of the loose category of discourse analysis, which gave me the tools I needed to treat viewer talk as text and to study it, not for what it "really" meant, but for how it worked to construct identities for both viewers and characters.

Readers completely unfamiliar with cultural studies and social construction literature may wish to put Chapters 3 and 4 aside and return to them after reading some of the analysis, which I hope gives concrete examples of this difficult theory.

In order to focus my examination of discussions that were sometimes wide-ranging, I look especially at viewer talk about the female characters, and about the viewers themselves as female. (The way talk constructs male identity, also an important topic, would be a fertile topic for future research.) As it turned out, the data I generated are not so very different from the conversations analyzed by, for example, Brown (1994). What I hope will be the contribution of this study is the way it uses poststructuralist theory and discourse analytic methods to reinterpret this type of talk. Often sounding casual and trivial, though sometimes passionate and engaged, this talk would certainly be regarded as unimportant by the young speakers, who were astonished that I could do such a project "for school." Nevertheless, as Leeds-Hurwitz (1993) has pointed out, even minor details are worthy of serious study. A social constructionist analysis of such talk can show how it might be interpreted as active and resistant, even while it is hegemonically winning consent to repressive female identities.

Because the discourse of psychology is such a powerful one in our culture, I will frequently re-emphasize that the social constructionist paradigm sets aside considerations of what viewers "really" think. Instead, I examined the transcripts of what they said to find out how they discursively constructed themselves and others within situations and contexts. While I can supply biographical context for some, but not all, of the viewers, I did not delve deeply into their backgrounds, because I wanted to focus on their talk about the show, rather than their talk about themselves. A factor that has been consistently deemed important in other studies (for an overview, cf. Press 1991) is the level of education of the interviewees and their parents. Accordingly, in places I note the viewer's type of education, distinguishing, for example, between those who attended preparatory schools and those who went to public high schools, between Ivy League, other college, and no college education, and I sometimes mention parents' education. However, this study cannot offer any "effects" claims; it can merely note patterns of responses among different age groups or educational backgrounds as worthy of future research.

Using the social constructionist perspective, then, the questions became, what female identities were seen as appropriate and/or encouraged as viewers talked about *90210*? What options were hidden? And what identities were made so natural that they were accepted as real and immutable—not just impervious to change, but so naturalized that one wouldn't think of changing them? Moreover, following the social constructionist treatment of agency as discursive, poststructuralist feminism suggests that I define agency as talk about female identity that challenged the status quo and broadened the identities females could potentially assume in our society. This led me to analyze talk about females with an eye towards ways it did—or did not—perpetuate the values of patriarchy and capitalism, and to ask what the role of the television text was in generating and guiding—or not guiding—this talk.

What I concluded was that, by and large, talk about *90210* did in fact work hegemonically to perpetuate a dominant notion of female identity—pretty and nice, defined not on her own merits, but in relation to a male—that feminists have argued is oppressive to women. In some ways, it seems hard to believe that these notions persist, almost half a century after Simone de Beauvoir drew attention to the ways patriarchy disadvantaged women. The opportunities and identities available in the 1990s so overwhelm those offered women even a generation ago that this abiding conservatism is particularly disheartening. Time and time again, I heard viewer talk working to explore identities that challenge the patriarchal definition of womanhood, then retreating to close down these alternate possibilities and re-establish a conservative status quo.

For example, the paradox of the active viewer enthusiastically perpetuating oppressive values can be seen in something as seemingly trivial as talk about the characters' appearance, which is the topic of Chapter 5. I found that this talk worked actively and pleasurably to position the speaker as an "expert" member of the community of viewers. But at the same time, this expertise worked to reify and perpetuate dominant notions of female identity (to present them as normal and "real") and to conceal ways in which these identities can be oppressive. This chapter also introduces the idea that consent to the status quo was won as talking about *90210* constructed a certain way of attending to self. Viewers attended to the show in ways determined by their own experience (active reading)—and the meanings they made revealed the text to be wonderfully polysemic—then cycled back to attend to their own identities and lives using values set out by the show (hegemonic reading). This cycle is central to the way I argue the hegemonic process worked in talk about *90210.*

Chapter 6 extends the themes introduced in talk about appearance to help understand conversations about the characters. Through a discussion of the way "realistic" was constructed in discussing a polysemic text, this chapter adds to the ideas of community and expertise the notion that talk about the show created a discursive community between viewer and character(s). This discursive community with characters, which sometimes took precedence over real-life communities, functioned importantly in the cycle described above of attending to self/attending to the show.

Chapter 7, which examines talk about the show's plots, suggests that this cycle between self and show was particularly noticeable and important as viewers memorized, regurgitated, and analyzed fictional narratives, discursively blending them with self-narratives. I argue that the cycle was concealed from viewers as they positioned themselves as "authors" of the viewing experience, doing what I have called "playing pundit" in the manner of television commentators. As they spoke in this "pundit" voice, they attended to the show based on their individual experiences—but then cycled the show's narratives back into ways in which they constructed and understood their own lives.

Inspired by this discovery, Chapter 8 expands understanding of the way the authorial voice—the discursive positioning of the self as author of one's identity, as described in the chapter on social construction—worked hegemonically. I examine how viewers' talk about television effects, which combined personal observations and desires with concurrent debates over television violence, worked to attach certain meanings to their viewing experience of *90210* and to conceal others. For example, all viewers said watching television did not "really" affect them; at the same time, some viewers, typically the younger ones, unproblematically acknowledged they learned behaviors and attitudes from television shows including *90210*, and all viewers acknowledged they changed their work, school, and personal schedules to accommodate their viewing of *90210*. I argue that this discourse of the autonomous self concealed the important role talk about the show played in the enculturation process.

In the context of this contradictory way of speaking about the effects of television, Chapter 9 analyzes some of the topical issues (abortion, drug addiction) raised on the show and discusses ways in which the viewers spoke about them. Of particular interest to me was the expression of moral judgments about these issues, as well as the presence or absence of critical discussion about issues and outcomes. I found that, while viewers said the issues were interesting, they did not discuss them critically or with any intensity. Substantive discussion—or even the few minutes' thought that producers expected the show to generate—was closed off as viewers retreated to an "us-them" morality protecting their community with the characters.

The intense negotiation I expected to see around issues was reserved for conversations about dating—who is dating whom, who should be dating whom, who they wanted to be dating whom, etc.—talk that is analyzed in Chapter 10. Disturbingly, I found that, as viewers talked passionately about this absorbing topic, they worked to construct, reify, and perpetuate existing gender norms and divisions in a way that feminists have argued is disadvantageous to women. In this type of talk, my analysis comes to grips most clearly with notions of activity and agency as they work to perpetuate existing gender roles.

A similar argument is made about the pleasurable process of guessing what will happen next on the show, the topic of Chapter 11. Here, viewers worked actively to read producers' minds—and, in so doing, vibrantly perpetuated cultural norms and stereotypes. These were active viewers, positioning themselves as in control of the meanings they made—meanings that can work to disadvantage them. The very process of predicting which outcomes producers would choose limited the possibilities available, closed off alternatives, and reinstantiated dominant notions of female identity. This chapter demonstrates perhaps most clearly the microworkings of the hegemonic process in talk about the show.

In conclusion, as summarized in Chapter 12, this study combines three literatures, cultural studies, social construction, and poststructuralist feminism, to revisit the issues of agency, pleasure, and community vis-à-vis girls' and women's television viewing. This theoretical combination permitted me to focus attention on whether talk about *90210* accessed alternative female identities or worked hegemonically to perpetuate dominant ones. It found that, for these *90210* viewers, talk about the show was an important player in the hegemonic process as viewers reproduced dominant notions of female identity while discursively positioning themselves as empowered and in control of their viewing experience.

Conducting this study and wrestling with this analysis has convinced me that the process of discursive identity construction is one of the key ways that television and other cultural forces intersect with our lives. I became convinced that, as we talk about dominant cultural meanings—seriously or sarcastically, enviously or mockingly—we reify and perpetuate them, continually giving them authority and currency. And this process involves activity, whether the identity constructed is in line with dominant notions or whether it interrogates them. Even dominant identities require active exploration and instantiation to remain so. I have realized that mastering dominant cultural rules can be hard work. And, as Foucault (1965) has pointed out, deviation from norms is the definition of madness. One might argue that enculturation is an important and necessary part of growing up, and that television is an admirable tool by which to bring this about.

All analyses are positioned, and the reader should understand that I have spent much of my life struggling with the identity issues raised here. An academic achiever who grew up in the progressive 1970s, I always expected I would find satisfaction in work as well as in personal relationships. Indeed, in my several careers as musician, journalist, and college professor, I have found arenas in which I can nurture and serve others while retaining an individual identity apart from these professional roles. In my jobs I have encountered communities of both care and respect—something I did not encounter as a married woman, and therefore I have chosen not to remarry, though I enjoy close friendships and a long-term, committed relationship. In thus rejecting the culturally accepted roles of wife and mother because of their identity implications, I continue to grapple with issues of dating, appearance, and so forth raised by both the show and the interviewees, and I have struggled against the double-edged sword of interrogating gender norms while taking advantage of the ways in which they sometimes privilege me.

Thus, as a researcher, I drew on the contexts in which I found myself to open up viewer talk to readings not available to the speakers. As far as I could, in the course of this book, I have tried to make my own opinions transparent. Naturally, many of the data are open to multiple interpretations, and in a number of places I explore some of the varying possibilities. Where I am more definitive, it is because the conclusion was supported repeatedly in the data. Still, readers no doubt will find additional meanings here. It is my hope that this book will provide a thought-provoking springboard for future research.

Chapter 2
Watching *Beverly Hills, 90210*

They negotiated with brothers and sisters for shower time. They unplugged the phone. Some avoided Wednesday night college classes, no matter what the content; others simply left night class early. All the girls and young women I interviewed during the spring 1994 season of *Beverly Hills, 90210* reported making an effort, sometimes a considerable one, to protect their viewing time.

In a typical comment, one young viewer said that her planning on Wednesdays started "when I get home from school, so then I can make sure my homework's all done and stuff." Her usual school-night shower time was 8 p.m., but on Wednesday nights this had to be renegotiated to take into account the *90210* starting time. "So I get my shower before that. Like at 7 or 7:30." This required extra planning, first because she was a leisurely washer—"I take like a half an hour in the shower"—and second because bargaining with siblings was a complicated affair—"Everybody's like, 'I'm first in the shower, I'm second in the shower.' We all fight who's first or who's second."

Often, viewers insisted that friends learn their viewing schedule. As one older viewer said, "People usually know not to call if I'm home and it's a Wednesday night between 8 and 10." (The second hour was to watch *Melrose Place*.) This telephone restriction was a common pattern; viewers frequently reported that their friends "know not to call" if they just want to chat. However, in a solution common among younger viewers, whose mobility was limited on a school night, some developed the habit of watching *90210* and *Melrose* with a friend via the telephone—"We'd sit on the phone from 8 to 10 watching them together."

Another viewer described detailed arrangements she made to preserve her viewing experience: "I want to be able to hear every word they say. Sometimes I tape it as I'm watching it just in case anybody does walk in, um, I can rewind it again later and replay that part. I turn my ringer off, I won't answer the phone, I mean—and people know. Sometimes I'll leave a message, I go, 'You know what I'm doing. Why are you calling?'"

Two college students said they would "call in sick" to a sorority meeting in order to be able to watch the show. Others said the effort they made to watch involved important job choices and course selections:

G: How hard do you try not to miss an episode?
NICKY: We leave night school early.
SHERRY: Very hard—yeah, we leave night school early to watch it.
NICKY: I chose not to have a really good night job so I could.

While this behavior will be examined from another viewpoint in the chapter on television effects, here I will note that reports in the popular press indicated these patterns were far from unusual. *Beverly Hills, 90210* was part of a staggering number of girls' and young women's lives. And that was no accident: *90210* was a key element of a daring strategy in the network television wars. Its producers intentionally targeted a young audience as a way for the upstart Fox Network to gain a foothold in an intensely competitive marketplace. While this study is about viewers' discussion of the show, it is instructive to note that the girls and young women's attention was deliberately and consciously wooed by producers embroiled in a high-stakes contest. Further exploration of the theoretical connection between the show's content, the concurrent political economy, and advertising could certainly yield interesting insights (for a perceptive overview of the way advertising fuels television's recycling of consumer messages, cf. Jhally and Lewis 1992). This chapter works only to contextualize the viewers' experience and provide background so that readers unfamiliar with the show can more easily understand the subsequent analysis. This introduction overviews the genesis of the show and describes the growth of its popularity; points out some conventions inherent in the genre through a run-down on the characters and typical plots; positions the show in a history of women's depiction on television; and acknowledges my own "take" on *90210*.

The Fox Network and the Youthful Audience

Debuting in October 1990, *90210* was a key part of the feisty young Fox Network's strategy to infiltrate the oligopoly of network television.[1] Though its success seems less surprising in retrospect, when Rupert Murdoch's News Corporation Ltd. formed the Fox Network in 1986, the odds against its survival were seen to be overwhelming. The big three networks—ABC, CBS, and NBC—had preclusively shared the national

1. Fox went on the air in October 1986 with *The Late Show Starring Joan Rivers*. The following spring, the network added two prime-time series on Sunday nights, which were carried by 105 owned and affiliated stations.

commercial broadcast television audience among themselves for decades. Their rule had been entrenched since the 1950s when the networks' radio operations declined and they made a relatively smooth transition to dominate the new medium. The big three controlled major markets through owned-and-operated stations that absorbed the biggest cities' scarce VHF frequencies, which for many years could reach the largest audiences. In smaller markets, scores of loyal network affiliates appropriated the best, often the only, available frequencies and ensured that each of the big three could reach virtually every household in America, cozily dividing the audience among themselves in a fairly simple tripartite battle of positioning.

A successful newcomer network somehow would have to gain a foothold in several of the largest cities and then, one at a time, persuade smaller stations to convert to affiliation with it, abandoning relationships that had lasted in some cases for decades and formed key components of local station identity. Long-documented audience behavior—tuning inertia—would further disadvantage an upstart. Moreover, Fox's entry occurred during a period of network decline. Competition from independent stations airing syndicated programming, from cable networks, from superstations whose reach was enlarged by cable, and from new media such as movies on videocassettes and pay-per-view, reduced the three over-the-air networks' share of viewing households from 92 percent in 1977 to 62 percent in 1991 (Cary 1992). Advertising revenues were stagnant at best. Fox was trying to gain a slice of a pie that was not only tenaciously held but shrinking.

However, a number of economic factors combined to give Fox its entree, and the clever strategy of targeting young audiences kept it competitive. Paradoxically, the very factors underlying the broadcast networks' decline gave Fox its opportunity. The proliferation of cable customers tended to equalize the reach of VHF and UHF stations, so a player with several major-market UHF stations now could be a contender. The former independent Metromedia stations Fox owned in New York, Los Angeles, Philadelphia, and other cities, some of them on the UHF band, provided such an infrastructure. Moreover, the multiplication of channels and media meant channel surfing was replacing tuning inertia.

For its bold gambit, Fox targeted youth, garnering headlines with its stated purpose of taking young people seriously. As *TV Guide* reported in 1992:

An entire network, Fox, was created with the idea of targeting its programming (*Melrose Place, Beverly Hills 90210*) to those under the age of 35. . . . [A]lmost the entire Fox lineup . . . garners praise on almost every campus. "Fox is gutsy and trendy, and the kids are excited by that," says Dr. J. Gregory Payne, chair of the Communication Studies Division at Emerson College in Boston. (Cary 1992, p. 30)

Fox's senior vice president of research and marketing, Andrew Fessel, called college students "the opinion leader audience. They're the first to explore the dial" (Cary 1992, p. 27). Though they watch even less than other young adults (17 hours a week versus 22 hours for average adults 18–25), college students watch more selectively (Farhi 1994).

90210 actually was Fox's second program to bring the youth strategy into play. The first was *The Simpsons*, an irreverent cartoon dissecting a dysfunctional family in a way that resonated with young viewers. It premiered on Sundays in January 1990, and in August of that year it moved to Thursdays, head-to-head against NBC's perennial ratings leader, *The Cosby Show.*

The youth-oriented prime-time soap opera *Beverly Hills, 90210* first aired later that year. Produced by Aaron Spelling—who had co-produced such popular fare as *Charlie's Angels, Fantasy Island, The Love Boat, Starsky and Hutch,* and *Hart to Hart—90210* filled a time slot on Thursday nights after *The Simpsons.* In its first season, overall ratings were not outstanding—for the week of March 4–10, 1991, *90210* was ranked 74th of 89 prime-time network shows, with a 6.7 rating and 10 percent share of audience (Ratings roundup, 1991). However, only a year after its debut, *90210* was described by the *New York Times* as "perhaps the most popular show on television among the youth of the 1990s" (Weintraub 1991). In 1992, a startling 69 percent of American female teenage viewers watched this show (Sessums 1992). In the 1993–94 season, when my study was conducted, *90210* was the most popular show among all viewers aged 18–34, according to *People* magazine (Feb. 21, 1994).

90210's original Thursday night time slot put it in direct competition with *Cheers*, the top show among college students, which Roper College-Track found attracted 33 percent of male college viewers and 21 percent of female. However, *90210* managed to garner 9 percent of the men and 20 percent of the women, making it the fourth most popular show among collegians after *Cheers*, Fox's *The Simpsons*, and *The Cosby Show* (Cary, 1992). One of the characteristics that distinguished *90210* was the fact that it alone of these four shows was not a comedy.

By 1993, *90210* was airing in 30 countries in Asia, Western Europe, Latin America, and Australia (Fitzgerald 1993). The following year, countries in Central and Eastern Europe were added to the list (Robins 1994). Syndication of reruns was slated from the beginning to start in fall 1994 (Russell 1992), shortly after I completed my study; the package ultimately was entitled "The Brenda Years," referring to the controversial character who departed the show during the 1994–95 season. By the spring of 1995, reruns could be seen six times a week in some American markets, along with the weekly Wednesday night broadcast of new episodes.

Like many breakout hits, *90210* spawned imitators. Some other ensemble shows aimed at young viewers, like NBC's *The Round Table* and Fox's *The Heights*, *Models*, and *Class of '96*, proved outright failures. Others, like MTV's documentary-style *The Real World* and NBC's sitcom *Friends*, proved enduring successes. One of the earliest successful emulators was Fox's drama *Melrose Place*, executive-produced by *90210*'s Spelling. A portrayal of a set of twenty-something yuppies swapping partners in a California apartment complex, it seemed to viewers a sequel— the story of *90210*-type characters several years later. *Melrose* premiered in July 1991, filling the time slot right after *90210*. Initially a hit, it held much of the lead-in show's audience, but quickly its ratings "faded like a Southern California tan in winter" (Zinn 1992). In the 1993–94 season, during the time my study was conducted, the audience picked up, according to *People* magazine ("Hot property!" 1994), reaching the No. 2 slot among 18- to 34-year-olds (*90210* was No. 1). This turned out to be a peak: By the spring of 1995, *Melrose* had moved to Monday night, and though its audience demographics continued to be desirable, its ratings had slipped again. *Melrose* captured barely half of *90210*'s stable and respectable 17 percent share of total audience (*People's Choice* 1995).

Fox's focus on youth to gain its programs a foothold with audiences was backed by solid economic reasoning. The network came on the scene at a time when the once-monolithic television audience was being segmented into specialty audiences that advertisers could target more efficiently (cf. Robichaux 1994). As with print magazines, advertisers could avoid "waste circulation" by supporting programs aimed at particular demographic subgroups. The young audience was a potential gold mine; youth comprised an attractive marketing cohort the networks had largely left to MTV and the video stores (Landler 1992). Few marketers yet had focused on the post-baby-boom subgroup that would become known as "busters" or Generation X (born between 1963 and 1974), or on its successors. Though "largely ignored by U.S. media, businesses, and public institutions," this contingent, consumers in their late teens and early 20s, annually spent $125 billion, the Roper Organization estimated (Zinn 1992).

In contrast, the big three networks' homogeneous audience had aged, right along with such programmatic icons as Angela Lansbury and Dan Rather. And by the late 1980s, advertisers had begun to see reduced value in older audiences, as the *Washington Post* explained:

Prime-time TV advertisers routinely discount aging viewers, paying rock-bottom prices to sponsor programs popular among them. Conversely, they pay a premium to advertise on programming that draws the young. Network officials and advertisers say the orientation toward youth does not reflect an inherent bias against older people. Rather, they call it the logical outgrowth of a fact that goes against stereotypes: Young people don't watch that much television, and older people do. Thus, when a 30-year-old actually tunes in, his or her attention can be sold at a higher price than if a 60-year-old is watching. (Farhi 1994, p. A1)

As one illustration, Farhi pointed out that at a time when *The Simpsons* ranked only 49th in overall Nielsen ratings, the youthfulness of its audience meant the price for a 30-second advertisement on it—$160,000—was the same as for the No. 2-ranked show, *60 Minutes.*

This was the setting in which young audiences experienced *90210.* Sponsors obviously courted youthful, mainly female viewers. Commercials during the time this study was conducted regularly promoted feminine health and beauty products (Teen Spirit shampoo, Loreal Hydravive shampoo, Sunflowers perfume, Playtex tampons, First Response pregnancy tests); clothing (Levis jeans, Playtex lingerie, Payless shoes, No-Nonsense Great Shapes pantyhose, which "trims your tummy, slims your hips, shapes your thighs"—in contrast to the next category!); junk food (McDonald's, Pizza Hut, Wendy's, Domino's Pizza, Snickers and Rocher candy bars); and low- to mid-priced cars (Chevrolet, Volkswagen, Honda, Toyota). House ads promoted the network's other shows, especially *Melrose Place* and the show following it on Fox stations, the local *10 o'Clock News.* (Frighteningly, when the show went into syndicated reruns in 1995, more than half the advertisements during some 5 p.m. weekday airings targeted children, promoting toys, amusement parks, and sugared breakfast cereals.)

This is not the place for an extended analysis of the incestuous link between programming and advertisers. The point here is that everything conspired to convince young viewers that *90210* was especially for them and their interests. As one viewer said, "It's like a teenage TV show. . . . Because all the other TV shows are like for grownups, and they're kind of boring." *90210*'s considerable demographic and economic importance made it a worthy object of study.

90210 as a Prime-Time Soap

Young viewers liked the show not only because they saw it as for and about them, but also because of its format as a prime-time soap, combining the closed-ended and essentially static narrative structure of the ensemble drama with soap opera's ongoing, serial format. This section will examine the ways in which *90210* skillfully blended dramatic and soap-opera characteristics and conventions. By the time of the study, the show's scripts demonstrated a highly adroit and sophisticated combination of the attractive features of both genres. While this study will not focus on production processes or scripts from a textual point of view, readers might find useful brief descriptions of the characters and plots.

Characters

A good example of this masterful overlap of dramatic and soap opera genres can be found in *90210*'s treatment of characters. Vladimir Propp (1928/68), who might be termed the father of narrative theory, enumerated seven basic roles assumed by characters in fairy tales; Kozloff (1987) applied five of them directly to television action shows (hero, helper, dispatcher, villain, princess). As this list suggests, the prototypical dramatic narrative features a male hero and relegates the lead female role to that of prize; however, Propp was more concerned with the ways in which character functions remain stable, no matter who fills them, and that they are fundamental to the structure of the tale. In contrast, soap operas tend to focus on multiple characters, and to portray females as powerful (Brown 1994). *90210* nicely mixes the two genres as the plots follow a group of regular stars, four male and four female, with equal attention given to both genders. Soap opera conventions can be seen in the portrayals of males as "sensitive," in Brown's (1994) term (empathetic and caring, willing to listen to the concerns of the female characters); on the other hand, the dramatic character roles are filled in each subplot, with a general sharing amongst the crowd of hero, helper, and sometimes even princess.

Other narrative theorists have enumerated Propp's character types in different ways, but there is general agreement on the importance to drama of "stock" characters. This notion has been considerably explored in film theory, where, feminists have argued, female stock characters are only stereotypes (child/woman, whore, bitch, wife, mother, secretary or girl Friday, career women, vamp, etc.). In soap operas, on the other hand, while stereotypes are certainly present, female characters especially are more fluid. Indeed, a character sometimes changes inexplicably, depending not on psychological motivations, as with films and novels, but rather at the convenience of the plot or the actress playing the character (Fiske 1987).

Again, *90210* presents a skillful blend of stock characters who nevertheless retain a certain fluidity. For example, the original premise is that the show depicts the trials and tribulations of a stereotypically naive family from Minnesota, the Walshes, when they move to brash, snooty Beverly Hills. But this set-up disappears as young Brenda Walsh eventually outsnobs the snobs, while her snooty friend Kelly transforms from bimbo to wise woman. Nevertheless, during the period of my study, each character was generally associated with a stereotypical descriptor (the sources and ramifications of these are explored in the chapter on characterizations): Brenda Walsh (played by Shannen Doherty) was the bitch; Kelly Taylor (Jennie Garth), the sensitive one; Donna Martin (Tori Spelling), the ditzy virgin; Andrea Zuckerman (Gabrielle Carteris), the Jewish brain; Dylan McKay (Luke Perry), the rebellious multi-millionaire; Brenda's twin brother, Brandon Walsh (Jason Priestley), the smooth campus politician; David Silver (Brian Austin Green), the troubled musician; and Steve Sanders (Ian Ziering), the party boy, frat rat, and golfer. Other regulars included Brenda and Brandon's parents, Jim (James Eckhouse) and Cindy (Carol Potter) Walsh, often compared to the *Brady Bunch* parents for their comforting common sense and laissez-faire attitude. In the weeks during which my study was conducted, a minor character, Lucinda Nichols (Dina Meyer), gained prominence, first as Brandon's professor's wife who unsuccessfully attempts to seduce Brandon, later as the divorced teacher of a feminist seminar who has a torrid affair with Brandon. In the fifth season, after the study was conducted, Brenda was replaced by Valerie Malone (Tiffani-Amber Thiessen), who moves into the Walshes' home while recovering from the emotional strain of her father's suicide.

The reader may note that the female characters tend to be distinguished more by temperamental factors, the males by occupational ones—a mutually exclusive duality that will be explored later, but that already lays the groundwork for perpetuation of gender stereotypes. I should add that, in general, all characters relish free time with little parental supervision, especially with regard to sexual activity. They remain forever young, attractive, wealthy (with one exception), and modishly dressed.

In talking with viewers, I realized that their perceptions of the characters were considerably enriched intertextually. The theory of intertextuality suggests that any one text is read in relationship to others. Extending the viewing experience was the proliferation of *90210*-related licensed products. Marketed through the producers' agent, Hamilton Projects, these included books, magazines, calendars, posters, lunch boxes, cosmetics, dolls, trading cards, and clothing (Fitzgerald 1992; Kanner 1992). And a barrage of publicity carried by magazines, newspapers, and tabloid television shows constantly reinforced viewer interest in and knowledge about the show, interweaving the on-screen behavior of the show's characters with the off-screen exploits of its actresses and actors. The girls and young women I interviewed played down the commercial *90210* products but repeatedly demonstrated detailed knowledge of press coverage. While this study does not attempt to trace the effects of intertextuality, it should be noted that topics foregrounded in the press often echoed through interviews—a number of articles, for instance, analyzed the characters' hairstyles (Shaw, 1994a,b), and hairdos were a frequent topic of discussion among viewers (see the chapter on appearance). Moreover, the viewers themselves referred to articles they had read or talk-show appearances they had seen.

Perhaps the most interesting way this intertextuality appeared in viewers' talk was in the blurring of character with actor. As Fiske (1987) has pointed out, this procedure typically is encouraged by the press, especially with regard to soap operas, and is "an intentional illusion, a conspiracy entered into by viewer and journalist in order to increase the pleasure of the program" (p. 121). (For an exploration of this phenomenon, cf., for example, Hobson 1980.)

Unquestionably the lightning rod for titillating publicity was Shannen Doherty, who played Brenda. *People Weekly*, in naming her one of "The 25 Most Intriguing People" of 1993, summarized the actress's self-destructive behavior ("Shannen" 1993), which included repeatedly showing up late for rehearsals (Fink 1994); feuding with co-stars and partying wildly ("Shannen" 1993); quickly breaking off an engagement with Chris Foufas (Sloane 1994); getting into a shoving match with another actress at a Los Angeles nightclub ("Shannen Doherty may return," 1994); dropping out of presenting an Emmy after a last-minute rehearsal brouhaha (Gliatto, Tomashoff, and Sandler 1992); assaulting her next fiance, Dean Factor, and having a fling with Judd Nelson ("Shannen" 1993); writing $31,000 in bad checks, owing $14,000 in back rent, and impulsively marrying Ashley Hamilton after a two-week courtship ("Shannen" 1993). (The marriage lasted five months.) Under a tidal wave of bad publicity, Doherty left the show after the season during which I conducted the study; rumblings of this impending departure provided an undertone to many of my interviews.

Meanwhile, the character of Brenda behaved similarly. Once the innocent Midwesterner, Brenda soon is patronizing her schoolmates. She gets involved with, and ultimately loses her virginity to, the rebel Dylan, with whom she then tempestuously breaks up. With a later boyfriend, Stuart, she impulsively elopes, cancels the wedding, then in a fit of temper breaks off the engagement in front of Stuart's father. (*Soap Opera Digest* noted, "Life imitated art when Brenda tried to elope with Stuart," Sloane 1994.) Brenda demonstrates a fuse as short as Doherty's, as this interview of Doherty by Liz Smith (1994) relates:

LS: There was a feeling, as the show went on, that your character became nasty. Did you or the scriptwriters collaborate on any changes?

SD: No. It was just sort of handed to me. All of a sudden this girl from Minnesota just turned into the Beverly Hills—
LS: Bitch?
SD: Yeah. In one sense it was good, because she was a bit more realistic than the other characters. Look, everyone has a nasty side—this little side that can get very mean. Or very wrapped up in a lifestyle. Especially when they're young. And my character experienced all of that. (1994, p. 13)

This interview demonstrates the way Brenda/Doherty as "bitch" was supported intertextually. However, there was also intertextual support for a read of both actress and character as strongly independent, speaking her mind, defending her point of view (see the chapters on characterization and dating). The actress, who as a child appeared on *Little House: A New Beginning*, said, "That show changed my life. Michael Landon was the one who said to me, 'Always stick up for yourself. Never let anybody walk all over you. Be a strong woman'" (Smith 1994). The combined Brenda/Doherty persona was the target of the gleefully negative *I Hate Brenda* newsletter, which ripped into the actress as well as the character. ("No defendas" 1993). Only one issue was ever produced, but 25,000 copies were sold (Sloane 1994). This study will not try to separate Brenda and Doherty surgically; I simply note the process as part viewers' experience of the show.

An even more clearcut case of a performer's life becoming intertwined with a character occurred for Carteris. Much publicity was generated as, before becoming pregnant she cleared the idea with producer Spelling. He agreed to have the parenthood worked into the scripts of character Andrea (Lipton 1994), who wrestles with the idea of having an abortion. Unmarried, career-minded Andrea is "exactly the kind of young woman who would have made the agonizing but very real choice of abortion a believable and powerful drama for *90210* to pursue," commented an *Entertainment Weekly* writer (Schwarzbaum 1994). Instead—as viewers I interviewed readily predicted on the basis of Carteris's pregnancy—the scripts had her get married and deliver the child, leaving abortion "the last pregnancy-related taboo left on TV" (Schwarzbaum 1994).

Off-screen relationships of other performers also were widely discussed in teen magazines and, as will be seen in interviews, resonated through viewer experience of the show. Doherty and Perry were involved for a time; later Thiessen and Green made a match (Goodman 1994). When added to the partner-swapping that occurs on screen, the romantic intertwinement would seem to require a scorecard, though most viewers could spew specifics without visible effort (see the chapters on relationships and dating). And the age of the actors and actresses intertextually contributed to their believability for the viewers I interviewed: most were under 25, some under 20; Spelling was a precocious 17 when the show started.

As will be seen in the analysis chapters, all this intertextual information stirred into the scripts' fertile blend of soap opera and dramatic conventions to enrich and enliven viewer talk about the characters.

Plots

Like the scripted treatment of characters, *90210* plots also incorporated both soap opera and dramatic elements. Fundamental elements of dramatic narration were isolated by Propp (1928/68), and his ideas have been refined by a number of important theorists, including Barthes (1977), who suggested that dramatic narratives are governed by rules in the same way as spoken grammar. Relevant here is the idea that a drama begins with a certain stasis—often called equilibrium or virtuality (a situation opening a possibility)—into which a disturbing element is interjected, often called disequilibrium. The drama ends with either a return to equilibrium or a move to a new equilibrium, usually but not always with a goal achieved (for a clear summary of this tradition and its application to movies, cf. Bordwell 1985).

The rigid format of serial television dramas imposes a limited structure on possibilities for disequilibrium and new equilibrium. As Kozloff (1987) put it,

It seems to be true that popular cultural forms are more rigidly patterned and formulaic than works of "high art." . . . One can practically guarantee that each week on *Star Trek* the USS *Enterprise* will encounter some alien life form, members of the crew will be separated from the ship (which will be placed in jeopardy), one crew member will have a romantic interest, all will be resolved through the crew's resourcefulness or high-mindedness. . . . On *Perry Mason*, Perry will take a case that looks hopeless while the prosecutor gloats; Della Street and Paul Drake will uncover crucial bits of evidence; Mason will break down witnesses on the stand, exonerate his client and uncover the real killer. More generally, one can rest assured that harmony will be restored at the end of each sitcom, children will be taught a moral lesson at the end of each domestic comedy, crime and detective shows will include a chase, and dastardly villains will inevitably be vanquished by their own dastardly inventions. (pp. 49–51)

On *90210*, such dramatic formulae are much in evidence. Plots revolved around a central problem handled in different ways by different characters, and especially in the early days were resolved by the end of the episode. It is appropriate to mention here that the "problems" often were carefully selected with the idea of educating the young audience members. From the beginning, the show aimed to depict in an educational way issues presumably facing many teens in order to guide viewer thinking. "We didn't want to do one of those high school series of ditsy kids running around outsmarting their parents," producer Spelling has been quoted as saying. "We didn't want to do silly things. We wanted to deal with real issues. We wanted to do a drug show, but we've seen teenage drug shows 16 times, so we showed a mother being on drugs and the effect it had on her child" (Weintraub 1991). Though most plots have vapid elements (*who* will model in the mother-daughter fashion show?), there generally is an effort to depict an underlying social issue (in the fashion show episode, a mother's substance abuse).

This strategy was expected both to attract viewers and to educate them. In contrast to most of the comedies with which *90210* competed, its scripts introduced such issues as abortion, teen pregnancy, breast cancer, date rape, AIDS, racism, and smoking. And the strategy worked: "We somehow struck a chord," Spelling told Weintraub. Producers also hoped viewers could learn from the show's content: "We can have some impact (a) to entertain and (b) when it's over, to get them to think about what they've seen, for maybe about five seconds," producer Charles Rosin has said (quoted in Simonetti 1994, p. 39). In the same way, actresses stated in interviews that they were aware of their social responsibility as role models. Tori Spelling, whose character Donna is the core cast's only virgin, commented: "It's great to have a model like her on TV to counteract the idea that you can't be cool unless you sleep with your boyfriend" (Cunningham 1994). Actress Doherty (Brenda) also was conscious of imitation by her teenage admirers (Murphy and Bailey 1991). For example, she used her position as a contemporary who speaks the language of teenagers to narrate a polished video about birth control.

In the first years, the dramatic problems introduced at the beginning of an episode always were neatly resolved, following dramatic conventions, in the one-hour time slot. "*Beverly Hills, 90210* generally ends with a complete resolution of the crisis of the day, thereby providing a reassuring, upbeat ending" (Simonetti, 1994). By the time of my study, problems sometimes stretched over multiple episodes, but they still uniformly reached a tidy resolution.

Thus in its plots *90210* departed from soap opera format, which resists narrative closure, cohering more closely to dramatic conventions. However, like daytime soaps, *90210* featured more than one plotline. (Indeed, Kozloff 1987 has argued that multiple plots are characteristic of television shows in general, in part to compensate for the lack of suspense built into the relatively static dramatic structure.) By the time of my study, *90210* writers were adept at constructing three or four plot lines an episode to reinforce a theme; for example, in a show on diversity, one character discovered his friend was gay, another encountered a blind person, and a third went on a date with a black man.

Soap opera plots tend to hinge on relationships between people, particularly family and romantic relationships; certainly the latter provided a constant subtext for *90210*, as is explored in the chapter on dating. Moreover, soaps tend to use time in ways that parallel actual time, and *90210* conformed to that criterion in a meta-narrative sense: While individual scenes were standard, fast-paced prime-time fare, the characters aged in real time. Over the course of several seasons, *90210*'s scripts followed the ensemble from grade to grade, accompanying the characters in real time from their sophomore year of high school through graduation and into college. One series of summer episodes even depicted their lives during summer vacation. (My study was conducted during the spring of 1994, the fourth season, when the characters were college freshmen.)

Recent narrative theory has pointed out that the dramatic format—equilibrium, disequilibrium, equilibrium—is never completely transparent or free from political agendas. Rather, some theorists say, narratives by their very form necessarily serve certain political interests over others, and reinforce certain "realities" over others. As Joseph Turow summed up the position:

Production firms tend to create cultural models that actually portray the right of [dominant] organizations and institutions to which they belong to remain powerful in the society, to control resources and hold leverage. Police shows on television portray the police as rightfully in charge. Situation comedies show going to school as a necessary part of growing up. . . . Despite depictions of social problems, most mass media in a society rarely challenge the nation's dominant institutional forces to the point of raising realistic alternatives. Rarely, for example, do United States television programs seriously portray solving the nation's armament problems by completely dismantling the military, or reducing a viewer's own monetary difficulties by stealing and then mocking the police. (1992, p. 154)

Even the framing of what counts as a "problem" and the depiction of a particular solution cannot avoid preferencing certain values over others (for an interesting application of this theory to a variety of social and media contexts, cf. Mumby, 1993). The dramatic structure particularly of television dramas, with their reassuring, upbeat return to the status quo, clearly use the fictional narrative to reinforce certain values. With a show such as *90210*, which ostensibly attempts to educate, this theory is particularly noteworthy.

In *90210*'s case, the solutions offered to problems are firmly "politically correct," emphasizing tolerance and valuing education, achievement, and individualism. On the surface, these are values with which many of us agree, and we might feel that we could do worse than to expose our young people to such notions. On the other hand, there are ways in which even these values work to maintain existing power relations that do not advantage women. As Mumby (1993) put it, "I see the recent controversy over so-called political correctness as in part an expression of the tension that exists between those who want to maintain a monopoly over the rules for what counts as legitimate knowledge and those social groups who have been largely disenfranchised in terms of their ability to shape our understanding of the world" (p. 2). In the opinion of many critics and myself, *90210* never probes issues or interrogates mainstream values in sufficient depth to yield fresh insights, and the scripts tend to back off before challenging any cultural currency. Reviewer Caryn James applauded the show's "mix of realism and melodrama" but noted that it "is ultimately so reassuring" (James 1991). "The problems never look so bad after a baking in the sun," noted reviewer Richard Zoglin (1991).

A variety of standard dramatic techniques kept the issues at a safe distance: "On *Beverly Hills, 90210,* bad things happen to minor characters only," wrote Marie-Claire Simonetti in an analysis comparing the show with the similar but less cautious Canadian show *Delgrassi Junior High.* "If they do affect main characters, they either happened to them in an extra-diagetic past (as Dylan's alcoholism) or almost happen to them" (1994, p. 41). Actor Priestley agreed: "Everything is *almost* happening. You know, [Brenda] *almost* got pregnant. [Kelly] *almost* got raped" ("Luke" 1994, p. 20). Ultimately, the show celebrated "the pursuit of dreams, persistence, individualism, hegemony and materialism" (Simonetti 1994, p. 42).

Indeed, *90210*'s handling of sensitive issues, including its presentation of non-mainstream points of view, fit nicely into Barthes's theory of inoculation, developed to apply to news stories but equally applicable here. As summed up by Fiske (1987), the theory compares the social body to the physical body.

Literally, inoculation is the process in which the physical body takes into itself a controlled dose of a disease that threatens it in order to strengthen its defenses against that disease. Figuratively, the metaphor refers to news's convention of allowing radical voices a controlled moment of speech that is nominated and inserted into the narrative in such a way as to ensure that the social body is strengthened and not threatened by the contrast between it and the radical. (p. 291)

As my analysis chapters show, I was concerned with the ways in which *90210* narratives "inoculated" viewers against non-mainstream female identities, or as Fiske and Hartley (1978/90) put it, the way the text presents these "radical" voices, only to have them "clawed back" into reinforcing acceptable mainstream interpretations, in this case, of femininity.

Women on Television

Andrea Press (1991) has provided a history of women's depictions on television that helps situate female identities on *90210*. She argued that prefeminist television of the 1950s and early '60s (*The Honeymooners, I Love Lucy*) showed women who remained in the home but nevertheless had important friendships with each other. These women conspired in an active resistance against men, resistance that in its continual failure perpetuated both their femininity and domesticity. Feminist television of the late 1960s and early '70s, in contrast, carried the dual message that it was possible for a woman to be sexy to attract men while engaged in exciting work for themselves as well as for men's admiration. It also worked through the tensions of women's new freedom from the home by establishing the community at work as a sort of pseudo-family, as on *The Mary Tyler Moore Show*. On postfeminist television in the '80s, women were given a work identity, but the emphasis was on their family role (*The Cosby Show*); further, the theme of collective resistance was not nearly so prominent as it was in many prefeminist shows.

"Perhaps now that we can no longer take the family for granted, television cannot afford to be so cavalier in offering multiple, comic depictions of women's dissatisfactions and rebellions," Press suggested (p. 38). She lamented the loss of female solidarity, pointing out that on postfeminist television, a woman might experience a problem because she is a woman, but she will solve it because she is a resourceful individual. There is no public or collective action. Indeed, the problem may even seem that of an individual, rather than that of women as a collective group. Traditional femininity—both glamorous and maternal—returns to center stage. And women are shown as having no problem balancing work and family. "Unfortunately, postfeminist television idealizes the family at the expense of more feminist insight into women's struggles within it" (p. 46).

To this litany I would make an addendum: Generation X television of the 1990s, at least as represented on *90210*, returns to the prefeminist war between the sexes, but conceals women's inferior status with an appearance of equality. Once again, we have the clearcut gender roles that characterized such prefeminist shows as *The Honeymooners*. As Simonetti (1994) put it, on *90210*, "sexism is blatant in the fact that boys will be boys (with their desire to watch strippers and obsession with sports) and girls will be girls (with their interest in dance, gossip, and fashion)"

(p. 40). And these gendered activities provide the prefeminist solidarity so missed by Press in post-feminism television, with the added ostensible message that the genders are separate but equal. Roles are indeed prescribed for each, but each is equally valuable (if anyone can swallow the notion that gossiping is equal to playing sports).

However, a key subtext of *90210*—explored in the chapter on dating —is that ultimately a woman is defined by her relationship with a male. As Reilly (1996b) maintains, media images reflect "a culture that counts marriage as the only solid proof of a woman's worth":

> In the media, purposeful, happy, feminine women are typically married. . . . In the media, there is usually something wrong with a woman who doesn't achieve marriage early: Frequently she's unattractive, certainly she's selfish, often she's dizzy, sometimes she's crazy. . . . Media's ever-single women most often fit the profile that ever-nasal Fran of *The Nanny* embodies. "Oh, I'm not gay," she announced earlier this year. "I'm just pathetic." (p. 105)

As Reilly suggests, "On TV, in movies, on the self-help shelves, the search for marriage is the avocation of choice for ever-single women" (p. 110). And *90210* provides an addendum: she must use passive-aggressive tactics to attract and keep a man. Thus, ultimately, the women are superficially presented as equal to males, but in many ways they relegate themselves to the prefeminist role of inferiors, incomplete or at least marred if they don't have a man. This role arguably infects Generation X television more virulently than prefeminist television because the gender inequalities are unstated. The insidious ways in which this concealing of inequality perpetuates a disadvantageous situation has been described by Jhally and Lewis (1992), who demonstrated how *The Cosby Show* worked to conceal for both black and white viewers the ongoing problem of racism in the United States by presupposing that it had been solved, or had never existed, at least for the Huxtables.

As will be explored in later chapters, these aspects of *90210* cause me to find it not only objectionable but worrisome. It is appropriate here to reiterate that, unlike many researchers studying viewers of specific shows, I am not a fan of *90210*. My urgent, concerned, and even angry voice will be heard throughout this book.

I must admit, I do appreciate the show's many strengths, including its focused acting and seamless production quality. In the course of my research, I have replayed some scenes dozens of times, and I never tire of the skill, efficiency and narrative momentum they demonstrate. With cuts seemingly timed to viewer's heartbeats, editing propels interest forward. It's hard to take your eyes off *90210*.

But my own experiences as a single woman challenging traditional female roles in both domestic and professional spheres lead me to object strongly to a text that both naturalizes dominant notions of female identity and conceals how difficult it can be to break out of those molds. As I point out throughout this book, the show does present alternative lifestyles, but—following the dramatic formula, or Barthes's inoculation theory—it then works carefully to discredit them.

In one episode, for example, Kelly's mother gives a speech at a school event in which she comments on ways that gender stereotypes limit women's modeling careers. She argues that options for women in fashion modeling significantly diminish as they approach 40, while the same is not true for male models. To me, this seemed no more than a simple truth voiced with a certain justified—yet controlled—anger. However, on the show, the statement is greeted with hostility by the fictional audience, which works to discredit the message by stigmatizing the speaker —she is divorced, alcoholic, and coked-up. Kelly is overwhelmed with shame; her mother (predictably) is speedily packed off to a detox center, and the equilibrium is restored. Offered but discredited is the idea that there is a double standard on appearance that disadvantages women.

Perhaps it is to the producers' credit that any dissenting voices were built into the show. An example during the time the study was conducted was the minor character of the divorcee Lucinda (Dina Meyer), mentioned earlier. Her dream is to complete a research project, a film about African women. She is independent, talented, smart, and artistic. Of all the characters, she was the one who interested me most (not surprisingly). Ultimately, however, I cannot praise her. As necessitated by the double forces of ideology and narrative, every episode in which she appears incorporates moments when her voice is discredited and her behavior can be read as selfish and insensitive.

Perhaps a stronger presence is the outspoken, down-to-earth Andrea. Ambitious, talented, and driven to succeed academically, Andrea speaks for the hard worker impatient with frippery. As mandated by the demands of network television, however, her persona typically is undermined by her marginalized status: with her simple clothing and glasses, Andrea is Jewish, poor, intellectual, "other." In the fashion-show episode, Andrea tells the beautiful, rich, popular Kelly with admiration that she is "strong," and Kelly pays the dressed-for-fashion-show Andrea the ultimate compliment: "I never realized you were so pretty." This vignette epitomizes the trap of the show: The alternate voice, the "other side," is present, but it is subsumed under the emphasis on, and seductive attraction of, the gossip-and-fashion world of Brenda, Kelly, and Donna.

Thus, I personally could not watch the show or think about it without interrogating its perpetuation of dominant notions of female identity, a process that I strongly believe quietly undermines women's potential by relegating us to a world of relationships and appearance and by presenting us as incomplete without a man. Nevertheless, as I studied my video-taped episodes of *90210*, I clung to the hope that this show—a milestone in programming history watched by millions of girls and young women—accomplished something better for them. Maybe, I thought, as fans ardently watched and talked about the show, they opened important meanings that remained closed for me.

In my determination to understand my young friends' complex, multi-layered and pleasurable viewing process, I turned first to the mass communication literature to learn what others have concluded happens when women watch television. The next chapter discusses this research, some of which bolstered my hope that the *90210* experience could be a positive one.

Chapter 3
Cultural Studies: Agency, Community, and Pleasure

In sifting through reams of material written about the ubiquitous and mysterious "idiot box," I decided to base my analysis on the cultural studies research tradition because it has focused on the interaction of both females and young people with media. Founded in Great Britain, this school pioneered the move to study television viewing, not quantitatively in the laboratory, but qualitatively in the busy, messy settings of everyday life. In pondering cultural studies analyses, however, I realized that the school was divided in at least one fundamental way. These researchers disagreed profoundly over whether and how media empower or oppress. Some argued that watching television shows and reading magazines and romance novels—and talking about them—disadvantaged women and young people by perpetuating existing patriarchal and capitalist power structures. But others maintained that these media encounters could strengthen media users by building community and helping them take charge of their lives. Some writers even started in the negative camp, then moved to the positive one.

As this disagreement suggests, behind both fears and hopes about what happens when we watch television lies a concern with what many authors call agency—with whether we can initiate changes in our lives, and in the meanings we make of events and power relations, or whether cultural forces shape what we value and thus where power resides. Are women active in our enjoyment of soap operas or romance novels, or are we manipulated by the patriarchy into valuing certain female behaviors over others? Do we exercise agency as we take time for ourselves to watch and read, or are we co-opted into substituting this behavior for any real fulfillment of needs or improvement in our condition?

Cultural studies targets two arenas in which to study agency: The generation of community and the production of pleasure. Some researchers expected that subcultures would filter and reshape media and cultural messages, giving individuals agency over and ownership of the meanings they made. And these researchers suspected that taking pleasure in media texts—often in ways not anticipated by producers of the texts—gave users agency in their media experiences. However, others maintained that this very activity and enjoyment worked ultimately to reproduce a culture that disadvantaged women and young people.

This chapter overviews cultural studies' treatment of agency, particularly with regard to community and pleasure. I start with the work of hegemony theorists, in whose bleak view media users work actively to perpetuate a status quo that disadvantages them. I then discuss work of researchers who celebrate the active media user.

Agency, Resistance, and Hegemony Theory

The issue of agency has for cultural studies researchers been inseparably linked with resistance to dominant social mores. British Cultural Studies was initially identified with the Centre for Contemporary Cultural Studies at Birmingham University. Founded by Richard Hoggart in 1963 (for a more complete history, cf., for example, McGuigan 1992), the school was fueled by a deep resistance to cultural elitism and an interrogation of traditional literary canons. As articulated in Hoggart's (1957) *The Uses of Literacy*, these researchers treated mass culture as a legitimate focus of study, asking how subcultures gave individuals agency to resist and interrogate existing power structures, especially in their media encounters. Members of this school saw themselves as speaking for, and with, some of those thought to be disadvantaged in Western society—women, youth, and the lower class.

Early researchers wanted to celebrate resistance to elitist or "high" culture, particularly as this culture was codified and transmitted through formal education. But despite this somewhat biased framing of research questions, early cultural studies findings did not support the expectation that subculture and mass culture fueled effective resistance to dominant ideologies. Two researchers who looked at the operation of subcultures in the lives of lower-class youth, Willis (1977) and McRobbie (1978), found that, while these young people appeared active and resistant, their activity ultimately worked to prevent them from bettering their situation.

Willis studied disaffected "lads" in a working-class school, who had developed a culture of defiance that seemed to help them control an otherwise demoralizing situation. These youths built a lively and rebellious community, united by what Willis heard as an active language of resistance. They empowered themselves by adopting what at the time were considered counter-culture identities (drinking, smoking, having sex, and generally refusing to conform to classroom norms) in their re-volt against education. Willis was forced to conclude, however, that this very resistance worked to their disadvantage: in reality, a good educa-tion provided the key to getting a good job and hence to gaining any real economic power. While the youths seemed to challenge and even interrogate elitist culture, their resistance ultimately cemented their fate in the lower echelons of manual labor and perpetuated the capitalist systems that oppressed them.

McRobbie (1978, 1981) conducted a number of similar studies with working-class girls and came to basically the same conclusion. In her companion piece to Willis's work, McRobbie (1978) looked at working-class girls in their own revolt against education. She found they used romantic fantasies and built a community around best-friend relation-ships in order to cope with the limited opportunities immediately avail-able to them. However, as for Willis's lads, these coping strategies, especially resistance to schooling, co-opted the girls into perpetuating oppressive conditions and diverted them back into subordinate roles:

Marriage, family life, fashion and beauty all contribute massively to this femi-nine anti-school culture and, in doing so, nicely illustrate the contradictions inherent in so-called oppositional activities. Are the girls in the end not simply doing exactly what is required of them—and if this *is* the case, then could it not be convincingly argued that it is their own culture which itself is the most effec-tive agent of social control for girls, pushing them into compliance with that role which a whole range of institutions in capitalist society also, but less effec-tively, directs them towards? (p. 104)

Similarly, McRobbie's (1981) look at working-class girls reading the popular British teen magazine *Jackie*, depicting traditional romance tales, found that the girls were "active" consumers of fantasies fueled by the magazine, not just dupes of the text. But their freely chosen con-sumption of *Jackie* worked to reinforce their subordinate status in the patriarchy.

This notion echoed through a study in the United States conducted by Janice Radway (1982). She was working out of a reader-response background, which questioned literary canons in the same way that cul-tural studies research did, and although her study was not informed by cultural studies findings, it paralleled them in ways that make it impor-tant to talk about here. Radway interviewed women in a Midwestern city who read popular romance novels, and highlighted a cyclical relation-ship between media use and patriarchal culture. The women Radway interviewed recognized their subordinate roles in that culture, and they perceived their choice to read romances as, not just an escape, but pri-marily an act of defiance. However, Radway maintained, these readers did not seem to be aware that they chose and enjoyed books that re-inforced their current subordinate status. In a conclusion that was strik-ingly similar to the findings of Willis and McRobbie, Radway maintained that women turned to romance novels as a protest against their current situation and out of a longing for something better, but the books served to reinforce their acceptance of their existing lot. In reading fictional romances, a woman found "a strategy for making her present situation more comfortable without substantive reordering of its structure rather than a comprehensive program for reorganizing her life in such a way that all needs might be met" (p. 215).

This cycle in which resistance perpetuates the status quo was inter-preted by some cultural studies researchers using hegemony theory. Developed by the Italian Antonio Gramsci in the 1920s and 1930s and rediscovered and made popular in the 1970s (e.g., Gramsci, 1971), hege-mony theory sought to explain the widespread acceptance of, even en-thusiasm for, fascism in Italy among those whose very freedoms fascism curtailed. Suspecting that the operations of ideology were more com-plex and insidious than in the Marxist model, Gramsci outlined a theory that described how relations of domination are concealed, and how the consent of the dominated to their lot is won rather than coerced. Forces in power did not simply impose their will; rather, they naturalized the "reality" of their control and won the consent of the oppressed to their lot. As Willis put it, "One of the most important general functions of ideology is the way in which it turns uncertain and fragile cultural reso-lutions and outcomes into a pervasive naturalism" (p. 162). Or, as Deetz (1992) explained it:

Gramsci . . . argued that the willing assent of the mass was engineered through the production of the normalcy of everyday-life beliefs and practices. Rather than an elite wielding visible control, "organic intellectuals" (e.g., journalists, teachers, writers) produce a variety of cultural forms that express and shape values, actions, and meanings and reproduce hidden forms of domination. The site of hegemony is the myriad of everyday institutional activities and experi-ences that culminate in "common sense," thus hiding the choices made and "mystifying" the interests of dominant groups. Dominant-group definitions of reality, norms, and standards appear as normal rather than as political and con-testable. (p. 62)

Hegemony theorists emphasized that the process of naturalizing the status quo, hiding the oppressive aspects of existing power structures, and inviting the oppressed to consent enthusiastically to their lot, does not proceed smoothly and seamlessly. Instead, these theorists argue, it is inherently problematic, unstable, and contested. The consent of the oppressed must be won and rewon continually by the forces of domination. Moreover, resistance to domination can appear in a plethora of forms, which then engender new systems of control. Both the hegemonic forces of control and those forces that would resist them, Gramsci believed, are constantly being revised and negotiated.

In American mass media research, Gramsci's ideas were cogently applied to the construction of what counts as news by a number of researchers (e.g., Efron 1971; Altheide 1974, 1987; Tuchman 1978; Gitlin 1980; Bennett 1983; Parenti 1986), who showed how the media elite are deeply invested in preserving existing political and economic power structures. Despite journalism's traditional "watchdog" role, these studies showed how things as simple as news routines, for example, worked to naturalize a worldview that perpetuated the status quo (for an interesting expansion of this theory, cf. Turow 1992). In cultural studies, Gramsci's theory permitted investigators to theorize a complex interaction between culture and individual: An active viewer/reader can work to co-construct, transform, and often resist dominant cultural meanings, but her activity serves to rewin her consent to the dominant ideology, especially the patriarchal and capitalist status quo.

The hegemonic naturalization of disadvantageous race relations is clearly illustrated Jhally and Lewis's (1992) study of fans of *The Cosby Show*—although the authors did not harness hegemony theory per se. Using methods similar to mine, except that researchers did not view the program with the interviewees, Jhally and Lewis conducted 52 focus groups of black, white, and Hispanic viewers, subdivided by social class. *Cosby*, a sitcom that was enormously popular with both blacks and whites, followed the domestic experiences of a black doctor, Cliff Huxtable, his lawyer wife, Clair, and their children, in the context of affluent circumstances and typical family problems almost never foregrounding race. (Will Cliff win the lawn bowling game against another doctor? How can young Theo be persuaded to do his homework?)

Jhally and Lewis initially hoped that *Cosby* could provide a much-needed role model of African-American familial and financial success, despite the restrictions of sanitized content and a normalized upper middle class lifestyle:

Despite these constraints, what *The Cosby Show* has confronted, many have argued, is the deep-rooted racism of white Americans who find it difficult to accept racial equality. Michael Dyson [1989:29], for example, has suggested that one of "the most useful aspects of Cosby's dismantling of racial mythology and stereotyping is that it has permitted America to view black folk as *human beings*." Here, at last, are media representations of successful and attractive black people whom white people can respect, admire, and even identify with. (p. 5)

However, Jhally and Lewis concluded, the show ultimately worked to cement the very racist and capitalist barriers they had hoped it would crack. These authors were not informed by hegemony theory, but their findings convincingly show how normalizing of the capitalist power structure can work to disadvantage blacks and perpetuate their frequently inferior status within it. Black viewers liked *Cosby*'s upper-class setting, characterized the show as "realistic," and praised its silence on economic and racial problems. In the process, however, they concealed the real power relations of capitalism and racism that keep most blacks in the lower echelons of income. Viewers, in talking about *Cosby*, perpetuated their subordinate status within existing economic systems:

Requiring upper middle class status as a mark of normalcy creates a world that forces black viewers to accept a value system in which they are the inevitable losers. A value system based upon social class (upper equals good, lower equals bad: a notion with a sinister Orwellian ring) devalues most black people, for whom a high-income life-style like the Huxtables' is quite unattainable. Black viewers are thus caught in a trap because the escape route from TV stereotyping comes with a set of ideologically loaded conditions. To look good, to look "positive," means accepting a value system in which upper middle class status is a sign of superiority. This is more than crude materialism; for a group that has been largely excluded from these higher socioeconomic echelons, it is cultural and political suicide. (Jhally and Lewis 1992, p. 122)

Although the authors do not use the word hegemony, they show how black viewers, in praising *Cosby*, often actively and pleasurably worked to perpetuate a disadvantaging capitalist, racist society—and to conceal the fact that they were doing so.

The hegemonic reproduction of dominant ideology in the lives of women television viewers was harnessed in a sophisticated and compelling study by Andrea Press (1991). Explaining that "ideology refers generally to the terrain of ideas so centrally constitutive of our world-views that we fail to notice what they are," she pointed out ways that television as a naturalized part of our culture is especially likely to work hegemonically to reproduce that culture:

Television, which some may analogously describe to be such an integral part of our lives that we also fail to notice it as we might fail to notice a necessary piece of living room or bedroom furniture, provides, in the context of our private experience [in the home], a constant stream of social images that impinge upon our view of the world and upon our very definitions of who we are. Television's unobtrusive nature . . . may make it effective in the same way ideologies are effective: unconsciously, both structure our conceptions of self and the social world. (p. 16)

Press used hegemony theory to understand the influence of television on the ways women articulated their identities and formed their ideas about what is normal and real. Moreover, she extended that notion to look at the intersection of social class and television viewing, suggesting that television helped solidify the domination of certain classes over others, and finding that this process works differently for women of different classes.

Middle-class women, Press suggested, identified with television characters and used that identification actively to work out problems in their lives. In so doing, they were likely to accept and attempt to perpetuate television's portrayals of both physical and behavioral ideals for women in what Press called "gender-specific hegemony." Even as they called television shows "unrealistic," were critical of them, and felt superior to them, they accepted the norms underlying the programs. "For middle-class women, therefore, television is both a source of feminist resistance to the status quo and, at the same time, a source for the reinforcement of many of the status quo's patriarchal values" Press concluded (p. 96).

Working-class women, however, tended to judge depictions of middle-class life uncritically as realistic lifestyles they said they themselves could achieve, even when their own personal experience seemed to counter this assumption. Therefore, Press suggested that these women experienced "class-specific" hegemony, in which wish-fulfillment about middle-class life, rather than closeness of fit between experience and image, served as the basis for perceptions of "realism." Press suggested that watching television worked to hide from working-class women a critical consciousness of their own situation and hence discouraged political mobilization to change the situation. In her interviews, she found these women expressing an optimistic (and to Press, unjustified) belief in their own upward mobility.

Like early Radway and McRobbie, Press concluded that women of both classes often found themselves frustrated with their family and/or work situations and dissatisfied with culturally available outlets to handle these feelings. Watching television both could allow women to express their frustration and could permit them to cope with it better. Their viewing thus functioned both as an expression of resistance and as a means of perpetuating the system.

And Press went a step beyond previous authors to conclude that activity that ultimately works to perpetuate the status quo cannot be counted as agency:

If women's tendency to resist hegemony through creative interpretations of television truly stops in the kitchen, then this evidence of resistance must be counted as something else. Theorists of resistance must develop some means for assessing the political effectiveness of the resistance they chronicle. (p. 177)

She emphasized that agency must be linked to interrogation of, if not changes in, culturally based power structures—a tall order for researchers who now must seek to prove that link! This suggested to me that, if I really wanted to make a case for viewers' resistant reads of *90210*, I needed a concrete, operationalizable way to show links between read of the show and interrogation of culture. This necessity first started me thinking about using discursive agency—treating talk as action, as explored in the next chapter—as a convincing and precise means of empirically linking television viewing and real life.

Hegemony theory has been refined by Condit (1994), who emphasized that dominant ideology should be theorized as a temporary coalition of multiple voices, rather than as a unified force:

A variety of groups forge concord by accommodating to each other's interests. This does not mean that an ideal, fair, or just concordance is produced, because some groups have disproportionate rhetorical advantage and some groups are not invited by the mediators into the concordance at all. Nevertheless, the hegemonic worldview that arises does so on the basis of a plurivocal set of interests, not a single dominant interest. (p. 226)

This notion is useful because it allows us to theorize the presences of marginalized voices that blend in with, but are discredited by, more powerful and legitimated ones. Multiple voices do indeed shape how we experience our culture; however, they speak with differential power relationships. Resistance can be both voiced and marginalized, both primed and then defused, so that it ultimately harmonizes with the hegemonic concord. Since I already suspected that *90210* spoke to viewers in multiple voices, and that a variety of discourses would emerge in their talk about it, I seized on these ideas as a way of making my analysis of this talk more subtle and layered. It was important to evaluate which discourses were offered but discredited, and which were naturalized.

The Polysemic Text, Resistance, and Pleasure

Another way of conceptualizing this variety of voices was taken by a branch of cultural studies research that celebrated the ways that television's multiple meanings can be read resistantly. Running parallel with hegemony theory's rather bleak picture, which focused on ways in which media encounters worked to win females to an acceptance and perpetuation of an oppressive patriarchal and capitalist society, were a number of studies that celebrated the resistant half of the glass, especially as it empowered women through pleasure and community. As McGuigan (1992) has pointed out, "pleasure, albeit ideologically implicated, exceeds the problematic of hegemony" (p. 68). While this is not the place to review the ways in which Freud, Lacan, Foucault, and Barthes have informed theorizing about pleasure (for overviews, cf. Fiske 1987; McGuigan 1992), I wish to make the point that pleasure, like agency, has been seen as simultaneously active and disempowered; both a form of subjection and a form of resistance; both stemming from collective, shared experience that is potentially the springboard for action, and as working to perpetuate oppressive social forces.

For cultural studies researchers looking at women watching television, pleasure, especially communal pleasure, was often seen as empowering. Much of the cultural studies research built on Hall's "encoding/decoding" model of viewers encountering a "polysemic" text, so it is important to outline briefly those ideas here. The idea that television texts are polysemic—that rather than delivering a univocal message, they can be read many ways—was a seminal one. Television text contains multiple meanings, these theorists argued. As Fiske (1987) explained polysemy:

> To be popular, the television text has to be read and enjoyed by a diversity of social groups, so its meanings must be capable of being inflected in a number of different ways. The television text is therefore more polysemic and more open than earlier theorists allowed for. (p. 66)

Or, as Hobson (1982) put it, "The message is not solely in the 'text,' but can be changed or 'worked on' by the audience as they make their own interpretation of a programme" (p. 106).

In his "encoding/decoding" model, Stuart Hall (1980) identified three types of "readings" potentially available to viewers of a polysemic text, positions that have remained important conceptually: dominant, negotiated, and oppositional. He emphasized the way "naturalized" television codes let the viewer seem to experience meanings directly; television news, for example, is so coded as to seem unshaped by production constraints and decisions. Moreover, a particular decoding that prefers dominant meanings is legitimated. However, such codes are not closed to negotiated readings, which contain a mixture of adaptive and oppositional elements, or to oppositional ones, in which the message is decoded in an alternative frame of reference.

Fiske (1987) refined Hall's theory, brilliantly incorporating into mass media theory the postmodern notions about the role of language in constructing meaning. Fiske drew on an impressive list of structuralist and poststructuralist theorists to theorize viewing as, not just a simple process of absorbing a univocal meaning, but rather a complex and contested event. "We can then characterize the television text as a site of struggle between the dominant ideology working to produce a closed text by closing off the opportunities it offers for resistive readings, and the diversity of audiences who, if they are to make the text popular, are constantly working to open it up to their readings" (Fiske 1987, p. 94). This reinforced my intuitive notion that what I wanted to study was the audience's reading—as expressed in viewer talk about *90210*—rather than simply the text itself, or my jaundiced read of it.

Here it is relevant to mention briefly an early application of Hall's theory by David Morley (1980), even though he studied mostly males watching a news show rather than females watching entertainment television, and he was not concerned with pleasure. However, his premise—that the social situation of the viewer could predict whether the content of the show was given a dominant, negotiated, or oppositional reading—relates to my study of girls and young women from different backgrounds watching a prime-time soap.

Morley's results were complex and contradictory. Neither class nor social position predicted type of reading; instead, direct personal experience was an important inflector in negotiated and oppositional readings. Moreover, he expected that viewer awareness that certain meanings were preferred would automatically engender resistance, but this theory did not hold: even if a viewer thought a newscast was biased, Morley found, he or she might still agree with its point of view.

While I was still determined to document educational background as a rough approximation of class, following Press (1991) among many others, Morley's findings suggested that personal experience might play a role in viewers' "reads" of *90210*—a notion that was not the primary focus of my study, but which my data turned out to support in a number of interesting ways.

A number of researchers drew on the idea of the resistant reader of a polysemic text to demonstrate that active female viewers, who take pleasure in their viewing despite the dominant ideology, indeed exercised agency. Because of what Fiske called television's semiotic excess—"there is always too much meaning on television to be controllable by the dominant ideology" (p. 91)—these researchers saw some viewers not only as active in terms of "working on" texts, but also, within certain bounds, able to make a variety of resistant and negotiated readings, which these researchers counted as agency. These investigators concentrated on ways that women's pleasure in media experiences could be legitimated and celebrated, in contrast to hegemony theory's emphasis on ways in which this process implicated viewers in perpetuating the status quo. For example, Hobson's (1982) early study of women watching the British soap opera *Crossroads* emphasized the women's sense of cultural possession of the program and the way that watching it asserted the women's right to control, if at least in part, the culture of the home.

Indeed, McRobbie, whose early work emphasized the disempowering aspects of media use for lower-class teenage girls, moved in later work to celebration of female pleasure vis-a-vis media. In a 1984 essay, McRobbie rejected her earlier hegemonic critique of *Jackie*, arguing instead in support of girls' ability imaginatively to transform patriarchal texts. In writing about girls, young women, and dance, she argued that although dance has often been seen as subject to dominant, oppressive male gaze, it can also be interpreted as "part of a strategy of resistance or opposition; that is, as marking out one of those areas which cannot be totally colonized" (p. 134). For this reason, she argued that films such as *Fame* and *Flashdance* are open to feminist readings in that they present strong-minded, determined females whose interest lies in achievement through hard work rather than through romance. Certainly the camera lingers on the female bodies dancing, but this gaze is open to multiple meanings. A woman also can enjoy her own body dancing.

Pleasure as resistance to patriarchy also interested Ian Ang (1985), who looked at women's reactions to the American prime-time soap *Dallas*. Her findings present a good example of the ways researchers were torn between the bleakness of hegemony theory and the celebration of resistance as they studied their data. While acknowledging the disempowering aspects of the *Dallas* text, she chose to highlight viewer resistance.

Ang argued that women's enjoyment of *Dallas* stemmed from a special sort of recognition of elements of their own lives in the show's characters and events. While admitting the "external unrealism" of the show, with its improbable plots and complicated relationships, women found in the text an "emotional realism," Ang argued. The melodramatic elements of the show represent a metaphorical "lumping together" of emotional events that do occur, albeit with less frequency, in individual lives. Ang concluded that the pleasure of *Dallas* consists in the recognition of ideas that fit in with the viewers' imaginative world: viewers "can 'lose' themselves in *Dallas* because the program symbolizes a structure of feeling which connects up with one of the ways in which they encounter life" (p. 83).

Like McRobbie, Ang valued that pleasure. However, like early Radway, she could not help noting that the central structure of feeling in *Dallas* revolved around the female characters' always-unsuccessful revolt against the status quo, and she was forced to acknowledge that women's "recognition" of their world in *Dallas* could work to reinforce the patriarchal culture in which they lived:

[T]he melodramatic sentimentality of *Dallas* is ideologically motivated by a sense of the essential impossibility of a fundamental alteration in the very structures which should be held responsible for all the trouble and unhappiness. This induces feelings of resignation and fatalism—sentiments which are not exactly conducive to resistance to these structures. (p. 123)

However, Ang chose to interpret female viewers' recognition of the futility of changing oppressive conditions as rather innocently enriching the lives of viewers:

[I]n so far as the imagination is an essential component of our psychological world, the pleasure of *Dallas*—as a historically specific symbolizing of that imagination—is not a *compensation* for the presumed drabness of daily life, not a *flight* from it, but a *dimension* of it. For only through the imagination, which is always subjective, is the "objective reality" assimilated: a life without imagination does not exist. (p. 83)

Ang argued that women's readings of a television show need not be measured in relation to their political power implications: "Where cultural consumption is concerned, no fixed standard exists for gauging the 'progressiveness' of a fantasy" (pp. 135–36).

Studies like Ang's inspired other researchers to take daytime soap operas more seriously. Researchers began to conclude that watching soap operas could contribute to resistance to patriarchy. For example, Fiske (1987) argued that soap operas, whose generic characteristics he said are specifically female in their emphasis on such things as relationality and openendedness, value aspects of American culture that are usually delegitimated. Because the soaps take seriously important aspects of women's experience in our culture, the genre empowers female viewers, he maintained.

This view echoed through a number of soap-opera studies. As Williams (1992) put it:

Should soaps and romances be viewed as pits holding some hope for women's so-called rising above themselves? Perhaps the women are all right as they are! Looking deeply into the multitudinous, dynamic, dialectical soaps, and the responses of their watchers, suggests that soap operas may be a profound reflection, and an ongoing source, of their viewers' very well mounted self-esteem. (p. 120)

Watching soap operas put women in a position of agency, researchers said. These researchers saw women watching soap operas as in control of their viewing experiences, and as actively empowered by them.

Discursive Pleasure, Community, Resistance, and Hegemony: Brown

To this approach, Mary Ellen Brown (1990, 1994) added the notion of a community of viewers, which, in using talk about soap operas to critique the patriarchy, could serve as a springboard to challenge existing power structures. Her study is theoretically significant for the ways in which it valued women's pleasure, incorporated Foucault's theories of discourses and built on Fiske's notions of polysemy, while at the same time revisiting hegemony theory and adding a political action component.

Brown drew on the poststructuralist claim that political struggle and negotiation take place on a discursive level. She argued that women find pleasure in soap operas and are empowered by them precisely because these shows enable women to produce a discourse that disrupts the dominant ideology. In her 1990 article that preceded the 1994 book, Brown maintained that talking about soap operas constitutes a resistive discourse, which she defined as a way of talking in which subgroups acknowledge their position of subordination. In this type of talk, women can freely reference the fact that they are defined by dominant groups in ways that do not necessarily represent their own perception of their world, and propose solutions about how one "gets by" in relation to the rules of the dominant culture. When women talk about soap operas, she maintained, they produce a resistive "feminine" discourse that disrupts patriarchal values. And the pleasure of feminine discourse often comes from its ability to make fun of dominant practices and discursive notions: "By playing in this way with the conventions of the dominant discourse, feminine discourse constitutes itself as 'other' to it, and displays a potential resistance" (1990, p. 190).

Thus, Brown concluded in both the 1990 article and in the 1994 book, even though women do participate in patriarchal culture, they are not victims of it. By watching and talking about soap operas, women break patriarchal rules about what counts as important and valuable: "This breaking of the rules is a source of pleasure, and the act of taking that pleasure entails defiance of dominant reading practices which attempt to shape the construction of meaning in our culture" (1990, p. 198). This resistance is slightly different from that of the women Radway studied. While Radway's romance readers saw the act of reading as resistant, but did not resist the patriarchal texts, Brown's soap opera viewers gained pleasure from a resistant reading of a text, mocking traditionally "feminine" characters and laughing heartily at the rules of patriarchy:

I have found that women in soap opera groups have a space to experience great joy through laughter at both soap operas' excessive portrayal of women and the excessiveness of the contradictions in women's actual lives. This raucous laughter is an affective response that becomes a transgressive act. It forms a contradictory and knowledgeable position from which to offer an emotional critique. In effect, these fans speak with their bodies, which is a tangible experience of their resistive pleasure. (1994, p. 177)

The 1994 book expanded this discursive theory by giving a more detailed analysis of the way soap operas work and by bringing in the concept of hegemony, including Louis Althusser's (1971) notion of "hailing." Althusser suggested that pleasure involves identifying with an ideologically constructed "subject," an idealized self in full harmony with the dominant ideology. He maintained that individuals enter into an imaginary relationship with this patriarchal and capitalist "subject," which "hails" her. This "hailing" is accomplished through the discursive construction of a social position for the individual—a way of talking about oneself that simultaneously constructs and limits one's alternatives as a human being. As Deetz (1992) put it, "the 'subject' is always an image or constructed self rather than an individual in a full set of relations to the world" (p. 136). An Althusserian reading of Ang's findings and McRobbie's experience might argue that women misrecognized themselves in the "melodramatic sentimentality of *Dallas*," and that they were "hailed" into pleasurably perpetuating the patriarchal and capitalistic status quo.

Brown agreed that the experience of being hailed by a soap opera, which "fits nicely into the type of feminine culture that is constructed to support dominant or hegemonic notions of femininity" (p. 59), can be pleasurable.

Whatever one may think of that place and the concerns it involves—home, relationships, emotional dependency—it is the place constructed for women in patriarchal and capitalistic discourse. Hence in the cultures of which I speak, whether or not we live in this space, we are still hailed by it; that is, we recognize a kind of subjectivity, or space in which we are supposed to fit, constructed by our culture for us even though we do not occupy it. (p. 174)

But, she said, there is also pleasure in resisting that hailing. In watching soap operas, women enjoy recognizing themselves and their place in the patriarchal culture, but they also relish resisting that space. Thus, in addition to working to keep women in their place, soap operas open a space for women's resistive pleasures. In talking about soap operas, women forge enjoyable oral networks, support groups that allow them to test social boundaries and explore behavioral possibilities within patriarchy: "The most important political aspect of soap opera fanships is the creation of oral networks. To the extent that soap operas do this, then they may be considered important for women's cultural survival in dominant culture" (p. 176). This talk can give rise to radical changes in consciousness that enable women to develop the "critical oppositional look, to become a spectator in the position of agency" (p. 181). Women can find emancipation through "the constant awareness of contradiction and the struggle to secure a place for the voice of the female spectator who speaks as well as sees" (p. 182). Talking about soap operas can help groups of women become politically active on other fronts.

The Dilemma

As cultural studies researchers observed women enjoying television shows, they interpreted what they saw in radically different ways. And indeed, as I began to analyze my data, I also grappled with the viewers' sense of agency, community, and pleasure derived from watching *90210*. I needed to judge whether the empowered sound of their voices as they talked about the show counted as agency; I worked to make sense of the communities that were constructed around talk about the show; I struggled to understand the meaning—if meaning there were!— to the seemingly uncomplicated pleasure these girls and young women experienced while watching the sheer beauty of the *90210* characters and riding the plot roller coasters. Moreover, as Ang suggested, these viewers also recognized an emotional way that *90210* "realistically" connected with ways they encountered life, and it began to appear to me that this recognition added a dimension to the ways in which they attended to their own lives.

I had to make a decision about how to interpret these findings. Following McRobbie's later work, one interpretation of this pleasurable viewing experience amid a welter of consumerism is that it offers the viewer ways to feel good about and indulge herself, to enjoy her own body and actively to explore possibilities for it. Moreover, it certainly is possible to suggest, with Ang, that a recurring imaginative struggle with an essentially unchangeable status quo provides at least an innocent, at best a valuable addition to these viewers' lives. As quoted above, "Perhaps the women are all right as they are!" Clearly, *90210* took seriously an aspect of these viewers' experience, as Fiske suggested, and as viewers talked about that, they felt empowered and valued. And, as Brown pointed out, talk about a television show was action, especially in the way that it worked to form community.[1] And for the viewers I

1. This review will not touch on studies of fanzines, fan clubs, and other organized fan behavior. Radway (1994) and Jenkins (1988) seem to offer good evidence that those who literally *produce* texts—romances or fanzines—indeed find through these materials ways of exploring and interrogating dominant ideologies. Indeed, this position represents an important shift in Radway's thinking, reminiscent of McRobbie's change of heart. In the

listened to, community was an important element in both power and pleasure.

I wanted to incorporate these aspects of the viewing experience into my analysis. However, it was difficult to reconcile the active, enthusiastic, pleasurable talk about a polysemic text with the ways in which this talk worked hegemonically to perpetuate dominant gender and consumer norms. The issue of agency with which this chapter began reappeared even more urgently in ways that these theories do not seem to resolve. When is a woman empowered by her pleasure, activity, and community, and when is she a victim of it?

Indeed, some theorists recently have criticized the celebration of the resistant reader and rejected the notion that resistance equals agency. McGuigan (1992) called this move a "drift into uncritical populism" (p. 70) and cited Fiske as a prime offender:

A satisfactory theory of television, I would suggest, needs to account for the multi-dimensional interaction of production and consumption at both economic and symbolic levels, giving due weight to textual diversity and audience differences, as Fiske rightly recommends. Yet, in practice, Fiske merely produces a simple inversion of the mass culture critique at its worst, thereby reducing television study to a kind of subjective idealism, focused more or less exclusively on "popular readings," which are applauded with no evident reservations at all, never countenancing the possibility that a popular reading could be anything other than "progressive." (p. 72)

McGuigan blasted Fiske for contributing to what he called the "new revisionism," where themes of audience empowerment, pleasure, and popular discrimination mark a retreat from more critical positions.

In a similar indictment of much cultural studies work, a critique that pinpointed the central contradiction over agency with which I wrestled, Grossberg (1993) acidly criticized studies in which "the assumption that people are active and capable of struggle and resistance becomes an apparent discovery, and the important empirical questions, of the concrete contextual effects of such practices, are left unanswered" (p. 95). Morley (1993) agreed that there is a "difference between having power over a text, and power over the agenda within which that text is constructed and presented" (p. 16). Indeed, Ang (1990) came herself to support this position, maintaining that "audiences may be active, in myriad ways, in

---

1994 article, Radway calls for a "new politics of the romance that could ally feminist critics with romance writers and readers in the project of defending daydreams like the romance as a space where important critical and utopian work gets done" (p. 217). This position will be examined more closely in the next chapter. Here, I will continue to pursue my interest in what counts as resistance on the part of ordinary readers. Like Brown, I want to look at ways in which talk about television shows works in the daily lives of viewers.

using and interpreting media . . . [but] it would be utterly out of perspective to cheerfully equate 'active' with 'powerful'" (cited in Morley 1993, p. 16).

After two decades of wrestling with the conflicting issues of agency and resistance, pleasure and power, community and activity vis-a-vis viewing, cultural studies researchers were still seeking a theory of agency that would reconcile them.

It was this difficulty that propelled me toward theorists who focused on discursive agency—on talk as action. I suspected that these theories had the potential to provide a more subtle way of thinking about agency, resistance, community, and even pleasure. In treating talk as both data and action, social construction allows the researcher to build a persuasive case for the connection—or lack thereof—between viewing and agency. Moreover, many of these theories address the notion of identity, an issue I suspected played a key role in viewers' experience of *90210*.

The central tenets of theories about the discursive construction of identity, and ways in which these theories reflect on the issues of agency and community, are discussed in the next chapter.

Chapter 4
Social Construction:
The Discursive Self

On turning to poststructuralist and postmodern theory with my research agenda in mind, I discovered—as in the mass communication field— a wide range of theories addressing the issues that interested me. As I delved into the literature, I decided to focus on the social constructionists for two reasons. (1) These theorists grounded their work on giants of European thought whose insights generated most postmodern and poststructuralist theory, and whose thought also lies at the roots of cultural studies work; and (2) they were particularly interested in the issue of identity. My initial intuition was that talk about *90210* involved identity work for teens and college students, and I became convinced that the ways social constructionists talked about identity would help clarify and solidify my analysis.

Social construction begins by questioning Western culture's notion that we each have a unique inner self that is the author of our private thoughts and feelings. While our ideas and emotions may be private in the sense of not necessarily communicated to others, social construction points to ways that culture and language "author" them, not solely we ourselves. Our inner life is not wholly the product of the autonomous self, but rather is shaped by the ways we have to express it, and by the communities that give it meaning. The pleasure or pain we feel around an event or object stems in large measure from the way it is valued in our community. A helpful example might be the way we take for granted our notions of what is appropriate. We can be outraged, disgusted, or embarrassed by inappropriate behavior. These sensations are "ours"—but they arise from a communal agreement on what is appropriate. American women sometimes feel intensely uncomfortable at the notion of the topless beaches that many Europeans take for granted. While our sense of discomfort and/or embarrassment can be powerful and meaningful, in an important way we are not the "authors" of these feelings. Instead, they arise in large measure out of a communal agreement on what these sensations are called and when they are appropriate.

Social constructionists emphasize the importance of language and other symbol systems in creating and maintaining "reality." Agreement on what is appropriate beach-wear is continually constructed, negotiated, and bolstered by, for example, media images and interpersonal talk. In this sense, then, symbolic representations including language work to construct our notion of what is real. Talk is action. As Edwards and Potter (1992) put it, "In saying and writing things, people perform social actions" (p. 28). Or, as Berger and Luckmann (1967) more picturesquely state:

Language now constructs immense edifices of symbolic representations that appear to tower over the reality of everyday life like gigantic presences from another world. . . . Language is capable not only of constructing symbols that are highly abstracted from everyday experience, but also of "bringing back" these symbols and appresenting them as objectively real elements in everyday life. In this manner, symbolism and symbolic language become essential constituents of the reality of everyday life and of the commonsense apprehension of this reality. (pp. 40–41)

Culture, language, and other signs impinge also on our identity—who we think, and say, we are. The self is a "construction" of language and communal meaning. This chapter begins by exploring the workings of this process, which I call the discursive construction of identity.

A key theme in this discussion, and one that will be central to my study, is the nature and importance of narrative in identity construction and community formation. Therefore, this chapter also explores some of the ways narratives offer us to construct ourselves and our world, and it gives an overview of some dominant narratives that structure Western culture. In addition, dominant notions of female identity within those narratives are outlined. Finally, I revisit the issue of agency.

Discourse, Self-Narrative, and Community

The discursive construction of self has been explored by a long line of theorists such as Wittgenstein, Adorno, Horkheimer, Saussure, Habermas, and Derrida. This approach directly challenges the traditional psychological practices that are cultural currency in the Western world, which posit an individual who is self-contained and separate from others, possessed of a unique inner life that can be revealed to others through the relatively transparent medium of language (for an explanation of this position, cf. Edwards and Potter 1992). Social constructionists challenge this psychological model. Sampson (1992), for example, went so far as to say that this "individual" actually was created by the traditional practices of psychology. The psychological "subject" of the European post-Enlightenment tradition is a discursive construct, Sampson argued; in studying it and reporting "facts" about it, psychologists not only create the "truth" they purport to find, but in the process perpetuate that "truth":

Psychology's subject is a character designed primarily to serve ideological purposes. . . . Psychology, in studying that character and presenting so-called "facts" about its qualities, helps contribute primarily to societal reproduction rather than truly to human betterment. (p. 2)

John Shotter (1993) expanded that position, challenging the traditional Western assumption that the individual has a private inner life that represents outer realities. We think of the meanings we make in our inner world as relatively unproblematically reflecting outer reality, he pointed out:

In the West, in our everyday, practical talk about ourselves, we take a great number of things for granted. And in our traditional forms of inquiry into ourselves and the nature of our everyday social lives, in psychology and sociology, we have codified these "basic" ways of talking into a number of explicit assumptions: for instance, we take it that we are self-contained individuals, having minds that contain "inner mental representations" of possible "outer" circumstances, set over against other such similar individuals, and against a social and natural background lacking such cognitive ability. (p. 4)

These outer realities, however, have meaning not in and of themselves, but in the context of a specific culture. Shotter suggested that all socially significant dimensions of life, including how we think and talk about our world, are co-constituted in interaction with others, not in the abstract. Like the concept of appropriateness, a given situation or behavior does not gain meaning from the private inner world of the individual alone. Instead, the meanings that comprise this inner world are culturally co-constructed—in part, in the language we have to express them:

It could be argued that in adulthood [people] . . . come to act individually and autonomously in terms now of their own inner mental representations. But even as adults acting all alone, people still face the task of making what they do relevant. . . . [I]t is the joint activity between them and their socially (and linguistically) constituted situation that "structures" what they do or say, not wholly they themselves. (p. 8)

Shotter argued that our culture presents itself to us in rational and individualistic terms. But the very discourses of science and individualism conceal their own role in structuring the sense we make of our world, Shotter maintained. Many of the meanings we attach to objects and events appear to be simple common sense, rather than communally constructed and reified (made to appear real and natural). Of course, topless beaches make us uncomfortable. This statement conceals the role of culture in constructing what counts as appropriate. We take for granted that we have unique inner realities and identities—and that we are the authors of our ideas about, for example, what is appropriate dress for the beach.

Shotter maintained that our individuality—our collection of traits, attributes, and inner mental states—is *not* the basis for the way we interact with others and the external world. Actually, he said, things work the other way around: Our identities are co-constructed by our culture, which offers us definitions, for example, of masculine and feminine, and rules about gendered behaviors. These definitions and rules are constantly being negotiated, but at any given time, existing norms inflect the meanings we make in important ways.

And language and other signs are an important location for this co-construction of identity. In Western society, we have certain ways of speaking about ourselves in relation to other people; these meanings help construct our identities. Who "they" are implicitly defines who "we" are, and vice versa. Shotter focused attention on unwritten cultural rules, the "practical moral knowledge" of what it takes to be human in our society: "In learning how *to be* a responsible member of certain social groups, one must learn how *to do* certain things in the right kind of way: how to perceive, think, talk, act, and to experience one's surroundings in ways that make sense to the others around one" (p. 46).

Social constructionists believe that identity does not flow from an internal well, an inviolate inner self, despite the fact that we habitually speak as if it did. Rather, they maintain, identity talk is a re-expression of self in terms that already have social currency. As Gergen (1991) put it, "To write or speak is not, then, to express an interior world, but to borrow from the available things people write and say and to reproduce them for another audience" (p. 105). Or, as Burman and Parker (1993) put it:

Language . . . has an immense power to shape the way that people . . . experience and behave in the world. Language contains the most basic categories that we use to understand ourselves; affecting the way we act as women or as men (in, for example, the sets of arguments that are given about the nature of gender difference deployed to justify inequality), and reproducing the way we define our cultural identity (in, for example, the problems and solutions we negotiate when we try and define who we are as a member of a minority group). When we talk about any phenomenon (our personality, attitudes, emotions), we draw on shared meanings. (p. 1)

This way of thinking about identity is full of possibilities for analysis of girls' and young women's talk about *90210*. It suggests that this talk can be analyzed, not for the psychological processes that underlie what the viewers say, but rather for the cultural taken-for-granteds that underpin the way viewers' talk orders and makes sense both of the show and of their own world. Talk about fictional characters and situations both produces and makes possible certain ways of being in the world and relating to others, certain identities, and the same talk conceals and closes off other possibilities. This understanding of the way in which interaction works to construct identity provides a lens through which to scrutinize active viewers working on texts to open up identity possibilities, and hegemonic texts winning consent of viewers to dominant notions of female identity.

In addition, social construction theory offers another take on community. In the last chapter, I described ways in which mass media researchers have argued that communities of soap opera fans provide social support for interrogation of dominant norms. Here, I will raise the notion of community to the discursive level. Using Shotter's (1993) suggestion that community has to do with a discursive construction of who "we" are, as opposed to who "they" are, I looked at ways in which viewer talk created community, not only with each other but also with the characters. This theory helped me foreground ways viewers discursively grouped themselves, not just with their friends, but with Kelly, Brenda, Donna, Andrea. The talk created and sustained new relationships between viewer and character that in turn cycled back into the meanings viewers made of their own lives. And in discursively grouping herself with a character, a speaker joins a community whose values are set by the text, even as the viewer takes authorship of the discursive link—it is *I* who have recognized myself in the character, not the producers and advertisers who have seduced me into normalizing this beautiful, youthful blonde, this upper-class lifestyle, and this preoccupation with gossiping, shopping, and dating.

To this discussion, Anthony Giddens (1991) added the notion of self-narrative, which he maintained is one of the most important processes in discursive construction of identity. Developing a self-narrative allows us to function in a world of possibilities, Giddens maintained. Citing Freud's psychoanalytic theories and D. W. Winnicott's sophisticated expansion of them, he defined this self-narrative as a practical consciousness that brackets the prospect of being overwhelmed by the complexities of our existence. Self-narratives bind and order meanings to construct a stable world and a coherent identity. "Self-identity is not a distinctive trait, or even a collection of traits, possessed by the individual. It is the self as reflexively understood by the person in terms of her or his biography" (p. 53).

A person with a reasonably stable sense of self-identity has a feeling of biographical continuity which she is able to grasp reflexively and, to a greater or lesser degree, communicate to other people. That person also, through early trust relations, has established a protective cocoon which "filters out," in the practical conduct of day-to-day life, many of the dangers which in principle threaten the integrity of self. Finally, the individual is able to accept that integrity as worthwhile. (p. 54)

This protective self-narrative is at once fragile and robust: "Fragile, because the biography the individual reflexively holds in mind is only one story among many other potential stories that could be told about her development as a self; robust, because a sense of self-identity is often securely enough held to weather major tensions or transitions in the social environments within which the person moves" (p. 55). Citing Erving Goffman, Giddens added that this cocoon also requires considerable maintenance. And the construction and maintenance of self-narrative is a continuous and reflexive process. We constantly remake the meanings of past, present, and future events and expectations.

Giddens extracted and scrutinized self-narratives specific to our culture by studying self-help literature. Primary among the narratives he pinpointed was the notion that the self is a reflexive project, for which the person is responsible. This reflexivity is continuous and all-pervasive, and is based on a narrative of development from the past to the anticipated future. Part of this narrative is the "ideal self," which he said forms a channel of positive aspirations in terms of which the narrative of self-identity is worked out. Giddens highlighted a central contradiction in this process (though he did not put it this way). We continuously and reflexively construct and reconstruct our self-narratives, treating our bodies as projects for which we are responsible, and doing what he called "colonizing" our past, present, and future—mentally ordering and valuing our memories, our current meanings, our hopes, desires, and fears. But at the same time we cling to a moral thread of authentic self-actualization based on "being true to oneself." Even though we are always reconstructing our self-narratives, we continue to maintain that we have an inner, authentic "self" to which we can be true.

I used this theory to study of ways in which viewer construction of fictional and cultural narratives work to colonize her past, present, and future by offering her specific ways of attending to her life, and concealing or closing down others. Social construction permitted me to examine ways in which "borrowed" cultural narratives of identity cycled through talk, although this borrowing was concealed by a discourse of authentic self-actualization—the "authoring" of opinions mentioned above. And the notion of the self as a reflexive project has important implications, for example, for the ways viewers talked about their own and the characters' appearances and personality traits. This talk combined with other aspects of the viewing process to provide an important way of both attending to the show and attending to oneself.

As these examples suggest, studying the mingling of fictional, cultural, and self-narratives, and the presence and function of the "authorial" voice, enriches a cultural studies approach to media experiences. The next sections isolate some specific cultural narratives that underpin Western culture.

Narratives of Community and Autonomy

Two important narratives that have shaped Westerners' understanding of our world, particularly in the United States, are those of community and autonomy. A clear example of the way these narratives underpin the lives of Americans was presented by Bellah et al. (1985), who talked with middle-class individuals across the country on the subject of their private and public lives. These authors came up with four meta-narratives that they said exist simultaneously in our culture but that sometimes clash with each other, causing deep confusion.[1] Drawing on historical writings, they called these narratives (1) the biblical tradition, in the words of founding father John Winthrop, which means "always having before our eyes our community as members of the same body" (p. 28); (2) the republican tradition, which emphasizes, in the words of Thomas Jefferson, "equal and exact justice to all men" (p. 31); (3) utilitarian individualism, epitomized by Benjamin Franklin, which emphasizes the importance of the American opportunity for individuals to get ahead on their own initiative; and (4) expressive individualism, exemplified by Walt Whitman, which seeks a life "rich in experience, open to all kinds of people, luxuriating in the sensual as well as the intellectual, above all a life of strong feeling" (p. 34).

These authors highlighted the contradictions inherent in these four traditions. In the voices of the people they interviewed, they heard both "the deep desire for autonomy and self-reliance combined with an equally deep conviction that life has no meaning unless shared with

1. Critics (cf., for example, Stout 1988) have suggested that the authors' methodology elicited these narratives. Nevertheless, the narratives remain interesting to me because they articulate ideas central to our society, whether or not these tales were of pressing importance to the particular interviewees credited with voicing them.

others in the context of a community; a commitment to the equal right to dignity of every individual combined with an effort to justify inequality of reward, which, when extreme, may deprive people of dignity; and insistence that life requires practical effectiveness and 'realism' combined with the feeling that compromise is ethically fatal" (p. 150). The narratives that are central to our culture present a key clash between autonomy and community that is imperfectly understood and hard to articulate. The solution, Bellah et al. suggested, is a rejection of individualistic language.

We believe that much of the thinking about the self of educated Americans, thinking that has become almost hegemonic in our universities and much of the middle class, is based on inadequate social science, impoverished philosophy, and vacuous theology. There are truths we do not see when we adopt the language of radical individualism. We find ourselves not independently of other people and institutions but through them. (p. 84)

The authors called for "a language in which we could all, men and women, see that dependence and independence are deeply related, and that we can be independent persons without denying that we need one another" (p. 111). They concluded that what is needed is the recovery of a "genuine tradition, one that is always self-revising and in a state of development" (p. 283), that is, the biblical and republican, with its goal of the common good. The alternative to individualism, they maintained, is the constituted self, which has encumbrances that make connection to others easier and more natural. This type of self is produced by a community of memory, which is "involved in retelling its story, its constitutive narrative" (p. 153). Through these communities of memory, individuals can exhibit a "form of individualism that is fulfilled in community rather than against it" (p. 162). A shared narrative of the past is key not only to creating community but to making autonomy possible.

These authors stopped just short of the social constructionist position that language co-constructs our identities. However, they emphasized that the way we speak about ourselves, and the narratives on which we base our lives, are key to who we are. And a central problem with the narratives dominant in our society lies in the conflict they construct between self and community. These authors maintained that we need to create a narrative that will permit us to fulfill our individuality through community. And the solution, therefore—although they did not specifically say so—can be seen as a shift in the language of the narratives we tell about ourselves. Agency is moved to a discursive level; discursive agency is changing the narrative. In this study, I argue that the language of individualism and the desire for community play an important role in concealing the ways talk about a television show can colonize our dreams and desires, thoughts and actions.

These issues also were addressed in a sophisticated manner by Gergen (1991), who provided perhaps the most comprehensible statement of the social constructionist take on dominant Western narratives. Gergen's thesis was that the proliferation of technology, especially in the fields of communication and transportation, has not only increased the amount of information we receive but has also expanded the potential relationships in which we can engage. Each day, he maintained, we absorb a multiplicity of different voices and viewpoints. These in turn endow us with a large repertoire of behaviors which, given the right conditions, we can enact. This situation is problematic, he said, because these varied behaviors are fragmented. Thus, for example, a white person may work alongside a black person every day and even hold a high opinion of that co-worker, and then attend KKK meetings at night, without perceiving a contradiction.

The reason for this perplexing fractionalization, Gergen said, is that twentieth-century culture continues to be dominated by two major vocabularies of the self that have been outmoded by technology. The nineteenth-century romanticist view, "one that attributes to each person characteristics of personal depth: passion, soul, creativity, and moral fiber," is necessary for deeply committed relationships, dedicated friendships, and life purposes (p. 6). However, in the modernist worldview, which Gergen traced to the beginning of the twentieth century, the chief characteristics of the self reside in our ability to reason: The self is rational, well-ordered, and accessible (p. 38). "Modernists believe in educational systems, a stable family life, moral training, and rational choice of marriage partners" (p. 6).

Our failure to recognize that the romanticist and modernist worldviews are not only contradictory but ultimately unsatisfactory has led to the fracturing of ourselves. Most people accept and live out aspects of either or both of these worldviews, even though social saturation has moved us into what Gergen called the postmodern world, which does away with the concept of an "authentic self" with constant, knowable characteristics. In the postmodern world, we carry others' patterns of being with us; given the right conditions, we can turn these patterns into action. "Each of us becomes the other, a representative, or a replacement" (p. 71). "The fully saturated self becomes no self at all"; we exist in a state of continuous construction and reconstruction; "anything goes that can be negotiated" (p. 7). Here, "one ceases to believe in a self independent of the relations in which he or she is embedded" (p. 17); the concrete entity of self disappears and is reconstructed as a relationship. To hold values is to close off options. "The problem with values is that they are sufficient unto themselves. To value justice, for example, is to say nothing of the value of love; investing in duty will blind one to the value of spontaneity" (p. 77).

In the postmodern world, Gergen concluded, a rich and meaningful life is found by "suspending the demands for personal coherence, self-recognition, or determinant placement, and simply *being* within the ongoing process of relating" (p. 133). Fulfillment is found as "the individual slowly disappears into the greater dance of communal life" (p. 110). Gergen finessed the problem of individuality vs. community by emphasizing the socially constructed nature of the individual and calling for a language that would permit us to talk about ourselves that way.

This rejection of autonomy and emphasis on the importance of community has interesting gender implications, since relationality has long been constructed as a female trait and, and such, devalued. The conflict between autonomy as a masculine trait and community as a feminine one has been articulated from a psychological perspective by Gilligan. In her early work, Gilligan (1982) was concerned to justify women's emphasis on relationality (i.e., community) over our culture's strong individualistic narratives (Bellah et al.'s utilitarian individualism, or Gergen's modernism). Citing Freud, Erikson, Piaget, and Kohlberg, among others, Gilligan argued that psychologists and scholars have defined identity formation in masculine terms, emphasizing separation and individuation over relationality and empathy. Kohlberg and Turiel (1971), for example, developed six stages of moral development, which show a development from a personal and social orientation (good is what feels pleasant, what satisfies one's own needs, or what preserves the social order) to a value for autonomy, individual rights, and an accord with "self-chosen ethical principles appealing to logical comprehensiveness, universality, and consistency" (p. 416). The mature male is autonomous and individuated, and by this yardstick women's development is seen as lacking or defective. As Gilligan (1982) described it:

The quality of embeddedness in social interaction and personal relationships that characterizes women's lives in contrast to men's, however, becomes not only a descriptive difference but also a developmental liability when the milestones of childhood and adolescent development in the psychological literature are markers of increasing separation. Women's failure to separate then becomes by definition a failure to develop. (p. 9)

Gilligan (1982) maintained that females develop in a way that is different but just as legitimate as males: For women, moral maturity and successful identity formation are reflected by an emphasis on relationship and care. The mature woman sees herself in a "dynamic of inter-dependence," in which she has a mandate to "act responsively toward self and others and thus to sustain connection" (p. 149).

Gilligan, Lyons, and Hanmer (1990) expanded on this theme by look-ing at ways in which the clash between community and autonomy is particularly difficult for adolescent girls. "Adolescence poses problems of connection for girls coming of age in Western culture, and girls are tempted or encouraged to solve these problems by excluding them-selves or excluding others—that is, by being a good woman, or by being selfish" (p. 10). Without explicitly putting it this way, Gilligan identified two narratives that clash in female adolescent development: the domi-nant narrative that "good" females put others first, and the utilitarian individualism identified by Bellah et al. emphasizing separation. Gilli-gan et al. put it this way: "For girls to remain responsive to themselves, they must resist the conventions of feminine goodness; to remain re-sponsive to others, they must resist the values placed on self-sufficiency and independence in North American culture" (p. 10).

In struggling with these narratives, girls lose contact with their own voices, the authors maintained: "Adolescence is a critical time in girls' lives—a time when girls are in danger of losing their voices and thus losing connection with others, and also a time when girls, gaining voice and knowledge, are in danger of knowing the unseen and speaking the unspoken and thus losing connection with what is commonly taken to be 'reality'" (p. 10). The authors observed with concern that the narra-tive of the autonomous individual in a world of abstract justice silenced the relational voice in the girls they interviewed, even though these girls felt relationality to be a moral imperative:

> If what is morally imperative for them, or what defines and sustains their "moral identity," is not valued or considered truly "moral" by the culture at large, one would expect a loss of trust in the self's perspective and judgment and the self's moral integrity. . . . The loss may be of a sense of self as a moral, caring self and of trust in a logic of interdependence and responsiveness derived from personal experience. (pp. 107–8)

Formal education, the authors said, played a role in the loss of the relational voice. The educational experience separates thinking from relationships and thus makes a division between classroom learning, which is valued, and powerful relational learning experiences, which is not. For this reason, the authors said, adolescent girls "often seem di-vided from their own knowledge, regularly prefacing their observations by saying, 'I don't know'" (p. 14).

Resonating with the views of Bellah et al., Giddens, and Gergen, Gilligan et al. (1990) called for a morality based on a balance between abstract and relational justice, which they called a counterpoint of justice and care. Rejecting the patriarchal dualizing of the two, in which the former is valued over the latter, they suggested that both should be valued in harmony: "We mark the orchestration of justice and care voices as a sign of moral maturity" (p. 322).

This work suggested to me that a focus on relationality versus abstract justice, as I listened to talk about moral issues, could be fruitful. However, I will differ with Gilligan's explanation. She was working with a psychological model of identity rather than a social constructionist one; thus, her interpretation of her findings was slightly different from the way I ultimately decided to handle such issues. She argued that, in separating justice and care and devaluing the latter, girls lost a "true" voice. Since social constructionists regard all voices as recirculations of cultural themes, I prefer to regard the "justice" voice as a certain way of being in the world that is culturally associated with males, and the "care" voice, that defines the self relationally, as one traditionally associated with females.

Nevertheless, Brown and Gilligan's (1992) look at the disadvantages of the extreme form of the feminine "care" voice is helpful for the ways it describes processes I too observed. In a study of 100 girls between the ages of 7 and 18, they emphasized the destructive aspects of idealized relationships, maintaining that pressure on the girls to be "nice" and to stay in relationships caused them to lose connection with their own feelings, especially the negative ones. The youngest girls strongly expressed negative feelings, but the older ones seemed careful to avoid conflict and to emphasize a self-narrative that is "nice": "Neeti seems to have taken in a conventional, authoritative voice and is modeling herself on the image of the perfectly nice and caring girl" (pp. 38–39). These girls were more likely to stay in relationships in which they were hurt, and more willing to silence themselves rather than to risk loss of relationships by public disagreement. And this desire to be "nice" was manifested in conformity: "'I hardly ever get into fights with my friends,' Judy says with pride, 'because we both usually like the exact same things and we do the exact same things.' . . . Indeed, liking and doing the exact same things seems to protect Judy from the danger of feeling strong feelings that she knows have the potential to disrupt and destroy relationships" (p. 126).

This work suggests that a dominant notion of what it takes to be female is to be "nice" and to sustain community and relationships through conformity and conflict avoidance. This mandate appeared frequently in the voices I listened to, as did concern with the complications and disadvantages of overemphasizing it. Treating relational morality as a "feminine" way of positioning the self helps highlight that cultural narrative of femininity. The next section explores other dominant narratives of female identity.

Female Identity in Western Culture

A number of feminist writers have pointed out the importance our culture attaches to gender identity and the ways in which this distinction disadvantages women. More than four decades ago, pioneering feminist thinker Simone de Beauvoir noted that femininity and womanhood have long been defined referentially—not as concepts in themselves but as departures from maleness. Woman "is defined and differentiated with reference to man and not he with reference to her," she wrote in *The Second Sex*, published in America in 1953; "she is the incidental, the inessential as opposed to the essential. He is the subject, he is the Absolute—she is the Other."

Woman not only is constructed as "other," she also is relegated to inferior status. As Butler and Paisley (1980) put it:

That "woman," "female," and "she" are variants of the masculine forms becomes clear to children as they learn to read and write. Children learn than neuter nouns are implicitly masculine; variants are required to denote women: "driver," "lady driver"; "doctor," "woman doctor." Exceptions to this rule are stereotypic or unflattering: "nurse," "male nurse"; "prostitute," male prostitute." . . . The lifelong experience of women is to encounter themselves as linguistic variants or, in a literal sense, nonentities. (pp. 35–36)

One important way this "otherness" is signaled is through clothing. As Leeds-Hurwitz (1993) has noted, semioticians have used clothing as the "example of choice" to explain how non-linguistic phenomena may be read as signs (p. 108). From this point of view, clothing is seen as "a tool of the social construction of self and others" (p. 111). "People respond to individuals differently because of the way they are dressed; in cultures where gender identity is considered critical information, it is marked clearly through clothing"—even from infancy (p. 115). In our culture, many people, as Spence and Sawin (1985) reported, cite "dress and care for appearance" as important properties of "femininity." These respondents listed as "feminine" traits the "way they dress, frilly dresses, cares about appearance, pretty hairdo, neat, clean, china doll look" (p. 46), but they did not list comparable descriptions of men in defining "masculine."

These descriptors suggest that being "pretty" is an important aspect of female identity, a notion that complements Gilligan's psychological observations that girls feel an obligation in our culture to be "nice," avoid conflict, and sustain relationships. I will refer to these ideas often as "dominant notions of female identity": being pretty according to an externally imposed standard that does not promote good health or self-esteem; being nice and avoiding conflict, even if this passivity is ultimately destructive; and foregrounding relationships.

And all of these notions contribute to the idea that the ultimate purpose of being a woman is to attract a man. As Weedon (1987) put it:

> As women we have a range of possibilities. In theory almost every walk of life is open to us, but all the possibilities which we share with men involve accepting, negotiating or rejecting what is constantly being offered to us as our primary role—that of wife and mother. Whatever else we do, we should be attractive and desirable to men, and, ideally, our sexuality should be given to one man and our emotional energy directed at him and the children of the marriage. This message comes to us from a wide range of sources, for instance, children's books, women's magazines, religion, the advertising industry, romance, television, the cinema and current tax and social security arrangements. (p. 3)

This particular cultural narrative was examined in depth by Reilly (1996a), who spotlighted the intensity of the marriage expectation. She traced the representation of single women in television and movies, demonstrating the recurrent message that if a woman isn't married there is something wrong with her. Her summary culminates with the character of Alex in *Fatal Attraction*: At the end of the movie, "the camera lingers on an Ophelia image of her floating dead in the water, then pans over to a portrait of the Gallagher family, intact and healthy; here is the marginal woman and there the married woman says the camera. *Choose one*" (p. 30). In psychological language similar to Gilligan's and summing up much the same point, Reilly quotes psychologist Mary Pipher:

> She says that adolescence for a girl is a kind of personal Armageddon, a time when a girl must choose what self actually means. According to Pipher, the adolescent girl faces an unpleasant choice: she can continue to be herself and be unpopular, criticized for being too fat, too plain, too different, too self-sufficient, too outspoken, or too smart—or she can abandon the identity she's had for twelve years and become someone else, someone thin, someone painstakingly well-dressed and well-coiffed, someone quiet, group-oriented, uncertain, and unthreatening. Pipher believes that this painful, media-driven hazing process—the "crucible," she calls it—forces many young girls to their emotional and psychological knees as they prepare for the adult female role. In order to be feminine, to be liked, loved, included in the group, accepted as a woman, chosen by boyfriends, and courted by potential husbands, the young girl splits into two pieces. The first pieces is the *real self* she grew up with, which may eventually disappear; the second piece is the *false self*, which she needs in order to achieve the things that girls are supposed to achieve. And a primary achievement is, of course, a fairy-tale wedding and a happily-ever-after marriage. (p. 43)

This literature prompted me to think about the role talk about *90210* played in reifying and perpetuating, or interrogating and resisting, these dominant notions of female identity. (Indeed, Reilly explicitly cites the show as implicated in the reproduction and perpetuation of these notions!) If adolescence is a key time for identity formation; if this formation takes place on a discursive level; and if media play a part in this process, then a social constructionist analysis of talk about a television show like *90210* can shed light on the microprocesses—the "how"—of this formative activity.

Feminism and Agency

It must be admitted that the social constructionist approach, while it is valuable for the ways it directs attention to the discursive features of identity, encounters problems when it runs up against the notion of agency. The most useful move social constructionists have made in this regard is to locate agency discursively. Giddens's (1979/90) theory of structuration—which he defined as the process of production, reproduction, and transformation of structures—emphasizes that structures can be not only constraining but also enabling. Thus, a self-narrative, for example, is both produced by, and is the medium of, human action. Transforming, reconstituting, or reinstantiating structures therefore open the possibility of agency. This notion seems to undergird both Bellah et al.'s (1985) and Gergen's (1991) call for new cultural language and narratives.

Feminists have strengthened this notion by suggesting that repeated discursive constructions of alternate subjectivities—alternate ways of being female that resist aspects of the patriarchal culture not in our interests—count as female agency. As Weedon (1987) explained it, the culture offers women acceptable identities, subject positions, through which to define ourselves, and language plays an important role in this process:

Language, in the form of an historically specific range of ways of giving meaning to social reality, offers us various discursive positions, including modes of femininity and masculinity, through which we can consciously live our lives. A glance at women's magazines, for example, reveals a range of often competing subject positions offered to women readers, from career woman to romantic heroine, from successful wife and mother to irresistible sexual object. These different positions which magazines construct in their various features, advertising and fiction are part of the battle to determine the day to day practices of family life, education, work and leisure. (p. 26)

For Weedon, discursive agency means rewording and reconstructing cultural narratives, redefining the potential subject positions offered to women, so as to allow us to choose another option when a situation is disadvantaging. Discursive agency creates narratives that open up new identity possibilities for women. Weedon (1987) called this process gaining access to multiple subject positions, or ways of being. She specifically focused on the discursive aspect of agency:

Once language is understood in terms of competing discourses, competing ways of giving meaning to the world, which imply differences in the organization of social power, then language becomes an important site of political struggle. (p. 24)

For Weedon, discursive agency must be harnessed first and foremost to transform patriarchal discourses. This is accomplished through making alternative discourses available so that possibilities for change can be articulated. "Language in this sense consists of a range of discourses which offer different versions of the meaning of social relations and their effects on the individual" (p. 86). Like Bellah et al., Giddens, and Gergen, Weedon identified a series of dominant narratives (she called them forms of subjectivity). And she explicitly linked these narratives with power relations:

The forms of subjectivity open to us will variously privilege rationality, science, common sense, superstition, religious belief, intuition and emotionality. Whereas, in principle, the individual is open to all forms of subjectivity, in reality individual access to subjectivity is governed by historically specific social factors and the forms of power at work in a particular society. Social relations, which are always relations of power and powerlessness between different subject positions, will determine the range of forms of subjectivity immediately open to any individual on the basis of gender, race, class, age and cultural background. (p. 95)

She added, "Knowledge of more than one discourse and the recognition that meaning is plural allows for a measure of choice on the part of the individual and even where choice is not available, resistance is still possible" (p. 106).

Weedon concluded by calling for an increase in subject positions available to women. What we need is access to real-life choices that can help us confront situations that disadvantage us. For example, she discussed the patriarchal notion that a woman who dresses provocatively or goes out after dark alone is "asking" to be raped. This cultural narrative is reflected both in judgments about the dress and behavior of women and in the sentencing of rapists. Patriarchy offers women dominant discourses of sexuality—specific subject positions, or ways of thinking and talking about herself and others as sexual beings—that define males as naturally active and females as naturally passive, indeed, in charge of holding male sexuality in check. Alternate subject positions, in which women take charge of their sexuality and are legally and socially supported in their pursuit of those who violate it, can have important real-life implications both for rape victims and for all women, Weedon pointed out.

And, in a mandate that provided a key impetus for this study, Weedon suggested that fictional narratives can help establish alternatives. She pointed out that there are two important disadvantages to much fiction currently authored by, and targeting, women. First, she said, "much women's writing, not least of all romance, reproduces forms of discourse which place women firmly within patriarchal relations and encourage them to identify themselves with masochistic forms of femininity and of female desire" (p. 170). Second, she said, because much entertainment fiction is outside the canon of "literature," we do not tend to read it critically. Thus the narratives it tells seem more "natural"; the socially constructed nature of the values it expresses are more hidden. "The institutional marginalizing of popular fiction helps to further the myth that it is pure entertainment, a condition conducive to its ideological work" (p. 171).

Weedon called both for readers who interrogate such fiction and for fiction that pushes the bounds of patriarchy:

Women need access to the different subject positions offered in imaginative alternatives to the present, in humorous critiques and even by positive heroines. While we need texts that affirm marginalized subject positions, however, it is important to be constantly wary of the dangers of fixing subject positions and meanings beyond the moment when they are politically productive. We also need ways of reading which see texts for what they are—partisan discursive constructs offering particular meanings and modes of understanding. Feminist poststructuralist criticism can show how power is exercised through discourse, including fictive discourse, how oppression works and where and how resistance might be possible. (p. 172)

As mentioned in the last chapter, Radway (1994) also came to this position, revising her earlier stance on romance novels as working only to reinforce patriarchal power structures. In an important reflective essay, Radway maintained that romance novels could serve as a "principal site for the struggle over feminine subjectivity and sexuality and, I would argue, over feminism as well" (p. 213). This would be accomplished by novels that "construct a feminist position for white, middle-class women that would manage to envision for them autonomy and success as well as intimacy, relationality, and the opportunity for a restorative, limited dependence on a man" (pp. 219–20). Like Weedon, Radway emphasized the importance of fictional portrayals that challenge the dominant narratives of female identity and offer new subject positions for women.

This charge offered me a guide for looking at the text of *Beverly Hills, 90210* and at talk about it. An important aspect of my analysis, therefore, is an examination of the subject positions—ways of being in the world—that the show offered to females, and that the viewers constructed in their talk about it. Viewers are agents as they explore alternative subjectivities that are available in the text, and an examination of the microprocesses of this activity became an important aspect of my analysis.

Discourse Analysis

In order to operationalize this approach, which takes seriously social construction's emphasis on language as constitutive of our understanding of reality—of talk as action—I turned to work by a group of researchers whose methods fall into the loose category of discourse analysis. This term has been applied to a wide range of methodologies (for a good overview of various ways discourse has been analyzed, cf. Tracy 1991). As Burman and Parker (1993) point out, "it is very difficult to speak of 'discourse' or even 'discourse analysis' as a single unitary entity" (p. 3). However, these authors maintain, generally underpinning this approach is a concern with the way language constructs meaning:

What the different theoretical models . . . share is a concern with the ways language produces and constrains meaning, where meaning does not, or does not only, reside within individuals' heads, and where social conditions give rise to the forms of talk available. In its various forms, discourse analysis offers a social account of subjectivity by attending to the linguistic resources by which the sociopolitical realm is produced and reproduced. . . . All involve an attention to the ways in which language (as with other representational systems) does more than reflect what it represents, with the corresponding implication that meanings are multiple and shifting, rather than unitary and fixed. (p. 3)

Burman and Parker frankly confront the challenges and the advantages of discourse analysis, commenting, "Not only is the relationship between what is 'inside' and 'outside' language problematized by these approaches, but the very terms and tools of our inquiry and evaluation become matters of interpretation and debate" (p. 3). Nevertheless, this approach enabled me to treat viewer talk as a text to be analyzed, not for what the speakers "really" meant in some interior world, but rather for what it accomplished, specifically in terms of constructing identities.

It is important to reiterate that my analysis focuses on discursive identity construction, drawing on a paradigm that sets aside considerations of what the girls "really" thought in favor of highlighting the ways in which they discursively constructed themselves and others within situations and contexts. This approach accords a different kind of importance to what in other paradigms are considered intervening or confounding variables. Here all the talk generated is valuable as data. Following the social constructionists, my assumption is that nearly every statement implies identity, and talk that discursively constructs identities for "I," "me," "us," and "them" in one situation is as valid as an indicator of the potential to construct subject positions as that generated in any other situation.

Thus, in examining the transcripts of my interviews, as I read and reread the wonderfully varied and lively talk that I was privileged to record, I attempted to determine ways that meaning was both produced and constrained by asking the following questions:

(1) When talking about the show, what topics did viewers discuss, and what topics are ignored?

(2) Did the talk construct the television text as polysemic? In what ways?

(3) How did this talk work to construct female identity? (For the purposes of this study, discussion was limited to female identity, although ways that male identity is constructed are also important.)

(4) What kinds of female identities did the viewers construct? What identities were marginalized, absent, or hidden from their talk?

(5) What identities were available in the television text, and how were they made available? What identities were marginalized, absent, or hidden?

(6) Did viewers in their talk explore alternate female identities? If so, how? Were the notions of resistance and pleasure useful and/or applicable?

(7) How did the cycle work as the show offered viewers ways to attend to their own lives, and as their own lives offered them ways to attend to the show?

(8) Was there an intersection on moral grounds relative to the construction of community? How did the notions of justice and care play out in this talk?

(9) Were there patterns of talk across classes and ages? If so, what are they?

Using these questions as an entree, I was able empirically to connect talk about television and identity construction, to uncover the micro-processes by which this process operated, and to examine whether viewer talk constructed alternate subject positions (discursive agency) or worked to perpetuate dominant notions of female identity. These theories gave me a way to understand talk as action, and to see what talk about *90210* accomplished.

My analysis necessarily is positioned, and my findings naturally are open to multiple interpretations. It is my hope that not only my conclusions, but also this method of delving into television research, might prove provocative and perhaps even enlightening.

Chapter 5
Appearance: Expertise and the Community of Viewers

As *90210* fans and I settled down to watch an episode, one of the first things viewers did was to cheer or jeer a character's appearance—in particular, a female character's hairstyle or clothing. Viewing time was peppered with such comments, voiced in a striking tone of authority. Because of my interest in female identity, I decided to focus my analysis on comments about the women's appearance, which were unquestionably the most frequent.

At first glance, comments about appearance might seem superficial, or at least of marginal significance. Certainly, the viewers themselves regarded this talk as trivial. However, as I examined the transcripts more closely, using the social constructionist perspective, I became convinced that these comments worked complexly on a number of levels. Study of talk about appearance generated themes that will resound through this book. The comments created a pleasurable community among viewers that positioned the speaker as "expert," and this expertise worked unproblematically to reify and perpetuate the dominant notions of female identity described in the last chapter. In other words, this talk functioned hegemonically, winning pleasurable consent to a specific construction of the "pretty, nice" female and concealing ways in which this limited patriarchal identity can oppress women in the real contexts of our lives.

Community, Pleasure, and Expertise

Consider these typical excerpts from viewing sessions:

Show comes on.
KATEY: Didn't she used to have brown hair? It looks red.

* * *

Show plays. Brenda (talking about ring): "Brandon, relax. It's just on my right hand. Besides, Stuart insisted—"
ERIKA (interrupting dialogue): She looks awful bony.
CASEY: I don't think she's that pretty.
ERIKA: She's too pale.

* * *

Brenda (talking about eating meat): "We might as well eat our own young."
BOTH: Snigger.
KAREY: I actually like Cindy's hair right there. It looks good compared to other episodes.
MARION: Yeah. It doesn't look like a helmet anymore.
KAREY: Uh-uh.

* * *

Donna and David talking about his piano playing.
MARY: She has new hair. Cute.
CHRYSE: I liked the other kind better.

* * *

David talking about his music. Donna persuades him to take piano lessons.
KAITLIN: I like her sweater.

Seventh-grader Katey mused about a slight change in hair color; college students Marion and Karey revisited Cindy's hair when it used to "look like a helmet"; and high-school students Mary and Chryse blithely disagreed about Donna's new "do." On one level, this talk can be analyzed in ways similar to those used by, for example, Brown (1994). It worked to construct and maintain the viewer community; it provided a shared arena of experience and gave rise to a pattern of friendly talk that drew its strength from a topic of common interest; and it generated enormous pleasure as the talk flowed out, uncensored and sure of acceptance.

However, drawing on the social constructionist notion that we construct a certain type of identity by what we say, I examined how this talk positioned the speaker. I first found that this shared bond allowed another important pleasure: It positioned the viewer as expert. Viewers spoke as equals of the characters, even superior to them: Almost all of the observations about appearance were phrased unhesitatingly as declarative statements, and others' opinions were not explicitly consulted. Even Katey's question about hair color quoted at the beginning of this chapter was rhetorical ("Didn't she used to have brown hair?"). Katey didn't wait for anyone to answer and clearly didn't really expect a reply. Instead, she supplied her own response, following the question with a statement that trusted her personal perception and positioned herself as authentic source of knowledge, saying firmly, "It looks red." This confident, knowledgeable identity, a subject position probably unavailable to these girls in many other contexts, constructed them as knowing as much about appearance criteria as their friends—and more than the actors or directors!

Even a disparity of opinion about appearance, as between Mary and Chryse above, seldom resulted in conflict. At first, this seemed to indicate that the appearance-commentary community was built around a relative lack of emphasis on "right" answers. However, on closer examination, it became clear that the "right" answer was simply the act of commenting on appearance. These viewers clearly were all members of the same club, whose invisible lexicon of membership rules included not only attention to and expertise about appearance, but also knowing that appearance was important to talk about. Almost never did they talk about the background music, for example, except for the occasional mocking comment ("music, music, music!") during the stock soap-opera close-up at the end of a scene, and one time when viewers identified a rock group heard in the background. Similarly, characters' diction or speech patterns were never mentioned (with one notable exception described in the chapter on guessing), even though these patterns differed considerably from viewers' own. (For example, there was a noteworthy absence in dialog of such words as "like" and "so" that punctuated viewers' conversations.)

Moreover, the appearance comments almost never were sparked by dialog or plot lines. Indeed, as in Erika's comment above, such reactions often interrupted a scene; when compared with the show's dialog, they almost always were non-sequiturs. Curiously, characters on the show almost never comment on each others' appearance. In the early episodes, characters would sometimes be shown primping at the mirror, an activity often accompanied by self-criticism. By the time of the study, however, appearance was almost never mentioned.

Nevertheless, these viewers knew that comments on appearance were not only appropriate but applauded, and that knowledge provided an important community glue. As one viewer said, "This is what we do, we talk about their clothes."

Indeed, as this statement suggests, viewers also knew exactly *which* aspects to discuss: hair, clothing, skin color, makeup, and one specific facial feature, the eyebrows. In over 500 pages of transcripts, the words "teeth," and "nose" never appeared in reference to character's or actor's appearance, except in one specific incident dealing with a handicapped character that will be examined in the chapter on guessing. In terms of women's facial features, viewers targeted eyebrows alone:

Brenda enters.
JEANNETTE: Her eyebrows are so thick!
KRISTEN: But they're thick and puffy!
* * *
MARION: Brenda looks like (garbled). What's with that black eyebrows?
* * *
Donna crying because her dog died.
BOTH: Laughter
KAREY: Her eyebrows are scary.

In an interesting intertextual aside, in an interview with *TV Guide*, actress Shannen Doherty (Brenda) commented on her own eyebrows in the early episodes, saying, "I'm dying. [. . .] I look so different! Before I discovered tweezers!" (Smith, 1994).

Less frequent but definitely present were comments about makeup:

KAITLIN: She has so much makeup on in this one, though.
MARY: Yeah, she doesn't have makeup in the other one.
KAITLIN (addressing screen): That's not a good lipstick for you.

Other aspects of bodily appearance were never discussed. The women's eyebrows and a very occasional mention of weight, as in Erika's criticism of Brenda ("she looks awful bony") were the limits of the talk about physical features. Characters' height was never mentioned (one time I brought it up; the resounding silence that followed it helped me realize I had unwittingly broken a community rule). Moreover, the hours at the gym and salad bar that clearly lay behind the actresses' uniformly slender Stepford appearance aroused no speculation. To me, it is astonishing that Shannen Doherty, who plays Brenda, was reported in the Liz Smith article to weigh 92 pounds. Indeed, those in the television business say that thinness is an absolute bottom-line criterion to get cast on a show like *90210*: "I see a lot of actresses who are incredibly talented and very sexy, but if they are not thin enough, I can't bring them further," casting director Lindsay Chag told *People* (Schneider et al. 1996). However, the comments I heard about female appearance foregrounded hairstyles, makeup, clothing, and eyebrows—all aspects that in our consumer culture can be changed with relative ease and reasonable cost.

The text is implicated in this process. Very seldom were characters shown exercising; what the camera played up was the cosmetology. The frequent costume changes over the course of each episode made *90210* on one level a virtual fashion show. Moreover, hairstyles, eyebrows, and clothing did evolve over the course of four seasons, incidentally providing chronological clues that astute viewers tracked. As one young woman said, "We can like look at Donna's hair, or look at Brenda's hairstyle, and be like, 'Oh, that was from two years ago.'" These manipulations on the part of the producers and actors, while not part of the dialog or action of the show, certainly provided a subtext that foregrounded the specifically changeable aspects of appearance and the desirability of certain possessions. The text's decorative elements present a clear invitation to comment, which viewers eagerly accepted:

Show plays.
KATEY: That's a nice car.

* * *

Show plays.
ERIKA: Like I can't imagine a college student having an apartment like David has.

Viewers knew it was important to comment on appearance and consumer status—and they knew what aspects to target.

Along with this expert voice was a sheer and uncomplicated pleasure as they looked at so much personal beauty. As one viewer said, "Well, probably, the biggest attraction immediately was they're all good-looking people." In talking about Kelly as her favorite character, one viewer (whose hair was quite dark) rhapsodized about Kelly's blonde hair, while her sister praised Kelly's eyes:

MADDY: Yeah, I love her hair.
SANDY: I like Kelly's eyes.
G: (to Sandy) Yeah?
MADDY: I like her hair.
G: She has dark eyes, doesn't she?
SANDY: I thought they were green.
G: Oh, are they green?
SANDY: I think.
MADDY: I like her hair, 'cause I love the color of her hair.
G: Yeah?
MADDY: It's just so light. Mmmm, it's, like, not even dark. Just all light.

"Mmmm [. . .] not even dark. Just all light." A pure, sensual pleasure suffused this description. It was enjoyable for these viewers simply to watch the beauty of the characters, the shifting kaleidoscope of the way they moved and dressed and did their hair.

And, as this excerpt suggests, as viewers pleasurably commented on appearance in an expert voice, they naturalized certain appearances, but not others, as desirable for oneself. Interviewees said they would like to be as pretty as Kelly or Donna, or knew people who felt that way (the second excerpt below is from an interview with twins Marissa and Melanie, whose voices were so alike on the tape as to be indistinguishable):

G: Are there ways you wish you were more like her [Kelly]?
JEANNETTE: She's really pretty.

* * *

M: I know some people that try to look like, um, Kelly.
G: Really?
M: Yeah.
G: Why do you think they do that?
M: Because she's—
M: She's pretty.
M: Pretty.
G: Yeah.

They constructed for themselves Giddens's (1991) notion of the body as reflexive project, with media representations as the model. Indeed, one viewer explicitly said she used the show as a source of ideas about her appearance:

ESTHER: I always want to compete with other people. So when I watch television shows, it's like, "Oh, that girl's wearing this, I'll go try that."
G: Uh huh.
ESTHER: Or I'll go get the new haircut that they have.
G: Oh, wow?
EMILY: Like when Donna got her hair cut, that's when I got my hair cut.

This talk positioned the viewers as active, as authors of their meanings and behaviors. They stated a simple truth: Kelly is pretty. Never did they suggest that their definition of "pretty" came from anywhere except themselves, that this particular combination of height, weight, features, body shape, and hair color available to only a fraction of women on this planet came with any value implications. As they expertly "authored" their opinions, they perpetuated this system in which, as feminists have pointed out, we set ourselves impossible standards, then denigrate ourselves when we don't measure up.

Embedded in this talk was a fascinating and, to me, disturbingly contradictory relationship between appearance as superficial and able to be changed, as suggested above, and appearance as a key identity marker. Many of the viewers emphasized that, if they found a character attractive, they tended to like that character:

G: Do you have a favorite character?
MARION: I like Kelly.

G: Uh huh.
MARION: Without, without thinking too much about it the first one that springs into my mind is Kelly. So—
G: Uh huh. What do you like about her?
MARION: I think she's beautiful.

The sheer enjoyment of Kelly's beauty spread into a sense that one likes Kelly as a person *because* she is beautiful. In a more explicit example, viewers in the following conversation seemed to use "pretty" and "nice" almost interchangeably:

MADDY: I like Kelly.
G: Yeah? What do you like about her?
MADDY: She's, uh, she's nice.
G: Uh huh.
COLLEEN: She's pretty.

* * *

G: Yeah. What about Donna?
SANDY: I like her.
MADDY: She's nice.
COLLEEN: Yeah, yeah.
G: Do you?
MADDY: She's pretty.

One viewer made the collapsing of beauty, niceness, and identity even more explicit in her warm approval of Kelly:

JANE: I like, like the most characters, my favorite one is like Kelly. I like how she dresses. I like how she acts on the show.
G: Really? Do you um—like how she acts—you mean her acting or how she is, the character?
JANE: How she is.
G: Like can you give me an example what she does?
JANE: She's just so nice, that's all.
G: Yeah.
JANE: And I love how she dresses.

Another viewer clearly pinned the characters' likability to hairstyle:

G: Do you have a favorite?
KATEY: Um—probably Kelly too. 'Cause like she's the prettiest out of all of them. But sometimes Donna, she can be pretty. Like it depends on what her hair looks like.
ALL: Laughter.
KATEY: Sometimes she can *not* look pretty.

G: Yeah. And then you don't like her?
KATEY: Yeah.

Viewers never said they wanted to look like Brenda or Andrea, who are not only the show's two brunettes, but also (probably not coincidentally) the "bitch" and the "brain," as opposed to blonde Kelly and Donna, who are pretty and nice. As one viewer said, "I don't know—(G: Yeah)—I don't know anybody who tries to look like Brenda." A certain specific appearance was linked to a character's identity, her core self, implying that the former is an essential feature of the latter. "Pretty" equaled "nice"; "how she acts" blurred with "how she dresses." Katey flatly said she didn't like Donna when she had a certain hairstyle. And nobody wanted to look like Brenda, the bitch, or Andrea, the brain, even though, in the great run of humanity, these actresses certainly are among the top contenders for personal beauty (Doherty, who plays Brenda, had at the time graced more magazine covers than any of the other cast members, and even made an appearance in *Playboy*).

At the same time, however, viewers frequently spoke of their own appearance as only skin deep. Esther, who said she got her hair cut when Donna did, proceeded to draw a clear distinction between her core self and her appearance:

ESTHER: Shows do not affect people, really.
G: But wait, I thought you just said that—
ESTHER: Only if you want to change your appearance.

This comment will be examined more in depth in the section about television effects. The point here is that, in talking about the show, viewers (1) positioned themselves as "experts" on appearance, (2) made appearance a central identity marker; and (3) focused on aspects of appearance that can be changed with relative ease, and suggested that changing their own appearance to conform with standards set by the characters would not essentially change their identities.

It seemed to me, as I examined this talk, that the multiple layers revealed here provide a close-up look at one of the microprocesses of hegemony, whereby what is normal and "real" is so constructed as to win active consent to a disempowering status quo. And I suspected that this discursive concealing of the inherent contradiction in judging by appearance and in constructing appearance as mutable might help understand, perhaps work towards resolving, the clash between hegemony theorists and those who theorize the active viewer.

Agency and Dominant Notions of Female Identity

Community, expertise, pleasure, and ideas about ways to change one's own hair and clothing—one could argue that talk about appearance offered these viewers numerous ways to construct themselves as empowered. These viewers forged the vibrant, accepting, and pleasurable community observed by Ang (1985) and Brown (1994), a community interpreted by those researchers as a positive source of mutual support and a possible springboard for political action. Forging a community around knowing what kinds of comments were expected, viewers accepted each other in amicable unity while sometimes being quite critical of the characters.

In addition, they actively culled ideas from the show. Eighth-grader Esther's comment about getting a haircut, for example, seems full of agency. She explored a new possibility, then felt empowered to get a family member to drive her to the hair salon and probably pay for a new haircut. Her viewing helped her to "compete with other people"—surely an active role. Her talk constructed her as an agent.

However, when analyzed from the point of view of discursive identity construction, this talk takes on a different cast. If agency is defined, with Weedon (1987), as the discursive exploration of female identities that challenge the status quo, then this talk is not agency. Instead, it perpetuates dominant notions of female identity—a woman is defined by her appearance, and she must conform to specific standards—and that are both consumerist and patriarchal.

For example, the active-seeming talk that constructed the viewer's own appearance as endlessly mutable appeared in the context of a stream of advertisements for clothing, health products and beauty aids. This talk gleefully accepted a commercially motivated invitation to participate in a specific culture that suggests identity can be polished and problems can be solved by changing hairstyles, makeup, clothing, and other accoutrements.

And perhaps most provocative for hegemony theory, the expert voice naturalized and concealed the commercial and patriarchal side of both invitation and acceptance. The examples cited here make clear the preponderance of the word "I" that resounded through the interviews. It is "I" who judge what is pretty, not the show, or the producers, or the culture that wins me to it. Viewers never questioned each other or themselves about how they came to form their opinions or motivations. A justification was neither required nor even expected. Judgments were presented as coming directly from the viewer, as somehow belonging to her and being imposed by her, with her unique background and knowledge, on the show.

Never did viewers suggest that their intricate knowledge of cosmetology (frankly unavailable to me!) was in large measure learned from the media; never did they question the media definition of "pretty," or their own unproblematic equating of appearance and identity. In discursively positioning themselves as agents in their ability to judge beauty and purchase beauty products, viewers concealed ways in which the experience of community and pleasure perpetuated the patriarchal and capitalist system. Of course, I comment on Kelly's beauty; of course, I like her and want to look like her; of course, it is I who author this desire, not the producers, camera work, lighting, etc., that seduce me into wanting it, or our patriarchal and consumerist culture that is invested in my consent to the "reality" of these pleasures and desires. This finding recurs throughout examination of talk by viewers of *90210*: viewers actively explored dominant notions and enthusiastically expropriated them, constructing themselves as authors of these desires and pleasures.

While I will argue throughout this book that this process exemplifies the microworkings of hegemony, it is worth reiterating a point made in the introduction about the adaptiveness of enculturation. It is indeed useful to know our society's norms, goals, and dreams. And I don't want to position myself as above the joys of shopping or getting a new hairdo—I myself am certainly an enthusiastic consumer. But I began to feel disturbed even about my own behavior in this regard as I realized how our consent is won to the naturalness and rightness of this particular female identity, which simultaneously closes down or marginalizes other options and silences any interrogation of the status quo.

Attending to Self, Attending to Show

Linked to this concern about the role of talk about *90210* in naturalizing a specific "pretty, nice" identity is another somewhat disturbing theme that weaves throughout this book: the discursive cycle created as viewers attended to the show based on their individual backgrounds, but then attended to their lives in ways offered them by the show.

In my early thinking about the relationship of viewer background and "read" of the text, I came down heavily on the side of Morley (1980) and Fiske (1987) in thinking that what viewers brought to the show was stronger than the meanings the text made. At first, it seemed that viewer background was all-important in the ways she attended to the characters—or, put another way, the show was certainly polysemic in the area of appearance.

For example, in one clip that I showed to most viewers, Donna has on a red beret that almost inevitably drew comments. A small sampling:

RUTH: That outfit's the worst.
COURTNEY: I know.

* * *

SANDY: I have the same hat.
[. . .]
COLLEEN: I know.
SANDY: Mine's better.

* * *

ERIKA: What is with the outfit? (Laughter)
CASEY: What? I like that.

In Sandy and Casey's world, the hat was attractive, likable; Sandy had even gone to a store and chosen one like it—but "better." In contrast, in the worlds of Courtney, Ruth, and Erika, a hat like Donna's was objectionable, "the worst." Although this study is not concerned to trace what the specific differences are that led some to praise and others to condemn, it is clear that viewer background provided a way of attending to Donna's hat. In their multivocality, these viewers certainly were not brainwashed by the television text in the specific judgments they made about character appearance.

However, on another level, they were deeply conformist. Actually, my purpose in showing the clip in which Donna wore the beret was to discuss the issue of drug addiction raised by the episode. That this dramatic encounter packed with ethical tension so reliably generated viewer talk about *Donna's outfit* took me by surprise. However, serendipitously it allowed me to see the community and expertise mentioned above—the way virtually all viewers "knew" to comment on the hat. Appearance is important for female identity, this community said, and we are authentic sources for judgments on this appearance. (Not surprisingly, the text does invite this read—the hat's bright red color, carefully reflected in Donna's lipstick, often gains emphasis through lighting and camera angle.) But even more, I realized that, even as their backgrounds led viewers to attend to the hat in various ways, their relatively consistent way of attending to the show offered viewers a way to attend to their own clothes. Viewer Sandy's hat acquired new meaning after she saw it on character Donna's head ("mine's better").

Once I began to suspect a cycle, I realized that examples of it abounded. Viewers delightedly accepted the show's invitation to foreground appearance, then enthusiastically cycled that way of attending to female identity back towards their own lives. In this next excerpt, two college students contrasted high school outfits in real life and on the show. Their talk demonstrated that their backgrounds and experiences gave them ways of attending to the show—but also how the show gave them ways of attending to their own lives:

ALISON: I've, uh, I've—we've sit there, like I used to sit there to watch it just to mock everyone out and—
ALL: Yeah, yeah.
ALISON: We'll do that. It gives you a way to make fun of what they're wearing and—
ERIKA: —see what they're wearing and—
(Garbled)
ALISON: —'cause they always wear the little slutty outfits, and it's just like, nobody in high school wears a mini-dress, you know—
ERIKA: We used to laugh at what they wear to school, you know—
ALISON: Yeah. We get out of bed we throw on some sweatshirt, jeans, and they're—
ERIKA: —all at class. They have their like mini-dresses on.

These young women "knew" that comments on clothing appropriately buttressed their community ("It gives you a way to make fun of what they're wearing")—and their lives gave them an authoritative way of attending to the outfits ("nobody in high school wears a mini-dress"). They knew the real score; they were superior to the writers, producers, and actors. There was even a moral superiority in the description of the clothes as "little slutty outfits," an aspect of female identity that will be explored more fully in the chapter on issues and morality.

But the flip side is that, even as these viewers explored a new subject position with what might be called agency, they accepted the text's formulation of that aspect of their lives: Their talk provided a way for them to attend to their own clothing. On one level, the sweatshirts they wore to class positioned them as in touch with reality, superior. However, there also was a certain wistfulness as their functional outfits were contrasted with the glamorous world of the television students. Their sweatshirts took on complex additional meanings in the context of a discursive community that generated expert comments about feminine appearance. The talk worked as a complex co-construction of self based on ways of attending to real life, ways of attending to the show, ways of discursively constructing community, and ways of positioning the self as the author of experience. Each supported the other in a cyclic relationship that generated pleasure and community while naturalizing an emphasis on personal appearance and clothing as an important identity marker.

One viewer even used her careful observation of the actors' appearance as a power move to construct herself as more perceptive than "most people." She commented on a stereotypically sexy move made in the show's opening montage by Jennie Garth, who plays Kelly:

ESTHER: Like in the credits I—you know, if you watch the beginning of it, or the end, you see Jennie, she walks like, she kind of wiggles—
G: Uh huh.
ESTHER: —right out of the screen, and it's really cute, and it really attracts me, and I don't know why. (Laughter) Most people don't notice that kind of stuff.

"Most people don't notice that kind of stuff," but Esther did. She used her painstaking attention to details of the credits to set herself apart, to construct herself as elite. And in saying she was a little different from most people because she noticed things they didn't, she attended to her own life differently. Talking about the show offered Esther a way of constructing herself as different, observant, unique. But it also, perhaps, contrasted her life with one in which women make such "cute" moves that she found so attractive—maybe even allowed her to explore the subject positions available in such a world. In short, the talk discursively constructed a particular identity in relationship to the television characters that worked pleasurably to perpetuate the show's norms of female appearance—and to conceal that process from the viewer.

This talk uncovered the microprocess by which naturalizing the status quo—accepting it as common sense—conceals and perpetuates power relations. Talk about appearance cycled the show's norms into ways of attending to the self and backgrounded the show's role in naturalizing those standards. The (to me remarkable) plethora of spontaneous comments about appearance almost always was naturalized as commonsensical—of course appearance is important to female identity. As mentioned above, one viewer said in a commercial break during viewing, "This is what we do, we talk about their clothes." This statement positions the viewer as separate from, and immune to, any real contamination through this talk. Just talking about clothes, this statement says, in no way implicates us in an endorsement of the value our society places on female appearance: We just talk, and we enjoy this talk because it positions us as superior, expert. And this expert voice worked hegemonically to conceal the naturalization of the text's standards.

The Whole Skinny Woman Thing

On one occasion, and only one, a viewer interrogated this cycle. Prep-school student Chryse, both of whose parents had advanced degrees, raised with her friends the disturbing issue of anorexia:

CHRYSE: Yeah, also for me, is the whole like skinny woman thing. It's like—
ALL: Really! (Garbled)
CHRYSE: —a big like issue in my life. Also just because, like, I feel like the whole like anorexia thing is so much bigger than anybody realizes. It's like, I don't know a single girl that I wouldn't consider like preoccupied with her weight—
MARY: They're totally obsessed with their weight. I don't—
CHRYSE: Yeah.
MARY: Except for [Kaitlin]. You're not obsessed. [Kaitlin's] the only person I know who's not obsessed with her weight. Everybody else I know is just like (sound), like that, all the time.
CHRYSE: Yeah, I mean, I feel like if I like look less at like the magazines and TV shows like that, then I don't feel as bad about it.
MARY: Yeah (garbled).
CHRYSE: But, it's really easy to just sit there and be like, you know, "Oh, she's really pretty, she's really skinny, she has like this long pretty hair, and she has all these nice clothes, and her face is perfect, I wish I could be like that."
G: Mm-hmm.
CHRYSE: You know like—
KAITLIN: Yeah, and I'm sure that happens—
CHRYSE: It's really easy to do that, even if you're like, "Don't do that, don't do that!" it still happens.
KAITLIN: Yeah, it's in the back of your head.
CHRYSE: It's impossible not to.

This powerful statement, unique in this study, truly represents an oppositional read. But its agency is colored by the suggestion that it is impossible to maintain and reinstantiate this position. Even though these young women were expressing a strong opposition to the necessity of appearing a certain way, a stance they knew was best for their mental and physical health, their voices resonated with disempowerment. "It's impossible not to" attend to one's life on the terms of the show, which values a certain type of appearance, Chryse concluded. If she watched less television and looked at fewer magazines, maybe she wouldn't "feel as bad," but, as Kaitlin said, that way of attending to self remains "in the back of your head." Chryse's resistance to "the skinny woman thing" may have crucial health implications for her ("I feel like the whole like anorexia thing is so much bigger than anybody realizes"). But the voice with which it was spoken took a disempowered stance ("Even if you're like, 'Don't do that, don't do that!' it still happens"). Her resignation contrasted disappointingly with the empowered howling, hooting, and hollering that accompanied her viewing of a show that promotes the very appearance criteria she knew she should reject.

Summary

Talk about appearances of characters and actors affords a glimpse of the ways in which talk about *90210* worked for these viewers (1) to build a community; (2) to position the self as at the center of experience—indeed, to give the self a privileged position vis-a-vis the characters, as expert and as superior; (3) to use one's own backgrounds to attend to the show; and, conversely, (4) to attend to one's own life in the show's terms. With the single exception of Chryse, as quoted above, none of the viewers questioned the notion that a particular, often impossible, standard of appearance is a vital part of a woman's identity; indeed, the viewers enthusiastically embraced the process of essentializing appearance and making judgments based upon it.

This issue of appearance highlights the ways in which we must continue to wrestle with the notion of agency. With often raucous, self-confident, authoritative voices, these girls and young women explored —indeed, stretched, amplified, and very occasionally challenged—the notions of appearance available in the television text. But this talk served mostly to perpetuate the idea—so condemned by feminists—that appearance is inextricably intertwined with identity. It is incumbent on us to be concerned with female appearance; our appearance is separate from our core selves; nevertheless, Kelly is pretty and nice, and I like her —and I want to look like her and in doing so, on a certain level, *be* her.

The girls' and young women's talk hegemonically concealed the ways in which they were hailed by an ideological subject—the pretty, nice, passive female. Rather, they constructed themselves as expert community members exploring possibilities for themselves and pleasurably weaving these possibilities into the ways they attended to their own identities and their lives. While they may have resisted certain specific portrayals of appearance, they did not resist the notion that a certain kind of appearance is central to female identity. They were swimming with the tide.

The next chapter applies these ideas to the way viewers talked about characterizations, and adds another element that will be important in the rest of the analysis—the way such talk created a community with the characters.

Chapter 6
Characterizations: Community with the Characters

Rivaling talk about appearance in its frequency and intensity was talk dissecting and exploring the characters' personalities. As I studied the almost overwhelming variety of examples of this talk, I again was initially struck by the way it demonstrated empirically the polysemy of the television text as described by Fiske (1987). Like talk about appearance, at first glance this talk seemed to support convincingly the notion that it was the viewers who "read" the text, not the text that determined viewer reading.

However, as I mulled over example after example, I ultimately came to the conclusion that this talk functioned in the same way talk about appearance, with an important addition. As with the talk examined in the last chapter, talk about characters worked to (1) establish expertise and community; (2) generate a cycle of specific ways of attending to the self and attending to the show; and in so doing, (3) operate hegemonically to reinforce certain ways of being female and not others. In addition, it worked (4) to create a community among viewer and characters that, while it seemed to empower viewers, also concealed ways it naturalized disadvantaging discourses. Once again, the issue of agency was complexly present. As in the previous chapter, I argue that to examine this talk is to uncover the microprocesses of hegemony at work.

Polysemy and Realism

The most polysemic of the characters proved to be Donna. Consider the variety in these five conversations:

DANIELLE: I like Donna too, 'cause like she's down-to-earth and every-thing—
G: Oh, yeah?

DANIELLE: —and she like [. . .] acts like a real person, like, not, not like a TV person.

* * *

G: What do you think of Donna?

JACKIE: I really don't like her that much. [. . .] She acts like she's like memorizing—she like—just memorize something. [. . .] It just doesn't seem real.

* * *

MARION: I think everybody hates her. [. . .] I can't stand her. [. . .] She's just dopey, and she's just goofy, annoyingly so, not charming goofy.

* * *

MADDY: I guess she's smart.

COLLEEN: Yeah, she's smart and nice and—

G: Uh huh.

SANDY: Yeah, nice and kind of funny sometimes.

* * *

KRISTEN: Um. I don't know. She seems sort of like, be like naive in a sense.

G: Mm-hmm.

KRISTEN: They really play her character as being like a naive airhead. You know?

It strains credulity, but Donna variously is "like a real person" or "just doesn't seem real"; she is "dopey" or "smart"; she is a "naive airhead."

The following comments by two groups of viewers with whom I watched the same episode, the one where Donna's dog died, illustrate the polysemy of the text with regard to Donna. The college students made hilarious fun of that part of the episode:

David and Donna.

NICKY: Oh Jesus.

NEWCOMER: Is the dog going to die?

NICKY: Lee—(Laughter) This is like *General Hospital.*

SHERRY: Just call the vet.

GRACEY: He has cancer.

ALL: Laughter.

(Garbled, something about animal rights)

NICKY: He's dead.

SHERRY: I'm sorry (sarcastic).

PATTI: This is ridiculous.

ALL: Laughter.

NICKY: I think he's dead.

PATTI: No longer with us.

SHERRY: That's nice. Have the dog die.

Donna crying.
ALL: Hysterical laughter.
[. . .]
SHERRY: Shouldn't they make sure that the dog stopped breathing?
ALL: Laughter.
PATTI: Call a doctor. Call a dog ambulance.

In contrast, two seventh-graders watched in empathetic silence; in response to questioning during a commercial one made these comments:

G: Is there any part of it that interested you?
PAM: The dog.
G: Yeah?
PAM: That was the best part.
G: What did you like about it?
PAM: Um, 'cause I like animals, so I guess —
G: Do you? Do you have a dog?
PAM: Mm-hmm.
G: What kind of dog do you have?
PAM: Collie.

Initially, the different identities viewers constructed for Donna seemed random, while the dog-dying episode seemed to demonstrate the not-too-surprising fact that what may interest a seventh-grader may appear risible to a group of college students. My own speculation is that Donna, at that point in the series, was intended in part to keep the youngest viewers interested. The only virgin among the main characters at the time of the study, she interacts more playfully than sexually with her boyfriend, David. As a surrogate for younger viewers, she is the one who asks the stupid questions (Take-Back-the-Night Rally Leader: "How many of you have ever been burglarized?" Donna: "Does having your purse stolen count?"). The subplots in which she is involved typically revolve around simple issues — over the course of several episodes, she adopts a dog, it dies, she is inconsolable, then her friends give her a new puppy and she is happy again. As sixth-grader Amanda said, "Like Donna and David, I think they're like the only ones that are like, like you, like you really can understand them."

To me, this accounts for the variety in the quotes above — the "goofy" behavior that so irritated college student Marion but was interpreted as "smart" and "funny" by sixth-graders Maddy and Colleen and ninth-grader Sandy. Viewer background shaped reading of a polysemic text. However, rather than asking what caused viewer "read," I prefer to ask what their reads accomplished. And close examination of the talk suggested to me that all the readings had one important point in common:

They worked to stay in the diagetic plane, preserving as much as possible the realism of the characters even if they questioned the events. The descriptors attached to Donna—"goofy," "smart," "funny," "naive airhead"—could be applied to a real person. Danielle explicitly praised Donna's realism while Jackie complained that she couldn't accomplish this link. Even the college students who acknowledged the produced nature of the show ("That's nice. Have the dog die") still treated *Donna* in terms that could be applied to a real person. The tone was light, sarcastic, trivial—but the construction of the situation remained realistic ("Just call the vet"; "He has cancer"; "Shouldn't they make sure that the dog stopped breathing?"). In their talk about Donna as a character, the older viewers who expressed so much impatience never suggested that Donna's "goofy" behavior was a production artifact of targeting a particular audience segment. Donna is "goofy" because that's how she is, not so that young viewers can understand her. While the interpretation of the characters varied widely, the effort to construct them as real was startlingly reliable.

This construction held true despite the fact that opinions varied as to what counted as realistic—the text was polysemic in this area as well. One group of viewers singled out Andrea:

PENNI: She's a great character, she really is. I really like her.
G: Yeah? What do you like about her?
[...]
PENNI: You never see her in bikinis.
SHERRY: She's very down to earth.
PENNI: Yes! She's the realistic one who doesn't have like the ribs showing.

Other viewers constructed Kelly as realistic and praised that quality:

G: Who is your favorite character?
KAITLIN: Oh, (laughing). Probably Kelly. Yeah. Kelly.
G: Why?
KAITLIN: Kelly or Donna. Well, Kelly because, I don't know, she seems like the most realistic one.

* * *

MARION: Even when, even when she [Kelly] was bitchy, though, I liked her, because she was the typical beautiful little rich girl who is really exclusive. [...] And even, even in that I thought she was just, to me the, to me the most realistic character.
G: Uh huh.
MARION: Because that's how, for the most part, that's how beautiful little rich girls were—

G: Yeah.
MARION: —they were very exclusive, you know what I mean?

Despite the variety in their judgments, what was consistent was that characters were judged to be "realistic," and this perception played a key role to viewer enjoyment of the show.

Constructing the Real

This finding is not in itself startling: Emphasis on "realism" of characters has been reported by other researchers (e.g., Hobson 1982; Ang 1985; Brown 1994). What struck me was the discursive work necessary to construct this perception. Even when viewers found it rough going, they stuck by their endorsement of character realism. As mentioned in Chapter 2, in early episodes, Kelly was the Beverly Hills snob and Brenda the naive Minnesotan. By the time of the study, however, there was general agreement that they had switched, Brenda becoming the bitch or snob, Kelly becoming nice. More consistently, Andrea was the brain and Donna was the ditz.

As mentioned, in my eyes all characters were treated relatively inconsistently (writers and actors might contend they were stretching the limits of the characters). For example, it was Brenda, in a typically Donna airhead move, who locked the keys in her boyfriend's car; Kelly becomes "bitchy" over Dylan's and Brenda's continuing friendship. Nevertheless, in each episode, characters get in at least a few zinger lines that help reinstate their stereotypes—Kelly will say something sensitive and Brenda something bitchy (*Kelly: "I know I was a bitch right when you needed me the most, and I really feel bad." Brenda: "Good."*).

Perhaps taking their cue from this intermittent reinforcement, viewers constructed the characters as realistic and stable, and they resisted the notion that the characters were changeable. Although viewers occasionally volunteered talk about changes in characters, this aspect was seldom foregrounded. As part of my prepared list of questions, I pushed them to talk about changes in the characters, and much of the talk about character changes was an artifact of my probing. (As one viewer said, in response to my insistence that she talk about these changes, "And it's so funny, 'cause it was so gradual that all of a sudden you look back and go, 'God, I remember when she was such a snob.'") However, despite the artificial nature of some of this talk, it is interesting for the ways it worked to conceal inconsistencies so that characters could be constructed as realistic.

Most viewers mentioned the same changes.

G: Do you think the show has changed in the time you've been watching it?

[. . .]

SUSIE: Kelly seemed really, really stuck up in the beginning, and she's not as stuck up any more.

[. . .]

AMANDA: Oh, David changed too.

G: Oh, yeah, how did he change?

AMANDA: Remember, he was a big dork.

G: Oh, yeah?

AMANDA: And then he became friends with them, and he tried so hard to be friends with them and everything. And then he finally became friends with them.

* * *

SANDY: He [David] like changed. Like, like a new person or something.

G: Huh.

SANDY: It's like all different and all.

G: And what did he used to be like before? I, I only just started watching it.

MIXED VOICES: He was pretty normal—didn't seem like the type to do that—

SANDY: When the show first started he was just like a little nerd—

G: Uh huh.

SANDY: —just kind of like try to of like, try to be cool—

COLLEEN: —and hang out—

SANDY: —and try to be with the like popular people.

* * *

M: Because I liked Brenda before. But now I like Kelly, 'cause Kelly always acted like a snob, like—

M: This princess.

M: But now she acts more like—

M: Now she acts more like a friend-y type person instead of like—

G: Yeah. She has kind of changed, hasn't she?

M: Yeah. Brenda acts more like a snob now.

* * *

COURTNEY: Brenda used to be—

RUTH: She used to be what?

COURTNEY: She's probably changed the most. Brenda. David's changed a lot. David was like—

G: What did he used to be like?

COURTNEY: He was a dork. They all hated him.

RUTH: Yeah, he was a dork.

Viewers worked to express character changes in ways that would make sense for real people. Just as viewers never referred to the necessity of appealing to a young audience to explain Donna's character, most tended to talk about changes in the characters from the point of view of human development. The variations in this process are particularly evident in the following exchange:

ERIKA: I think the characters have changed.
G: Oh yeah? In what way?
ERIKA: Kelly. Kelly was a real bitch in the beginning, wasn't she? Wasn't she real materialistic and—
CASEY: Yeah, she kind of was, but, yeah.
ERIKA: I think she was. Brenda has become bitchi-*er*.
G: Yeah.
ERIKA: They've alternated personalities, Brenda was very nice and naive and—
G: Uh huh.
ALISON: Yeah, in the beginning.
ERIKA: Yeah. Now she's just a bitch.
ALISON: But I think a lot of it's that they've established the character.

These viewers negotiated and explained the changes in the characters in several different ways. Erika was comfortable with the idea that the characters—qua characters—have changed; Casey was resistant to the notion that the characters have changed ("Yeah, she kind of was, but, yeah"); Alison constructed it that the characters changed initially, but now they are stabilized and firm. I probed a little to see how that construction would play out:

G: That's interesting, what you said. You mean they established the character and then they feel like they can move around in it a bit? or—?
ALISON: Well it just seems that like they—
ERIKA: You know more background—
G: Uh huh.
ERIKA: —and personality and all.
ALISON: Yeah, but I think that's just because like, when you start out as playing a role, you don't know. Like, as time goes on, there's a certain character established.

The changes in characters, initially constructed by Erika as an unguided and incomprehensible event ("they've alternated personalities") was negotiated into an ordered, even cumulative evolution ("as time goes on, there's a certain character established"). Casey was most comfortable with the latter, which she immediately seized and developed:

CASEY: Yeah, like just like in a soap opera, too, like when something will happen, and like something traumatic happens to this person, like say she was raped, like two seasons before—
G: Uh huh.
CASEY: —and you might not have watched before and everyone who has watched knows—
G: Uh huh.
CASEY: Like, "Omigod, she sees something happen of course she's going to run and tell the police"—this is like hypothetical, you know what I mean? [. . .] Things are just more understood and people know things and have that background, so they're able to move with it.

"People know things [. . .] so they're able to move with it." The right kind of viewer understands the realistic nature of these characters. If the viewer has "that background," then the changes in character can be explained and the variations in her behavior make sense.

This approach was a recurring one. Virtually all the viewers worked to explain changes in the characters as orderly and consistent—that is, realistic:

G: Has it changed or have, have the characters changed?
JEANNETTE: Uh, I think Kelly changed a lot. 'Cause she used to be, uh, she used to be really conceited—
G: Uh-huh.
JEANNETTE: All that stuff, like, "Oh, we're gonna get all these guys and—" (inaudible), you know. Now, she, she cares more about other people than herself.

Viewers constructed the changes in Kelly's character as the kinds of changes that could happen to real people ("Now, she cares more about other people than herself"). The emphasis was on constructing the characters as unified in their development, and, as such, consistent and realistic.

Occasionally, viewers reported deliberately ignoring inconsistencies, as in this conversation:

KAREY: Like we don't sit there and analyze—we had a roommate that—
MARION: —how ridiculous it is.
KAREY: —roommate that totally analyzed it to the hilt. Like I might say, "Oh God. Why is he with her? I don't understand why—" and that'll be the extent of it. Well—[Laura]: "Why do you think he's doing that? Tell me, why do you think he's doing that?" I'm like, "I don't know. This is a show."
MARION: —"show."
KAREY: And then it's finally like, "Hey, this is a show—"

MARION: Right.

KAREY: "—these aren't really this guy's thoughts."

MARION: She was like that with everything.

KAREY: I know.

MARION: [Laura]—[Laura] had no suspension of disbelief. (Laughter) She completely lacked that whole theory when it came to the media.

KAREY: She was like, she, I remember: "Well, what do you think he's—"

MARION: She was horrible.

KAREY: "—with her for? What do you think he's gonna do?" I'm like, "I don't know, watch next week." I'm like, "Jesus. It's a show, I'm enjoying it, don't take it away from me."

When pressed by their former roommate to explain the inexplicable, Marion and Karey cited the fictional nature of the episode ("Hey, this is a show"); Marion (an English major) produced the theory of suspension of disbelief, in which audiences deliberately accept or at least overlook unrealistic aspects of a production. Interestingly, however, their answer to their friend's probing was not, "Who cares?" or even "Why are you asking that question?" Indeed, Karey reported that she asked the same thing (in her words, "Why is he with her?") as the objectionable Laura (who reportedly asked, "What do you think he's with her for?"). Laura's offense was not that she attempted to delve into the characters' motivations and traits, but rather that she pushed too hard. She exposed the cracks and flaws in the ways Karey and Marion had worked to unify the characters, challenging their construction of the characters as realistic and motivated. Marion and Karey were forced to take refuge in the fictional nature of the show that they usually worked to ignore ("Jesus. It's a show, I'm enjoying it, don't take it away from me"). Constantly and persistently, viewers actively worked to preserve their sense of the characters as realistic, although to me the task sometimes seemed daunting.

One viewer even extended the construction of the characters as realistic to a comparison with real people:

COURTNEY: Our friend who, who lives there, who went to school in California, is named Cat, and her friends are like Brenda and Donna and Kelly.

RUTH: They're really like that?

COURTNEY: They're just, I mean—I haven't met them. I've seen pictures and I've talked to them on the phone. But—and, I can just—from what stories she says, they're a lot trash—well, some of them are a lot trashier than that. But, just like, you know, really obsessed with being thin and beautiful and (inaudible). And they're—I mean, they do drugs and they, they have sex freely, da-da-da-da.

Courtney unproblematically said that the characters are like real people; in the face of Ruth's challenge, she hesitated, but refused to back down. Unlike with appearance, where no support was needed to defend judgments, here viewers worked hard to buttress their construction of the characters as real.

Moreover, viewers objected vehemently to anything that detracted from the realism of the characters. When they were unable to overlook character inconsistencies, viewers expressed deep distress. For example, one pair of viewers discussed an episode in which Dylan is babysitting for his half-sister, who gets her period during the time they are together. These viewers relived their acute discomfort with the characterization of Dylan as "the sensitive brother type," which appeared unrealistic to them because it was out of sync with his other qualities and contradicted their image of a brother:

COURTNEY: Oh, my gosh, what can I say about that episode was when little girl got her period—
RUTH: Don't say that.
COURTNEY: And no—
RUTH: I called that before. I called that.
COURTNEY: She did call that. And we're like, "That is just the low—that's the new low." And we're just like, we're just like bracing ourselves for it—
RUTH: And then they bring her—
COURTNEY: Oh, come on, do it.
RUTH: —of course, they bring her to Mrs. Walsh.
COURTNEY: And Mrs. Walsh knows what to do. I mean, that's so funny. I mean, what brother wouldn't just freak and run in the other direction? He'd be like. "Aahhh." Oh, it's just so really—trying to portray Dylan as the sensitive brother type. I don't think so.
RUTH: (laughing.)
COURTNEY: That's so bad.

Their objection was that the "rebel" Dylan would never be the "sensitive brother"; indeed, this possibility caused them considerable discomfort: They had to brace themselves for a "new low"—it was just "so bad." Ruth even distanced herself from the emotional moment by retreating from the diagetic context and weaving in a self-narrative ("I called that before. I called that"). They did not ask themselves whether the plot was unrealistic or even uninteresting (points I might have been inclined to make); what jumped out at them was that Dylan's reaction was out of character and unlike the behavior of brothers in general: "I mean, what brother wouldn't just freak and run in the other direction? [. . .] Dylan as the sensitive brother type. I don't think so."

My point is that viewers discussed other aspects of the sh/ found unrealistic with ease, even saying that unrealism in these areᴜ. added to the attraction of the show. For example, most viewers called the characters' lifestyle, with its extreme wealth, "unrealistic." But they were not really bothered by this. Indeed, some even recognized the interest that the "unrealism" of riches lent the show:

COURTNEY: I mean, that apartment this, this year, I'm just like yeah, right. [. . .] That apartment would be that big, you know. No way, not after you see our double. But, I don't know, it's just like the characters are—I don't know. There's just something about them that you just like. [. . .]
RUTH: Yeah, I mean—I can't imagine living like—like, sure I'd like a new car or like nice clothes, but, I don't know, their lives aren't realistic. You can't—
COURTNEY: If they were realistic, no one would watch.

The "unrealistic" lifestyles actually added to the show's attraction for these viewers. Some viewers openly admitted that there was an element of wish-fulfillment in seeing what money can buy:

G: Are there ways that you wish you were more like them?
(Inaudible) (Laughter)
JOAN: Yeah, that's like the biggest [wealth]. I think that's what attracts too. 'Cause they have these nice cars. And it's like they always seem to go on vacation.
MEETRA: It's like no problem. "Oh well, we're going here." And they don't have to worry about the money to go do this.

Viewers could delight in the unrealism of the lifestyle, the clothes, the cars, the vacations. However, they could not tolerate unrealism in the characters. And sometimes they pinpointed "unrealistic" moments with astonishing consistency. Below, two junior high students, two high school students, and a college student, all from a variety of educational backgrounds, come to the same critical conclusion about a tiff between Dylan and Brandon that ends humorously with Dylan accidentally punching Steve in the face instead of Brandon, then all three going off amicably to eat brownies:

G.: What was the part that you didn't like the most?
PAT: I didn't like it when they tried to beat each other up, 'cause after they punched Steve in the face they all made up like it never really happened.
PAM: Yeah.

* * *

JACKIE: That doesn't happen in real life though, I mean you know like, your best friend hitting you and then hitting another best friend and then—
JEANNETTE: —they're are like all best friends again.
JACKIE: —best friends again at the end. That's not real life.

* * *

KAREY: Dylan and Brandon, that was kind of unrealistic to be like that. You know—
G: Yeah.
KAREY: And all of a sudden they were just over it, you know. No big deal.

In each of three groups, viewers said that the quick, humorous resolution to a fight that actually came to blows was not realistic. What is interesting here is not that they challenged the realism (to me, the entire show is unrealistic). Rather, it is important to note that (1) viewers chose to foreground this resolution to an interpersonal conflict as "unrealistic"; and (2) viewers objected strongly to this unrealism. These viewers asked themselves how *they* might resolve such a situation, and they concluded that it simply could not be resolved quickly. You could not "all of a sudden" be "just over it"—"that's not real life." Viewers worked hard discursively to construct the characterizations and relationships as realistic and expressed discomfort when they could not achieve this.

Most of the time, however, they were able to resolve inconsistencies and construct the characters as real. They seized on textual explanations for character traits, using them to bolster the characters' realism. In one episode, Donna was scolded by her parents for almost having sex with David. One viewer commented, "You know, that actually in a way this is really kind of good, because it totally explains why Donna is so submissive and childish." Donna was childish because she had controlling parents, not so that sixth-graders could understand her behavior.

I suspected that the insistence on constructing the characters as realistic, and the uneasiness when this could not be done, accomplished something important. As I grappled with the meaning of this activity, the first thing I concluded was that constructing the characters as realistic gave viewers another access to the "expert" voice heard in talk about appearance.

Realism and Expertise

Just as viewers constructed themselves as skilled judges of makeup, hairstyles, and clothing, so also did they speak as masters of what counted as realistic—and unrealistic. In the statements quoted above, in which viewers declared that some behaviors weren't realistic, they spoke with certainty and authority: Courtney scoffed at the notion of "trying to portray Dylan as the sensitive brother type," adding with certainty, "I don't think so"; Jackie asserted, "That doesn't happen in real life."

Unlikely as it may sound at first, this positioning as expertly detecting when characters weren't realistic worked in important ways to reinforce their construction of the characters as real: occasional unrealism was worth mentioning only because it jarred with the viewers' underlying construction of the characters as real. More frequent were confident, expert statements about the realism of the characters. Indeed, in one such instance, this expert voice temporarily confounded a viewer who (perhaps unjustifiably) was forced by me to confront her uncritical assumption of it. She attended Rider University, which at the time of the study was competing in the Northeast Conference basketball playoffs. In my desire to be meticulous in talking about all characters, I questioned her about a minor character, D'Shawn, a black basketball player who expects to be "carried" through his academic work:

Advertisements
G: I forgot to ask you what you think about that last character.
JOAN: D'Shawn?
G: Yeah.
JOAN: Typical.
G: What?
JOAN: Typical of some—
G: Really?
JOAN: Yeah. I mean we haven't seen anything like that at our school, but—
G: Yeah? I don't know if I'm allowed to ask that 'cause—you've got good basketball, huh?
JOAN: Yeah, yeah. I know, like, two of them, I know really well. You know. I've never seen anything like that.
G: Yeah.
JOAN: I mean they do get excused from a lot, seeing what's going now [the playoffs], but, you know, I've never seen anything like that before. But it's just like so typical, um, on TV, how they show it.
G: Oh. Oh.
JOAN: I think that's why they're doing it, too. They always have this where the sports person never takes their tests and someone else always does it for them.
MEETRA: And the big, you know, the big-time athlete breezes right through it.
G: Yeah.

JOAN: Or the coach will usually excuse it —
G: Mmm.
JOAN: —if you have that kind of coach, but—it's—it seems typical on TV.
G: Oh.
JOAN: And not real life. I mean, it might happen, but I've never seen it happen.

At first, Joan was comfortable characterizing D'Shawn as a "typical" athlete. When I reacted with surprise, she began to qualify that judgment, first to say she hadn't seen any athletes like him, then to conclude that such a character is typical of television, not real life. However, to the end she maintained that "it might happen." Her talk focused on constructing D'Shawn as realistic, even though she was unable to cite any real-life parallels, and she continued to work hard to maintain that construction.

Even when viewers foregrounded production processes with regard to character traits, they often used this analysis to reinforce their image of the characters as realistic. For example, during viewing, Marion and Karey discussed with hysterical laughter the way in which Andrea tells her boyfriend, Jesse, she is pregnant (she showed him a note with the words, "I am pregnant" on it). Marion was much struck by the propriety of Andrea's grammar in avoiding a contraction:

MARION: Why didn't she write "I'm"? (Hysterical laughter) I'm just sitting there—she wrote, "I *am* pregnant." Why didn't she write—
KAREY: Because she's so, um—
MARION: Um.
KAREY: —you know—
MARION: —that's like, "I *AM* pregnant." It makes it sound like they thought she wasn't. (Laughter).
KAREY: I *AM.* Don't think I'm *not* for a minute, because I *AM.*
MARION: If you were wondering—
KAREY: If anything so stupid were (Garbled) (Laughter). They say stupid things.
MARION: It's just the kind of thing that—
KAREY: I know. Because she's, it's totally her character. (Laughter)
MARION: Yeah.
KAREY: Her vocabulary and everything.

Though they saw Andrea's words as laughable, even "stupid," these viewers managed to justify the unnatural statement as bolstering the character's consistency. This type of analytical talk not only co-existed with talk that constructed the characters as real, but it also actually supported it.

And constructing the characters as real provided another forum for the pleasurable expert voice that often constructed the viewer a perior to the show. As with comments about makeup and hair, or in the conversation about the "little slutty outfits," viewers gained added enjoyment from this position. They condescended to the actors—"you don't have to be capable of Shakespeare to be cast on Fox"—and, calling the show "trashy" and "cheesy," implied they enjoyed the sensation of "slumming": "That's part of why we watch it, 'cause we're like—not necessarily that we think we're so superior or anything, but just like, you know, we know, we know what's going on. We know the score and, and they're kind of deluded in their own little sunny California."

And this expert voice concealed the ways in which any true critical stance was put on hold. The disclaimer above ("not necessarily that we think we're so superior or anything") gave permission for the pleasurable silencing of the critical voice, and allowed the active construction of the reality of the characters to proceed unquestioned. As with talk about appearance, the expert voice ("they're kind of deluded in their own little sunny California") seemed to relegate talk about characters to the realm of the trivial, concealing any work that it might be accomplishing.

Realism and Community with Characters

While an important aspect of constructing the characters as real was to provide a new forum for the expert voice, I suspected this process accomplished something more. As I examined the transcripts and tried to listen carefully to the girls' and young women's voices, I concluded that constructing the characters as real allowed viewers to create a discursive community with the characters, constructing links between themselves and the show, and comparing and contrasting themselves to Kelly, Donna, Brenda, and/or Andrea. I came to believe that this type of discursive community with the characters was one of the key arenas in which talk about the show intersected with viewer identity. (For a further exploration of this desire for community with relation to television shows, cf. McKinley 1996.)

Two different ways of accomplishing this community emerged. Some viewers (they tended to be younger, although I am not aiming here to make claims with regard to age) positioned themselves as observers, information-gatherers. They did not identify with the characters; rather, they observed them and "learned" from their behavior, as they might learn from an older sibling or schoolmate. Other viewers (typically the older ones) drew explicit connections between the characters and themselves in ways similar to those described by Press (1991).

An important prerequisite for making these connections was a construction of the characters as real. Many viewers seemed to be aware of the "stock" nature of the characters discussed in Chapter II, but they did not speak of the characters as determined by the genre. Rather than suggesting that producers drew on a culturally appealing range of characteristics with potential for dramatic interest, viewers often said they saw themselves in the characters, layering the characters' identities with the realism of the viewers' own traits: "They're so symbolic of these different things"; "I think we can find ourselves in all those people"; "They seem to symbolize different types of people":

KAITLIN: Brenda's like the bitch, and Kelly is the (inaudible) Donna as the ditz, and Brandon's like the all-American, and Steve is the jock. You know, it just seems like it, it's trying to, in a really weird way, represent everybody that—
CHRYSE: But, can't you guys kind of like see some of yourself in like a cross between like Donna and Kelly? . . . Like Kelly just seems like a kind of like a normal teenager, but with problems and [. . .] and Donna's just kind of like goofy and, and—I don't know.

Chryse cited qualities that she felt she possessed—sometimes she felt like a "normal teenager," sometimes she felt "goofy"—and drew connections between these qualities and those exhibited by the characters. This notion was echoed by another viewer:

KYLE: Donna has to deal with like, like, you know, not wanting to drink and not wanting to have sex, and like and all that type of stuff. I mean, that's something that like every, every teenage person goes through, I think. [. . .] I can relate to that. And I can relate to like, you know, Kelly's need to, like, always want to be beautiful and have like the, you know, the nice—nice boyfriend, and like the good reputation. That type of thing. But then, like, Brenda's the characteristic that she always wants to, like, you know, be her own person still, too, and be unique, whatever. So, like, you know, I mean there's definitely like, each of the characters [. . .] have their own thing.

In this way, the viewers discursively constructed a community with the characters. In drawing more or less explicit connections between themselves and the characters, positioning the characters with "us," viewers were indeed able to imaginatively participate in aspects of a character's experience and personality, and explore them in talk with their friends.

Several different types of talk worked to construct this community. For example, during viewing, frequent sympathetic and empathetic comments constructed viewers as in a friendship relationship with the characters that was manifested in two broad categories: reacting in tune with characters' emotions ("I hate her!" "That is so messed up!" "I wish somebody would just hit that guy!") and calling out advice to characters

("Throw the weight on her!" "Don't tell him!"). In the excerpt below, two viewers shared Brenda's emotions as she is booked in jail because she helped some animal activists break into a research lab. The girls entered into Brenda's feelings and called out reactions to the screen:

JEANNETTE: I feel bad for her. She doesn't deserve to be in jail.
JACKIE: Yeah, she didn't really know what was going on, they just told her to come up.
[. . .]
JACKIE: Oh, I'd be so scared in there!
JEANNETTE: Uh huh.
[. . .]
Warden: "Bail was preset at $50,000."
ALL: Ohhh! No way!!
Warden reads charges.
JACKIE: She didn't do that!

These rich reactions will be explored further in the section on morality. Here, the point needs to be made that these two girls were participating in a community with each other and with Brenda. They explored her subject position and its attendant emotions ("I feel bad for her"; "Oh, I'd be so scared in there!"). They constructed motivations ("She didn't really know what was going on") and hurled objections at the screen ("She didn't do that!").

Many viewers continued to build this relationship with the characters in talk apart from viewing. For example, one viewer said about David, "I think he's really stupid for doing that [drugs] and getting involved. But I'm proud of him because he stopped, you know." She constructed David as a real person of whom she could be proud. His triumph somehow reflected favorably on her.

Examples of this type of talk abounded. Sometimes viewers constructed a protective position toward the characters. When speaking of some of the issues that arise on the show, one viewer said, "You kind of get worried for them you know—when they do those things." In the following excerpt, two viewers discussed Brandon as if he were a friend in need of "fixing up" with a new date:

MEETRA: I wish we could just find one nice person.
JOAN: One nice girl for him. That's why I kind of wanted Kelly. But he always gets the bad end of the deal always. All these girls.

"I wish *we* could just find one nice person"—Meetra constructed herself as in the position to find a date for Brandon, as she might for the boy next door. Completely backgrounded are the facts that Brandon is not a real person and that his amorous liaisons are the constructions of writers and producers seeking ratings. The young women constructed instead a discursive community with the characters.

Perhaps the most interesting example of the way this community worked was the following comment by a college student, expressed to a chorus of delight from her sorority sisters: "If Donna and David have sex—(laughter)—that's like—I would be in heaven with that. No kidding (ovation). I would think I'M having sex." Light-hearted, casual, and transient—nevertheless, this talk worked to construct, maintain, and defend a close community, even intimacy, with Donna and David.

Attending to Self, Attending to Characters

While this type of talk has been reported in other studies (e.g., Hobson 1982; Ang 1985; Press 1991), I prefer not to interpret it in traditional psychological terms, as identification or role modeling. These processes are difficult to assess and indeed are often denied by viewers. Rather, I would like to focus on ways that constructing a discursive community with the characters offered viewers a way of attending to themselves—of discursively constructing their own identities. This process was particularly clear in the numerous instances when viewers drew explicit parallels—or contrasts—between themselves and the characters. Consider the following:

KYLE: Andrea was always like the, you know, the one who had to work hard. [. . .] She had her goals set to go to like Yale and kind of had to be like the smart one among all her friends. Whatever. Like, like, that was kind of—I don't know, like, like, you know, [me] trying to go to Princeton. Like that was kind of similar to my experience, you know, in high school.

* * *

KRISTEN: Um, I like Andrea.
G: And can you say why?
KRISTEN: I don't know, 'cause of like the way she is and the way she acts and—
G: Mm-hmm.
KRISTEN: —I just like her the best. [. . .] I guess, 'cause she's like, when she was in high school, she was like really into her work, and into like working real hard on like the activities she was into.
G: Mm-hmm. And that's like you?
KRISTEN: Yeah.

* * *

NICKY: I like [Brenda's] character, 'cause she just does whatever she wants to do. [. . .] I don't know—I guess like her personality, a little—

like I can be cocky and I just do what I want to do, and I don't care what other people think.

* * *

JOAN: I mean I am pretty aggressive. [. . .] So that's why I, kind of I guess, like Brenda cause she so aggressive and you know. I mean she's a snob and stuff like that, but it's like, I like that. She doesn't let, you know —like with her parents, she like fights about everything. And it's like— you know, that's how I am with my parents, I'll fight with them until—
MEETRA: —until the last length and she's still screaming at them.
JOAN: But it's like, you know then they do give me what I want, and I know I can get it from them. You know, so that's why I kind of like her. She kind of gets what she wants, too.

* * *

ESTHER: She's [Kelly]—when she sets her mind on something she sticks to it. I'm not like that. I just give up really easily.

* * *

JEANNETTE: She [Kelly], she has her ways of dealing with problems.
G: Mm-hmm.
JEANNETTE: I don't know. To me, I feel like I kind of avoid problems.
G: Oh.
JEANNETTE: And she will confronts them and solves them, but me, I avoid them.

The characters' personality traits—their ability to get involved in school activities or get what they want, their tenacity and problem-solving skills —gave viewers a touchstone by which to assess themselves. They felt good when they saw similarities, and criticized themselves when they didn't measure up. They evaluated themselves in terms set by the television text as they grouped themselves in a community with Andrea, Brenda, Kelly, Donna.

Indeed, viewers sometimes went to considerable lengths to defend this community with the characters. An example of this rich process is offered by the excerpt below, in which viewers referenced an episode where Donna's friends protested an administrative decision keeping her from graduating:

ALISON: I like Donna.
ERIKA: Donna's stupid.
ALISON: She is. But she's, she's never had a problem with any of her friends and—did they ever? They never like got mad at Donna. (Laughter)
G: Yeah, Yeah.
ALISON: She's just like standing there. She's standby.
CASEY: Yeah. Donna always had all the support.

ALISON: Yeah.
CASEY: "Let Donna graduate." (Laughter) "Let Donna graduate."
ALISON: No, no, what is it? Say, like, "Donna Martin graduates," or something (laughter). "Donna Martin graduates."
CASEY: You just like her 'cause she has the same last name.
ALISON: Yeah, she's a Martin, she's cool.
G: She's your what?
ALISON: (whose last name is Martin) She has the same last name.
ALL: Laughter.

Alison started by expressing a preference for Donna, which Erika directly challenged (clearly, Donna was not a part of Erika's community). Since Alison could not refute the charge "Donna's stupid," she shifted her ground, citing the relationship with the other characters, "They never like got mad at Donna." Casey took this idea a step further, recalling an episode when the students petitioned for Donna to graduate from high school after she was suspended at the eleventh hour for drinking. Alison then completed an unusual connection between herself and Donna through their last names. Throughout, viewers worked hard to defend and bolster their community with the characters.

Indeed, unlike with appearance, viewers reported arguing vociferously in defense of this community with their real-life friends who also watched the show. As one viewer said forcefully, "Mostly my friends don't like Brenda, and I always stick up for her. I always stick up for her. Yeah." In protection of her community with Brenda, she would fight with her real-life friends. Sometimes these arguments seemed to border on the unpleasant. When one viewer said, "I actually like—we had got in a fight about her one night too," there was an undertone of unhappiness over these conflicts. Disagreements over the show would not seriously threaten friendships, because, as Marion and Karey did with their roommate, differences could always be smoothed over with the comment, "Hey, it's a show." Nevertheless, the fact that the community with characters would inject a quality of confrontation into the community of viewers speaks for the intensity with which this connection with the characters was constructed and maintained. By constructing the characters as realistic and then identifying shared traits, viewers created a discursive link between themselves and those characters. And they were willing to defend this community, even at the cost of confrontation with other viewers—the community with the characters took a certain precedence over community with their friends.

Note that viewers were careful to say that they recognized traits in the characters that the viewers said they already possessed. Viewer identity was constructed as inviolate, but they said they liked to see characters that resembled themselves. However, I would suggest that—as viewers constructed a community with the characters, as they drew connections and disjunctions between the characters' personalities and their own— new meanings accrued to those traits that gave viewers important new ways to attend to their own lives.

This is an important and complex point. I am not suggesting that these girls and young women brought no real-life experience to the show, or that the show dominated their view of their lives. What these viewers were doing, however, was attending to the show out of their own backgrounds, then cycling back to attend to their lives with added meanings from the show. Thus the experience of the show co-existed with real-life experiences, each adding meaning to the other.

Although this study cannot make causal claims, I did observe a pattern in ways in which this cycle was accomplished that seemed to correspond to educational background (for a further exploration of this pattern, cf. McKinley, 1995). In an echo of Press's (1991) finding that working-class women experienced class-specific hegemony, in which they misrecognized themselves in the privileged lifestyle of the characters, a number of the viewers I listened to from less-educated backgrounds said that the show "reminded" them of their lives:

JOAN: And I just like how Brandon and Brenda, how they deal with their parents. I mean it's so funny. You know the way they talk about them. 'Cause that's kind of like me and my brother, how we talk about our parents. So that's what—when they sit there, 'cause they're, you know, twins. Um that just reminds me of me and him, how we talk about our parents. So, 'cause you all have these little—Like you and your brother, I mean, I can tell how you say things about your dad or your mom.
MEETRA: Yeah, like we joke around like mock my fath—. My brother will like, you know make fun of my dad. My dad has no idea. We'll be sitting at dinner, and he'll be doing something right in front of my father, or like he'll say something that's like—not like sarcastic, but, you know, something that's supposed to be funny. And my dad won't figure it out. And it's just like funny to me.
JOAN: And it's kind of like what Brandon and Brenda did in front of their parents. 'Cause they had no clue, you know. It's kind of things that (inaudible)—.
MEETRA: Just like that last episode when um, you know, when his [Brandon's] mom didn't realize that Kelly was going on this trip and Brandon's like, "Dad, explain to your wife what dating is." And I just starting laughing, 'cause she's just standing like, "What are you talking about?" I mean I thought that was funny.

These two young women saw their own relationships with their parents reflected in Brandon and Brenda's treatment of Jim and Cindy—and the real-life situation gained additional meaning. The community Joan felt with her older brother was cycled through Brenda and Brandon; perhaps the real-life relationship was even strengthened as Joan emphasized the fictional characters' closeness in age and, presumably, mentality ("'cause they're, you know, twins"). The way Meetra mocked her father gained new meaning when "it's kind of like what Brandon and Brenda did in front of their parents." The show intertwined with past, present, and future for these viewers, co-constructing their memories, the ways in which they spoke of their current lives, and the ways in which they thought about their futures.

In a similar example, Karey, who had just graduated from a state college, revisited—and perhaps slightly reconstructed—her high school years when she identified with Andrea:

KAREY: Her grades were always important. A lot of it reminds me of me, back in high school, when my grades were really important to me. And a lot of times when, I mean—not that I didn't have a good time, I always did—but I was always worried about what I would be doing, how it would look for me. I mean, "I have a reputation to uphold in the school and I, you know, can't be seen doing this, I can't be at this party."
G: Really?
KAREY: And I kind of feel like she's that way, also. So I guess a little, a little bit of it reminds me.

In contrast, some of the viewers from better educated backgrounds suggested that there were important ways in which they were *not* like the characters. Echoing Press's (1991) finding that middle-class viewers said television's portrayal was unrealistic, but that they adopted its behavioral and appearance ideals, these viewers explicitly articulated a distinction between themselves and the show but ultimately perpetuated some of its assumptions. As Princeton student Courtney, whose father had an advanced degree, said, "It's so, like, *nouveau,* I don't know. It's like different from what we grew up with, it's so like, lifestyles of the rich and famous, I guess. [. . .] It was just like so different." In fact, Courtney expressed surprise when her life *did* coincide in some ways with the show. She recounted an episode when the characters were pledging sororities: "I'll tell you one thing that was just so funny, though. It was, it was when they were rushing the sororities—(G: Yeah)—it was the same time we were rushing." In the excerpt below, I questioned her, thinking she was surprised at the coincidence of timing. That turned out not to be the case. Rather, Courtney was surprised at how involved she became in the episode—at the connection she drew between the show and her life. She found herself constructing a link between her life and Andrea's, who was almost rejected by a sorority, and this connection surprised her.

COURTNEY: I just found myself getting so serious about it, and I kind of surprised myself.
G: Because you were going through the same thing.
COURTNEY: Well, no, no, no. But just like taking, taking—
RUTH: —taking her side.
COURTNEY: Yeah, 'cause sometimes they're (inaudible). Other times you really find yourself, you know—
G: Mm-hmm.
COURTNEY: —living their, living their lives.

To Courtney, the distinction between her life and the show was so clear that any connection came as a surprise. Nevertheless, the association she made with Andrea served to add meaning to her own experience of pledging. Similarly, Marion, whose parents both went to college, suggested that her life was quite different from the show, but that it offered her an opportunity to explore the show's world vicariously: "You live kind of vicariously through them, [. . .] maybe wanting to be like them, or *be* them. [. . .] You wish you could be that way, maybe you wish you could be that strong, like Lucinda, or as pretty as Kelly, or have what Kelly has, like Dylan, do you know what I mean?"

The point is that, whether they said the show reminded them of their life or whether it was perceived as a contrast, the community viewers constructed with the characters offered them ways of attending to their own real-life experiences. Through the television text, Marion explored being strong like Lucinda or pretty like Kelly, then attended to her own life on the basis of these possibilities. Courtney's experience of pledging gained new meaning when Andrea pledged. And Joan looked to her present relationship with her friend Meetra, as well as her future, in terms of the show when she said, "I guess because they're all, like, best friends. [. . .] It's like that's what you want for yourself. Like me and her are always there for each other. But it's like that's what—you know, it's so nice to see that." Just as Sandy's hat (mentioned in the previous chapter) acquired new meaning because it was like Donna's, meanings in other aspects of life changed in the context of a community with the characters. Struggles with drinking and sex, with being your own person, having the nice boyfriend and the good reputation, all gained additional meaning when the speaker's community was expanded to include Kelly, Donna, Brenda, and Andrea.

Alternative Female Identities

A striking aspect of many of these comments about the female characters quoted above is the way they sometimes seemed to explore strong
female identities—to condemn the notion of the pretty, nice, passive
female, and to praise women who are aggressive, hard-working problem-
solvers. Kristen liked Andrea because "she was really into working hard
on like the activities she was into"; Brenda reaped praise "'cause she
just does whatever she wants to do" and "she gets what she wants"; Kelly
"confronts and solves" her problems. And condemnation was heaped on
Donna's head because she is "ditzy and dependent on what's-his-name."

Talk about the characters did indeed provide a forum for the exploration of alternative subject positions for females, at least for the older
viewers. This exploration can be traced, for example, in the way in which
viewers talked about female aggressiveness. I was at first puzzled by the
mix of reactions concerning this trait in Brenda. The younger viewers
all objected to Brenda's "snobby" qualities:

G: Um, let's see, Brenda.
PAM: Hate her.
PAT: I don't like her either.
G: Really? Why not?
PAM: Snob.

* * *

G: Tell me what you think of Brenda.
DANIELLE: I don't like her.
AMANDA: I think she's like really snobby.

* * *

MADDY: I don't like her. She's like snobby.

Here, there was a straightforward construction of female identity: If
females are pretty and nice, as pointed out in the chapter on appearance, you like them; if they're snobby you don't (I'm guessing these
sixth- and seventh-graders didn't want to say "bitch" in front of me). For
twins Melissa and Melanie, whose voices were indistinguishable on the
tape, the condemnation of snobbiness holds true for actors as well:

M: Brenda? Ugh!
ALL: Laughter.
M: I like Brenda's character, but I *don't* like Shannen Doherty.
G: Oh really?
M: 'Cause she's supposed to be like this big snob in her life or some-
thing. I read about it somewhere. And that's why I just don't like her.

G: So that sorta changed your opinion of her in the show when you read about her?

M: Yeah. See, like, when Dylan and Brenda broke up, I was kind of sad at first. But then I like was reading all this stuff about how Shannen Doherty is really this big snob. And like she doesn't even talk to people. And she really hates 'em and everything. She acts like such a prince all the time. You've heard that stuff in the news, how Shannen Doherty is like. Anyway, so, um—so I wasn't feeling so bad, and I was like happy.

As discussed in Chapter 4, Brown and Gilligan (1992) have suggested that girls of this age are preoccupied with the notion of being "nice," which these authors define as passive, silencing, and ultimately destructive to female identity. The issue of passivity and activity clearly is on the table here, and for the youngest viewers, the solution was simple: Be "nice." High-school students Jeannette and Kristen amplified this point:

G: Tell me about the other characters. Which ones do you like and which ones—are there some you don't like or you like them all?

JEANNETTE: Brenda.

ALL: Laughter.

G: Why?

JEANNETTE: I don't like her.

KRISTEN: I can't stand Brenda.

G: Why not?

JEANNETTE: Because she's a snob—

KRISTEN: She's stuck up.

JEANNETTE: She's got an attitude.

KRISTEN: Yeah, she expects to get everything that she wants.

"She expects to get everything that she wants." And naturally, this is an unrealistic expectation.

However, for the older viewers, the issue of activity and getting what you want wasn't quite so clear-cut. These viewers grappled in numerous ways and on many levels with the notion of feminine aggressiveness. A number of the older viewers openly celebrated characters they saw as having various strong characteristics which included (1) doing or going after what you want; (2) not caring what other people think; and (3) being different.

For example, one viewer constructed Brenda as a person who says what she thinks: "'Cause she's a bitch, and she's just like, she's so like aggressive, like she just says what she thinks. And I kind of admire that. And I'm just glad, I mean, I just like her character, I think it's a really good character that she can be that way." These statements imply that many females do not say what they think—just speaking out is a form of aggression that calls for comment when a woman does it.

In a similar way, another viewer constructed Brenda as a person who spoke with conviction, who meant what she said:

REBECCAH: And Brenda just seems kind of cool.
G: Uh huh. Anything else about her?
[. . .]
REBECCAH: Well, she says everything with conviction, you know that she means what she says. Whereas all the other girls seem to be, you can sway them either way.

Saying things with conviction—meaning what you say—is unusual enough in a woman to call for comment. It is a form of verbal aggression.

Other viewers praised characters who did what they wanted to do: "She's [Kelly] strong and very independent of the others, and she'll do what she wants and think how she wants." This construction takes speaking out a step farther—"she'll *do* what she wants and *think* how she wants." Apparently, this is not typical or predictable behavior for females, although some viewers saw it as admirable. Moreover, it calls for strength, as in this conversation about Lucinda:

KAREY: She's so strong, and I mean, um, I, I admire that, you know, she goes after what she wants.
G: Uh huh.
KAREY: Most people, you know, a lot of—I mean, I know I wouldn't be that way. It's kind of nice to, to see that, that, you know—
G: Yeah.

"She's so strong." Moreover, "She goes after what she wants." The cumulative effect of these comments is an overwhelming desire to think, act, speak for oneself—indeed, just to know what one wants, and not to have to pretend one isn't aiming to get it. Clearly implied here is the idea that most women don't accomplish that. None of these comments was ever applied to males. It was not noteworthy if a male knew what he wanted and went after it. But when females did, it was observed and commented on. In a resigned footnote, Karey commented, "I know I wouldn't be that way."

This issue also surfaced around the minor character of Emily, who (before the time of the study) dated Brandon, then had a nervous breakdown and was permanently incarcerated in a mental institution. As one viewer said, "She was one of my favorite characters ever. [. . .] I just liked her 'cause she was like different. She was cool. She was a rebel and she rode a motorcycle, and she had roots and didn't care. And she, and she was fun. I mean she was kind of messed up in the head, but who cares, she was interesting. I liked her." Emily flouted conventions of appearance ("she had roots"), of female accoutrements ("she rode a motorcycle"), and of female traits ("she didn't care").

Female characters who said what they thought, did what they wanted, and didn't care—in short, who were aggressive—painted a picture of female agency, even if against a background of defensiveness. Women are not supposed to be cocky and aggressive, viewers said, but, at the same time, "it's nice to see that." I became excited as I wondered if these viewers were exercising discursive agency, exploring a subject position that flouts convention and breaks the "pretty and nice" rules for female conduct by saying what they meant and doing what they wanted.

And this praise for the aggressive woman meant that some viewers deplored Donna's airhead qualities. Ruth and Courtney emphasized that Donna was "the antithesis of everything we stand for"; she was too "ditzy and dependent." The airhead was condemned as weak, ineffectual, and ultimately self-destructive. For example, foolish Donna can be "suckered" into giving David money that everyone knows he will use to buy drugs:

JANE: And David knows that she still likes him so—
KATEY: Yeah, but he doesn't like her. But he's like suckering her into money and stuff.

* * *

SANDY: I don't think Donna should of gave all the money to David.
G: Oh yeah.
SANDY: 'Cause—
MADDY: 'Cause—(garbled, background noise)
SANDY: —'Cause she was like—she looked at him and he gave—he had a certain look with him, whi—don't—"You're making a mistake, you know, you fool!"

And she will never get smart, viewers predicted; Donna will continue this destructive behavior pattern even after they graduate from college:

KRISTEN: Donna will still be saying, "David, stop doing drugs."
ALL: Laughter.
KRISTEN: Donna will, Donna will be—Donna will still be chasing after David—
JEANNETTE: He'll be telling her, "No stay away."
KRISTEN: —but telling everyone else that David's fine.

Donna is not only incapable of helping David with his drug addiction, she is actually deluding herself and others, "telling everyone else that

David's fine" and ignoring his injunctions to stay away. The ultimate result is self-destruction:

JACKIE: Not like Donna. Donna just like—
ESTHER: Like oh come on—
JACKIE: Sweet.
ESTHER: Too sweet.
JACKIE: Soft.
G: Yeah?
ESTHER: She's gonna get hurt here.

"She's gonna get hurt"—and she is completely ineffectual. Here, it is not
so much that Donna should stand up for herself, but that Donna should
get real, stop making a fool out of herself.

As I studied these comments, I wondered if this exploration of the
strong, cocky, aggressive woman could count as feminist agency—if I
had been wrong in my assessment that talk about female identity and
90210 could only work hegemonically. However, as I mulled over the
ever-present issue of authorship, and the way that cycled into an artificial duality in female identity options, I became less and less convinced
that agency was in fact being exerted.

Authorship

The viewers indeed worked in an expert voice to construct the characters as real, spoke of themselves as in a community with the characters,
and cycled this talk back into ways of attending to themselves, sometimes exploring the position of being cocky or aggressive. Concealed in
all of this talk, however, is the issue of authorship that I argued in the
previous chapter is closely linked to the hegemonic process. As with talk
about appearance, with the discursive construction of expertise came
a positioning of self as the source and author of one's viewing experience. Viewers never suggested that producers, writers, or actors had any
role in the development of their expertise. It was *they* who extracted
the meanings from the text, not the text that imposed meanings upon
them.

For example, consider the authority with which viewers spoke of the
changes in David, as quoted earlier in this chapter: "He was a dork.
They all hated him"; "Yeah, he was a dork"; "When the show first started
he was just like a little nerd"; "Remember, he was a big dork." It is important to note that, in the early episodes, David is repeatedly called a
"dork" and a "nerd" in the script. However, viewers never said the other
characters thought David was a dork or that the writers had chosen this
soubriquet for the character; rather, they easily accepted the character

definition offered by the text and positioned themselves as its author. Although clearly a co-construction process was going on, this fact was invisible in their talk.

Moreover, just as this talk concealed ways in which viewers read the characters on the show's terms, it also hid ways in which their own backgrounds cycled into their "read" of the characters. At the risk of seeming to imply a link between background and reading (something this study is not in a position to do), I would like to report another pattern that emerged: A number of college students from educated backgrounds reacted to Donna's dumbness and childishness with pain and embarrassment, while accepting and even praising Lucinda's sexual forwardness; the opposite held for two college-age viewers whose parents did not go to college. For example, consider the following reactions to "dumb" Donna:

Donna and parents.
KYLE: That was awful! She was just so dumb.
* * *
A woman asks if anyone has ever been burglarized. Donna: "Does having your purse stolen count?"
JOAN: That dummy!
MEETRA: She is. (Giggles)

Both comments constructed the viewer as in community with Donna. However, Meetra, who did not attend college and whose parents didn't either, and Joan, a Rider student whose parents did not attend college, reacted as to a friend, amused and slightly contemptuous. They were able to put themselves in a superior position vis-à-vis Donna ("That dummy!"). They objected to, but they could laugh at, her foibles. However, Kyle's writing, "That was awful! She was just so dumb" expressed the discomfort experienced when someone we know has embarrassed herself. Kyle, a Princeton student whose parents had advanced degrees, reacted strongly to the dumb blonde. As partially quoted above, so did Princeton students Courtney and Ruth:

RUTH: Never liked Donna.
COURTNEY: Not Donna, ucch.
RUTH: Oh, I hate Donna.
G: Why?
COURTNEY: Donna's the antithesis of everything we s—I stand for, anyway.
G: In what way?
COURTNEY: She's just so ditzy and—
RUTH: —dependent on what's-his-name.

For Kyle, Courtney, and Ruth, the dumb blonde was a hot issue; Meetra and Joan, whose parents did not attend college, were contemptuous yet comfortable.

Similarly, Princeton student Terry, whose father had an advanced degree, objected to Donna's childishness, a trait that did not really bother Meetra and Joan. At one point during viewing, Terry objected impatiently and exasperatedly on Donna's bright orange telephone, with a yellow ear outlined on the receiver: "It's like they totally give her all the, like the toys of childhood." In contrast, Meetra and Joan noticed Donna's immaturity, but it didn't make them uncomfortable. Rather, they could enjoy feeling superior:

JOAN: Donna, she's so dippy. Even the way her hair is, look at that.
MEETRA: She needs a brain transplant.
JOAN: I mean, it looks cute, but—
MEETRA: Yeah.
JOAN: It's like, grow up.

"Grow up, Donna." They condescended to her, but without the acute discomfort experienced by Kyle and Terry.

For Joan and Meetra, the hot button was the sexual aggressiveness displayed by Lucinda and another minor character, Laura.

Laura tells Steve she's been thinking about him.
MEETRA: The girl's annoying.

* * *

Lucinda flirting with Brandon.
JOAN: I do not like her. Yuk!

Joan and Meetra "do not like" women who are actively pursuing men. They objected strongly and emotionally to women who chase after men, just as Kyle objected to dumb women and Terry to childish ones. In contrast, Marion, both of whose parents went to college, praised Lucinda's forwardness:

MARION: And I like her.
[. . .]
G: What do you like about her?
MARION: Um that she—I think I like that she—she's very forward—
G: Uh huh.
MARION: —you know, it's like she knows what she wants and she doesn't—I can't say that she doesn't play games because she does play games but she, like she does it for herself.
[. . .]

MARION: But she seems to be—well she doesn't seem to be deceitful, you know, she seems like she's fun. And she is playing games, but she's making no—she doesn't pretend like she's not.

The text was indeed polysemic, and viewer background directed attention to characters differentially. Joan and Meetra condescended humorously to the dumb, childlike woman, but without passion; however, they vehemently rejected the sexually aggressive woman. The women from better-educated backgrounds emphasized being smart, mature, and strong and felt acutely uneasy with women who were otherwise.

While it is tempting to explore the ramifications of this relationship, that would be the subject of another study. What I want to note here is the way the viewers positioned themselves as the sources of these meanings. It was *they* who didn't like the aggressive woman or the dumb one, not their upbringing or the culture in which they lived, that guided these reactions; it was *they* who knew that David was a dork and Brenda a bitch; it was *they* who found themselves in the television characters, not the clever writers who seduced viewers into thinking they saw their reflections in beautiful Kelly and cocky Brenda.

And it was *viewers* who accepted that the alternative to being pretty and nice was to be cocky and aggressive, not the patriarchy that offered only this bipolar set of alternatives. As discussed in the chapter on social construction and feminism, Gilligan (1982) has written that women are offered in our culture two mutually exclusive modes of being: They can be self-sacrificing and ignore their own needs (pretty and nice, in the terms of *90210*) or they can be selfish (i.e., cocky, aggressive). As these viewers struggled to resist the "pretty, nice" mandate, the only other option they constructed for themselves was "cocky and aggressive," the other alternative offered by our individualistic, capitalistic society.

Though I was delighted to hear the rejection of "pretty and nice," the more I thought about these voices, the more I became convinced that I would be mistaken to applaud this elevation of "cocky and aggressive." The alternate subjectivity that many feminists would have women explore is the recognition that meaning is multiple, and that patriarchy's construction of femininity must be denaturalized. Radway (1994) called for a female identity that values intimacy and relationality alongside autonomy and success; Gilligan (1982) suggested that women have a dual responsibility to act responsively toward self and others.

Once again, I was forced to conclude that this talk was working hegemonically to preserve patriarchal categories—that contrast the "good girl" and the "bitch"; that suggest that ownership of one's sexuality is irreconcilable with caring for others; that insist that speaking in one's own voice is incompatible with preserving connection. This conclusion spoke to me with such force that I have allotted to it a considerable portion of the chapter on dating.

Summary

In their talk about character traits, viewers opened up a polysemic text in order to construct the characters as real and build a community with them. They brought their own backgrounds into play to work on the polysemic text, attending to specific aspects of the characters in idiosyncratic ways, but then they reliably recycled specific, generally agreed-upon meanings into the ways they attended to their lives. They sometimes used that community as a way of exploring the identity of the strong, cocky, aggressive woman—sometimes even risking challenging their real-life communities in the process—but this exploration was conducted along hegemonic lines delineated by patriarchy that, as the chapter on dating will argue, work to preserve the cultural notion that women's voices must be modulated if they are to relate to men romantically. Real interrogation of the status quo did not occur, and the process by which these characterizations were naturalized continued to be hidden.

The next chapter looks more closely at this cycle of attending to self and attending to show as it occurred in plot narration. Examination of the discursive construction of narrative uncovers a gold mine of ways in which the themes discussed here—community, pleasure, expertise, agency, authorship, and the relationship of self and show—play out, setting the agenda for the rest of the analysis.

Chapter 7
Narrative: Playing Pundit

In addition to talk about appearance and characterizations, the girls and young women I talked to often spontaneously recited plots. By their own reports, this happened frequently in their private conversations: When I asked what they talked about when they discussed the show, they typically responded: "I just mainly talk about what happened"; "Sometimes like, you know, we'll go out, and it'll be a couple nights [after] the episode's on and we'll just start, you know talking like, 'Did you see what happened that night?' and we'll just talk about what happened." Often this talk served to fill in gaps when viewers missed something: "We tell each other what happened. If I missed five or so minutes, if my phone rings and I'm on it, I'll be like, 'What happened during that part I was on phone?' [. . .] Just what happened on the show"; "Usually we talk about what happened [. . .] like if someone has missed it or something like that, kind of like a fill-in type of thing, and if you know, just like what happens, stuff like that."

In fact, my second interview with seventh-grader Jane provided a concrete example of this process. I asked her if she had talked about the episode we had watched together four days previously. She responded in language exemplifying the way her community collapsed its thoughts in perfect assurance of a common understanding: "My friend in 'C' [a school division] [. . .] asked me what it was about and I told her. [. . .] Told her that um—they got married and that she's going to keep the baby. And that they moved out from David. So I told 'em."

Underpinning this talk are the themes that have been explored in the chapters on appearance and characterization. Indeed, fertile new ways to understand these themes can be found in examination of plot recitations. In addition, this chapter introduces the rather disturbing way in which viewers handed authority to the text, "playing pundit" as they competed for most plots recited or best reading of producers' minds. As I worked to understand what this process could mean, I uncovered another layer of the *90210* experience: Talk about plots could link self-narrative and fictional narrative to accomplish identity work. Throughout this book, I argue that this blending of narratives is a central process of enculturation—and hegemonic perpetuation of the status quo.

Narrative, Expertise, and Community

On examining talk about plots, one of the first conclusions I reached was that, as with talk about appearance and characterizations, a primary function was to build and maintain community. As has already been seen, in some cases it was the community of viewers that was buttressed. As indicated by Jane's blind pronouns quoted above ("*they* got married, *she's* going to keep the baby, *they* moved out from David"), so much already has been shared in the viewer community that a verbal shorthand, cryptic to outsiders, was perfectly intelligible to others in the group.

More frequently, however, narrations solidified the community with the characters observed in the last chapter. This process can be seen in the following typical account. This viewer was describing a moment in which Dylan says he will "be there" for David, should David need help in kicking his drug habit, just as David supported Dylan when Dylan's father died:

CASEY: Last week, when, uh, um, David was really strung out—
G: Uh huh.
CASEY: —and Dylan went out and talked to him and goes, "You remember when you did this for me." And to like someone who didn't watch it all the time wouldn't remember. [. . .] But they didn't have to explain everything about like the father, the death, or anything.

Because regular viewers are a part of the community of characters, in the know, "they didn't have to explain." Long-time viewers will remember about "the father, the death"—everything. And this knowledge creates a pleasurable community between Casey and the characters.

Viewer enjoyment of this community with characters frequently was evident. For example, pleasure echoes through the following recitation of a complex moment where talk about the show reinforced both community with characters and community with friends, as two viewers inadvertently fooled an eavesdropper:

MEETRA: He thought we were talking 'bout real people.
JOAN: —real people. 'Cause the way we were talking about their names and stuff.
MEETRA: Cause we were just saying, you know, "Oh, I can't believe, you know Brenda did this," and it was just like—and he, I guess, never

watched the show, so he never realized that we weren't talking 'bout people.

JOAN: But he assumed that this was really going on. And he's like shocked.

MEETRA: Like these were our friends and they were doing things.

ALL: Laughter.

G: Um, what, what about that? I mean, do you talk about—as if they were real people, do you think?

JOAN: Yeah we do. We don't say, "On *Beverly Hills*," we just say, "I want to see what Kelly and (inaudible)—" you know, talk like they're real people.

MEETRA: And it's just like you know, it's you know, "I can't believe," you know, "Dylan did that to Kelly."

JOAN: Yeah. And he actually thought, he's like, "Well, what did he do?"

ALL: Laughter.

MEETRA: Said, "No. It's a TV show."

As reported by Brown (1994), constructing community through this type of talk gave these viewers both pleasure and discursive power. First, Joan and Meetra thoroughly enjoyed the way their talk constructed a real-seeming world for them. Their sense of community in this world was heightened by the fact that their friend had no access to it. A sense of "us-them" can be heard in the recollection that their friend was fooled—duped enough to ask, "Well, what did they do?" Second, a sense of glamour accrued through their relationship with this world. The friend assumed that "these were our friends"—and what friends! He was "shocked" that people would do such things—and no doubt intrigued as well. Joan and Meetra acquired a certain cachet through their relationship with Brenda and Kelly ("like these were our friends and they were doing things"). Finally, their sense of superiority over both the television characters and their friend added yet another layer. Not only did this talk permit them to enjoy the "in-crowd" feeling of membership, but also they felt superior to this television world—and they could make fun of their friend because he took it seriously. Secure within the community with each other and with the television characters, they could turn to their friend and condescendingly set him straight ("said, 'No. It's a TV show' ").

As with talk about appearance and characterizations, recitation of plots served to position the viewer as expert, knowledgeable, a member of a community with characters and other viewers—and sometimes superior to those communities.

And, as shown in the previous chapter, talk about the plots could strengthen the community with the characters at the expense of the community of real people. In this excerpt of an interview with three high-school students, ninth-grader Jackie had left the room to answer a phone call from her mother just as the rest of the group was negotiating its interpretation of the show:

JEANNETTE: Oh I got a favorite part!
G: Yeah?
JEANNETTE: When Brandon dissed Lucinda. (Laughter) I liked that part.
(Laughter)
G: Everyone hates Lucinda.
(Jackie returns from phoning her mother.)
G: (to Jackie) What was your favorite part of the show?
JACKIE: My favorite part was when Brenda came into the Peach Pit and told everyone about that, you know, and Kelly came out after her.
G: And what was the worst part?
JACKIE: The part where Brandon told off Lucinda.
ALL: What?!
JACKIE: That was the most boring part!
JEANNETTE: What? That was the best!
KRISTEN: He was deflected to the third degree, what are you talking about?
JEANNETTE: That was the best, the best!

Poor Jackie, the youngest of the three girls, probably would not have disagreed with her friends had she been in the room when Jeannette praised that moment "when Brandon dissed Lucinda." When the disagreement surfaced, the community of viewers shifted, pitting Kristen and Jeannette against Jackie rather than the three friends against the characters.

Narrative as "Playing Pundit"

As the above excerpt suggests, plot recitation often functioned competitively, strengthening the community with characters over the community with other viewers. Much of this type of talk arose spontaneously, and was often punctuated with the line, "Did you see that?"—a comment that created a hierarchy of who had seen what, and that constructed a forum for one-upping each other.

For some of the viewers, typically the younger ones, this aspect of the plot recitations was particularly noticeable. Focusing on mastering the plots allowed them to construct a discursive power for themselves, "knowing the answers" when it came to details of plot lines, able to "get it right."

For example, on Wednesday evening before viewing an episode, seventh-grader Jane began to tell her friend Katey what happened the previous week because Katey had been studying for a test and hadn't seen the show. The plot had concerned the Peach Pit, a diner:

JANE: Did you see it last week? Um. This guy who owns it, he had a heart attack. And Brandon took over. His [the owner's] — his um brother. He [the owner] had a heart attack, and he couldn't work and the place was closed, and they were losing a lot of money. So his [the owner's] brother took over 'cause he owned 50 percent. And then Brandon took in for Nick [the owner]. So the brother has 50 percent and so does Brandon.

The specifics of the heart attack, and the reiterated "50 percent," constructed Jane as knowledgeable and precise, expert. Interestingly, many of the details were wrong: The name of the owner is Nat, not Nick; it was Nat's cousin, not his brother, who co-owned the Peach Pit; and although Brandon indeed has been working there during Nat's illness, Nat still owns his 50 percent. Nevertheless, although she hesitated ("his — his um brother"), Jane continued to speak authoritatively. Katey's immediate response was to counter with her own "expertise," an association from a previous episode (although she reproduced Jane's error with regard to the name, calling the owner Nick):

KATEY: Oh. I remember when they were gonna rip it down.
G: The Peach Pit, really?
KATEY: Yeah. And then like Nick started talking about all of the — 'Cause (inaudible name) has like a lot of famous people's pictures. And the stuff he was talking about, all the people who went in there and stuff. And um — cause they were going to build like a shopping mall there or something like that. I remember that. It's a while ago though.

"I remember that," Katey said, emphasizing her own knowledgeability — and one-upping her friend in a discursive power move. A similar interaction occurred as Jane went on to narrate the latest development with David's drug habit. Jane told what happened last week, and Katey retaliated by associating the recent events with a previous episode about David's drug habit:

JANE: And he went back to the drugs.
KATEY: Oh, he did.
JANE: Uh, huh. 'Cause he went back to the night shift again.
KATEY: I though that was so stupid that um — Donna and David broke up.
JANE: They were back together, I think. Well, they were talking about it kind of in a way.

KATEY: I remember when she [Donna] went on the skiing trip. Was that the same episode where um—Kelly's sister got lost in the park?
G: I think it was. Wasn't it?
JANE: I don't know.
G (to Jane): Did you see that one?
KATEY: And 'cause David was like really high and he fell asleep or something like that.

In both of these transactions, the girls used talk about the show pleasurably to construct themselves as knowledgeable, knowing the answers. Numerous times during the two interviews, they tenaciously recounted details of previous episodes and/or predicted the future. "Did you see that?" they asked each other, seeking a shared experience, but also introducing a "test" element—I remember this, do you? In fact, they "played pundit" like commentators before an election: They competed, they showed off what they knew, and they quizzed each other.

Conspicuously absent was discussion of the issues the producers said they expected, as described in Chapter 2. Upon learning that David "went back to the drugs," Katey simply responded, "Oh, he did." She did not pursue the moral or ethical issues involved in David's drug use. Rather, she was more interested in dredging her memory for a parallel example, an endeavor in which she succeeded: "Was that the same episode where um—Kelly's sister got lost in the park? [. . .] And 'cause David [who was supposed to be babysitting] was like really high and he fell asleep." In light of producers' claims to make viewers think about the issues, the calm silence about the dangers of David's drug habit so intrigued me that I devoted a later chapter to the way this and other issues were handled. Instead, in much spontaneous talk about plots, the object seemed to be to cite as many episodes and describe as many storylines as possible:

JANE: I remember when Brenda and Kelly used to be best friends. And Brenda went to France was it?
KATEY: Yeah.
JANE: And um—um—and she was going out with Dylan then. And then Kelly got involved with Dylan. Did you see that?
KATEY: Yeah.

"I remember [. . .] Did you see that?" The speaker not only is expert, but also in competition with her friend, proving she is more knowledgeable.

Some of the older viewers, who narrated plots with equal enjoyment, "played pundit" in an even more subtle way. A sophisticated example occurred when three Princeton University students speculated during a commercial on the significance of a recent episode that took place in the 1960s. In that show, Brenda finds a diary recounting events during the Vietnam War. As she reads it we see the events reenacted, peopled in Brenda's imagination by herself and her friends, dressed in '60s outfits and speaking dated slang. My own take on the show was that the producers had fun nostalgically re-creating and playing with '60s stereotypes. (I watched it with a sixth-grader and a seventh-grader, who seemed quite uninterested, and a high-school student, who told me she was somewhat curious because she had studied the Vietnam War in school.) In the exchange below, however, Princeton student Terry wanted to see the events on the episode as a "preview" of what would happen in the present, a notion roommate Kyle vehemently opposed. The episode we were watching was a rerun, which explains the verb tense.

David and Donna talking about anniversary and waiting to have sex until they are married.

ALL: Laughter.

REBECCAH: Did they have sex this episode?

TERRY: No.

REBECCAH: Do they have sex the next episode? They still haven't had sex, have they?

TERRY: Actually, wasn't there something like last week, or no, two weeks ago in that retro—or whenever the retro thing was about her having sex with him and then him dumping her afterwards?

KYLE: Well, yeah, but that was, that was the '60s characters.

TERRY: Yeah, but everything else in those characters—

KYLE: No, no, no, no. No, no, no. It hasn't happened yet.

TERRY: I don't know.

KYLE: No, no, no. That '60s episode was just all the same characters, were just supposed to—I mean—

TERRY: Well, all the same characters had the same things happening to them.

KYLE: Not necessarily.

TERRY: Well, Kelly was going out with Dylan—

KYLE: Yeah, but—

TERRY: Brenda was jealous.

KYLE: Yeah, but—

TERRY: The only thing was Brandon—well, Brandon was a conservative prick.

REBECCAH: It wasn't meant to—I don't think the episode was meant for all of the people to end up like, to show like what was going to happen with all the people. I mean, I don't think, when they did that episode, it was meant to like tell us that Donna and David had sex.

TERRY: I don't know. I don't think it was meant to tell us that, but maybe that, maybe we were supposed to guess. I have no idea.

As in the argument between the high school students over what was the most boring/most interesting part of the show, this disagreement was carried on quite aggressively ("No, no, no, no. No, no, no. It hasn't happened yet"), dividing the viewer community against itself. Like a news show roundtable analyzing an election or a group of sports color commentators, viewers vied with each other to gain acceptance for their interpretations, each presenting herself as the most credible expert.

But what I have called "playing pundit" went beyond the issues of expertise and community that have already been raised. In addition, it necessitated intense and careful scrutiny of the text that importantly constructed that text as authoritative. As the Princeton students quoted above analyzed what they thought the producers were signaling about whether Donna and David will have sex, they focused on the task of memorizing and analyzing the text from multiple angles. "I don't think it was meant to tell us that, but maybe we were supposed to guess," Terry said. And of course, what we are "supposed" to do, we will do. Our job is to know as much as possible about plot twists and the motives behind them—and the bottom-line authority here is the text.

Constructing the Authoritative Text

Perhaps the most extreme examples of positioning the text as authoritative came from the younger viewers. Unexpectedly to me, all of them unproblematically indicated that they learned from the behavior of the television characters. Active information-gatherers seeking the expert position, they treated the show as a valid source of data about life. Consider, for example, the following exchange in an interview with two seventh-graders:

G: Do you think that TV affects you?
PAM: Yeah. I guess
G: Yeah, in what way?
PAT: 'Cause you kind of learn stuff on TV.
G: Mm-hmm?
PAT: Like how certain people act and do you want to act like them and stuff.

"Like how certain people act and do you want to act like them." For the younger viewers, television was a perfectly legitimate source of information about how people behave. And the girls worked hard to become experts in this area. Sixth-grader Maddy commented, "I like watching the end the best 'cause it shows how they solved their problems." This statement not only positions Maddy as waiting to find out the solution to the problem du jour, but also situates the television "answer" as worthy of note. In another example, two ninth-graders watched a clip about date rape (*Laura: "Is that date rape?" Counselor: "Yes. Don't be afraid to call it that"*). Esther immediately asked, "It is?" Jackie added, "I never knew that." In an adult, one might suspect sarcasm, but I heard these comments as perfectly serious.

As has already been observed, these girls "learned stuff on TV" through rote memorization. They said they concentrated on remembering what happened, rather than on asking themselves whether they would behave like the characters, or even what it would be like to *be* the character:

G: When you watch it, do you think to yourself what you would do if you were in that situation?
KATEY & JANE: Not really.
G: What do you mostly just think about?
JANE: What's going to happen next.
KATEY: Yeah.

These viewers seldom questioned the logic of events; they were much more likely simply to absorb and regurgitate. For example, eighth-grade twins Marissa and Melanie said they remembered the high-school graduation episode as their favorite, but not because they explored the identities of the graduates. Instead, they simply concentrated on remembering what happened:

M: They went up there, and they like slept over overnight on the campground—
M: Like they were telling, like, where they were going to go to college and stuff—
G: Uh huh.
M: —and she's like, "I'm going to go back there," and like all that.
G: So when you're watching it, are you thinking, sometimes, you know, like, what you might do what you graduate? From high school?
M & M: Not really. No.

Marissa and Melanie didn't picture how they would feel graduating from high school. They simply memorized things high school graduates do— sleeping overnight in a campground, telling where they were going to college. And once they had the details at their fingertips, they could speak with authority, one-up their friends, be expert.

Other viewers (typically older) tended to be a little more analytical, but the same curious disjunction occurred: They spoke in an expert voice, but at the same time, constructed the text as authoritative. When a viewer became confused, it was she, not the text, that was as at fault. In a typical example, one viewer recited the complex peregrinations of David and Kelly:

COURTNEY: He had the biggest crush on Kelly, and then their parents started dating, and Kelly was mortified that her mother fell in love with the father of one of the biggest dorks in the school. And then Kelly, of course, Kelly and David started getting to know each other and started getting close or, like, got to be friends, and he realized he probably couldn't date her because their parents would probably get married and so they, they accepted each other as—I don't know what the deal is now because their parents are divorced, but David still lives with Kelly and her mom or, or did live with Kelly and her mom. I just never understood that. And yet, and so he and Kelly are technically not related in any way, but—except for the fact that they have a half sister and they still call each other brother and—I don't know, it's very strange.

"I just never understood that." Courtney didn't suggest that the many-faceted, somewhat mercurial text might be confused or inconsistent. If she doesn't understand it, it must be her fault; the text is authoritative. But she also constructed herself as author of the experience: "*I* just never understood that." As mentioned in previous chapters, the expert voice authored the viewing experience.

A delightful real-life parallel occurred during viewing with seventh-grader Katey. A promotional advertisement for the 10 O'Clock News came on, including a clip of a fire in Philadelphia, that sparked a recitation from real life:

KATEY: Um—my mom's aunt's sister's daughter's husband was one of those guys who died in the Philadelphia fire. One of the two.
G: Oh, really?
[. . .]
JANE: Your mom's—how was it?
KATEY: My mom's aunt's sister's daughter's husband was one of the two guys who died in the Philadelphia fire. It was like kind of hard to understand.

Katey had carefully memorized this litany of relationships, although she didn't really understand it:

G: Well, I'm thinking, her aunt's sister—isn't that also her aunt then? Or is it different—
KATEY: No, because. Wait.

JANE: She was not on the same side of the family maybe.
KATEY: Yeah.
G: Oh, oh.
KATEY: I think 'cause—it was, I don't know, but I don't think that she was related.

It would be difficult to distinguish between this discursive treatment of a real-life relationship and Courtney's construction of Kelly and David's relationship on *90210*. And in the latter, Courtney gave the same authority to the television text that Katey gave to the real-life situation. Both confessed they didn't really understand the relationship ("Wait. I think 'cause—it was, I don't know," Katey said. Courtney commented, "I just never understood that. I don't know, it's very strange"). Neither questioned that the facts existed to be understood; Courtney never suggested that the television text was inconsistent, any more than Katey would suggest that the real-life relationship was a sham. Like sports commentators, both got kudos when they were experts and took the blame when they faltered.

This is such an important dissonance that I have devoted the next chapter, a discussion of the discursive construction of television effects, to an exploration of the ways that almost all viewers granted authority to the television text while simultaneously positioning themselves as authors of their viewing experience. The rest of this chapter examines what this careful attention to the text and these recitations and analyses might be accomplishing in terms of identity.

Linking Fictional Narrative and Self-Narrative

As I listened to these persistent and tireless efforts to memorize, regurgitate, and sometimes dissect plots and relationships—pursued with a doggedness that teachers dream of inspiring—I suspected that this enthusiastic activity was accomplishing identity work. The one-upping was somewhat unsettling, as the girls brought competitive and hierarchical values into their leisure time in the patriarchal manner that Gilligan, Lyons, and Hanmer (1990) have suggested silences relational voices. But it did not seem to me that this discursive rivalry alone could account for such perseverance.

As discussed in Chapter 4, theory suggests that narratives are one important way we structure our reality. It seemed very likely to me that, for these girls, *90210* plots, in addition to furnishing a forum to play school, provided these viewers an important way of structuring the reality of teenage life. And that chapter pinpointed self-narrative as an important identity component. For the viewers I listened to, recitations of *90210* plots not infrequently cycled back into their construction of self-narrative.

For example, as they looked ahead, many viewers (typically the younger ones) intermingled elements of the fictional narrative into the narratives they projected for themselves. In the exchange below, seventh-grader Danielle, whose mother went to college but whose father did not, seemed to have lifted her notion of college life from the show relatively unproblematically. Sixth-grader Amanda, whose parents went to Penn State, drew on her non-mediated knowledge:

G: Are you guys going to go to college, do you think?
AMANDA: Yeah.
DANIELLE: I am.
AMANDA: I am.
G: Yeah?
DANIELLE: I want to go to UCLA, and the reason I want to go there is because that's the only college I know that's in California.
G: And you want to go to California?
DANIELLE: Yeah.
G: Why?
DANIELLE: I don't know, it just seems nice.
G: From watching it, you mean?
DANIELLE: Yeah.
G: Yeah?
DANIELLE: And like, my dad was like trying to get me to stay back here, but I wanna go out there.
G: Oh, really?
DANIELLE: 'Cause he still lives in Florida.
G: Oh, wow, it's a long way huh?
DANIELLE: So, he's trying to keep me over here, and I don't want to stay over here.
G: Yeah. (to Amanda) Where do you want to go?
AMANDA: I want to go to Penn State.
G: Do you? Yeah? Do you know someone who goes there?
AMANDA: Well, my, both of my parents went there.
G: Oh.

Both girls had constructed self-narratives, colonized the future, in Giddens' (1991) words. And while the content differed, the narratives carried the same authority. Amanda linked hers to her parents' real-life experience, while Danielle unproblematically blended her narrative with the fictional one—but both were valued equally.

It seems likely that, as Danielle approaches college age, real-life information will reshape her early desire for UCLA. The point is not so much to ask whether the show will influence her actions (an always-questionable undertaking!) as to suggest that talk about the show cycles back into new ways of attending to one's own life—even if it is only to provide Amanda with the social power of an answer to the ever-puzzling question, "Where do you want to go to college?"

Similarly, the notion of living with friends in an apartment at college and going to the beach with them was maintained and incorporated into what seventh-grader Katey knew about a real-life institution, Temple University in Philadelphia, where she said she wanted to go:

KATEY: I'd want to live in um—they're not the dorms. They're like apartments but they're on the campus.
G: Or near sometimes. Depending on where you go.
KATEY: I think they have those for Temple. And that's what I'd like to do. Like and live with my friends and stuff. I think that'd be really fun. And then like you could go to the beach with them and stuff.

In my mind, living in North Philadelphia and going to the beach are somewhat tenuously linked. Katey, however, effortlessly blended the nearby university into the fictional college narrative.

The same blending occurred as Katey spontaneously talked about where she would like to live:

KATEY: I'd like to live in Beverly Hills?
G: Would you?
KATEY: Well, actually I would. But, like if Beverly Hills came over here, then it would be nice. 'Cause there wouldn't be any earthquakes or anything else.
G: Yeah, right. Yeah, there was that big earthquake.
KATEY: So if [her home town] became Beverly Hills, that would be nice. Live in a big house.

In a serious tone, Katey unproblematically combined what she knew about the real-life situation in California (earthquakes occur there) and about the fictional depiction of life there (everyone in Beverly Hills lives in a big house), then compromised by combining the two. Obviously, Katey knew she was speaking hypothetically. However, the material things she associated with the show and talked about with her friends had been woven into an agreeable narrative of what she would like for herself.

Fiske (1987) has pointed out that adult soap-opera viewers often cheerfully effect this blending of real life and character, as in the common practice of sending letters to a television station addressed to soap opera characters. He argued that these viewers are not "duped," but rather are pleasurably playing with the boundaries between reality and fantasy. The young viewers I listened to did the same in their blending of fictional and self-narrative, as in this conversation with sixth-grader Maddy:

MADDY: If I didn't go to college I'd probably be working at like McDonald's.
G: Uh huh.
MADDY: I'd probably see like, like, one of the *90210* people there. The ones that would probably be working there if they weren't on the show. They'd probably be like working at Burger King or something. If they didn't go to college.

Maddy understood that not going to college can mean a dead-end job, an important real-life truth. However, she lightheartedly blended that knowledge with the construction of a world in which the reality of her own prospects could overlap with those of uncommonly wealthy and attractive television personalities. Moreover, she blended character and actor narratives. I was asking what the characters would do when they graduate, and her response suggested that (1) if the characters didn't go to college they wouldn't be on the show; (2) if the actor were out of work s/he might have to get a dead-end job; and (3) this could parallel her own prospects. She enjoyed her joke—and she effected a subtle discursive blend of fiction and self.

Again, a key aspect of this process was the way it constructed the viewer as author of the experience. In their statements, viewers discursively positioned themselves as the sources of their ideas: "*I'd* like to live in Beverly Hills"; "*I* want to go to college in California"; even "*I'd* probably see like, one of the *90210* people at McDonald's." The statements were never, "The show makes me want to live in Beverly Hills"; "The way California looks on TV makes me want to go to college there"; or even "The show makes the characters seem so attractive that I wish I could see them in person." Viewers' construction concealed the show's role in shaping the blended narrative.

Attending to Show, Attending to Self Through Narrative

As with characterization and appearance, viewer background did intersect with ways of attending to the plots. A good example is talk about Brenda that occurred in the first minutes of an interview with Jackie. The ninth-grader had been through repeated operations and lengthy hospital stays to correct a congenital problem, and had endured much painful physical therapy ("the PT was horrible"). She said her favorite episode was one in which Brenda had a similar experience with hospitals and health care: "And, um, she's been through a lot of things, like the scare with breast cancer and everything. (G: Mmm) And it's just like—nice to watch her go through it. (G: Yeah) [. . .] And she had a lot of crying scenes and I think she did really well." Jackie found special interest in Brenda's brush with serious illness, even though she did not explicitly link it with her own experiences. Her self-narrative gave her away to attend to the show's narrative.

Similarly, in talking about the plethora of coincidences in the show, Marissa and Melanie honed in on an episode that had to do with twins: "Like the one where, um, Steve and, um, Brandon were like dating this one girl, but they turned out to be twins. And one had a date with one, and the other had a date with one. And he's like, 'That's the same girl I'm going out with.' It was so weird."

When I suggested that they, as twins, might have a similar experience, they vehemently disagreed:

G: So, you didn't think about, "Gosh, that could ever happen to us"? You said, "No."
M: Like best friends going out with different twin sisters.
G: Mm-hmm.
M: I was almost—this one thing—
M: The twins—
M: —twins like—it's like really—I'm like, "That could never like actually"—well, it *could*, but probably—
G: (encouraging) Probably will.
M: Like the chances of that are like one like—
G: Yeah.
M: —in one billion.

"Like best friends going out with different twin sisters. [. . .] The chances of that are one [. . .] in one billion." To me, the disclaimer is less interesting than the way in which an episode involving twins was noted and remarked on. Real-life experiences influenced the way the television narrative was attended to—and the narrative cycled back into ways viewers attended to their own futures, in this case, the possibility (or lack thereof) of dating best friends.

In a similar example of background cycling into viewing, Kristen, who chose to live with grandparents in New Jersey while the rest of her family lived in a distant state, paid close attention to an episode where Steve had a run-in with his father:

G: Did you have a favorite part?
KRISTEN: Steve fighting with his dad.

G: Really. Why?

KRISTEN: 'Cause I'm so glad that Steve got [paid] his dad back.

This scene was not salient or even interesting to Kristen's friend Jeannette, who lived with both parents and who had commented during viewing of this scene, "This is what's called the boring part of the show."

In the same way, college student Courtney said the affair between Lucinda, the professor, and Brandon, the student, fueled her imagination about real-life affairs:

COURTNEY: And also, it's, it's, it's just so funny because, I mean, (inaudible) imaginations. I mean, we all hear, I mean, some of us hear about, you know, the—

RUTH: Oh, yeah, pre—that's true.

COURTNEY: —the crew coaches who sleep with their, with their—

RUTH: A different (inaudible).

COURTNEY: —athletes. I know. Yeah. And we're just like, "Does it really happen?" You know, like you try to pretend like you're so shocked, but you're like, "Tell me details!"

"Does it really happen?" Courtney's experience with college gossip directed her attention to certain aspects of the polysemic text, and talking about the show's narrative added a new dimension to her real-life experiences. With the on-campus scandal, Courtney had to pretend to be "so shocked," but as she watched Lucinda, the college professor, have an affair with undergraduate Brandon, she asked herself, "Does it really happen?" And as she talked with her friends about sleazy Brandon and pushy Lucinda, she gained access to a way of talking about the alleged real-life affair—"Tell me the details!"

Interestingly, despite the variety of backgrounds that gave different ways of attending to narratives, certain plots were recalled with great consistency. One episode that stuck in viewers' memories occurred early in the series: David's friend Scott, who was playing with a gun, accidentally killed himself. This episode was cited as memorable by nearly all viewers. A small sampling:

PAM: Oh, I liked the one when David's friend died.

G: Mm, yeah.

PAM: I liked that one.

G: A lot of people say that one. (To Pat) Did you see that one?

PAT: Mm-hmm.

G: Yeah, what was—what made you remember that episode?

PAM: Um, I don't really know. I just—it—there was like, like different from all the rest. Like, you would never suspect it.

G: Mm-hmm.

[. . .]

PAM: His name was Scott. [. . .] I like, I always liked Scott. I always thought he was nice.

G: Oh, really?

PAM: So that's probably why.

* * *

JEANNETTE: Favorite episode.

KRISTEN: Um—

JEANNETTE: When Scott shot himself.

G: Oh, yeah.

KRISTEN: Oh, yeah.

JEANNETTE: That was—I watched that one with [Corinne].

G: Oh, yeah?

JEANNETTE: Yeah, 'cause we had—it was when I was in junior high, and we had youth group on Thursday nights?

G: Right.

JEANNETTE: So, right when it was on, she called me and she's like, when he shoots himself, she was screaming. That episode just sort of sticks in my mind. It was just, it was just, I was crying, I really cried at that one.

G: Wow.

KRISTEN: Yeah, it was really sad.

G: It was unexpected.

JEANNETTE: Right.

G: Yeah.

JEANNETTE: But the previews, they were like, someone is going to shoot themselves, commits, like, suicide—

KRISTEN: Yeah. No—but they like didn't say who—

JEANNETTE: Yeah.

KRISTEN: Or anything.

JEANNETTE: Yeah.

KRISTEN: And then for like the next five days she [Jeannette] tried to figure out like who it was.

JEANNETTE: Yeah.

G: Mm-hmm.

JEANNETTE: And there were all these arguments in my school. "Who's gonna get killed?"

G: Wow.

JEANNETTE: I was crying during that one.

KRISTEN: Yeah, I was too.

* * *

ERIKA: What we think is—I remember um, the one year that that kid, David's friend, uh—
G: Uh huh, uh huh.
ERIKA: —shot himself. We had a bet going. (Giggles)
G: Because you saw on the previews.
ERIKA: Previews. One of them was going to die. We bet which one was going to die.

Seventh-grader Pam, high-school students Jeannette and Kristen, and college student Erika all remember this episode (a coup for the producers!). (These excerpts also reveal how I became contaminated as an interviewer, offering such prompting short-cuts as "Because you saw on the previews"! This process of predicting from the previews is examined in the chapter on guessing.)

But perhaps more importantly, as viewers remembered the episode, they blended it with their personal reactions and histories. As they recalled the fictional narrative, they added to the pleasure of the recital by linking it to a self-narrative. For Jeannette, the memory remained detailed: the days of excited anticipation at school, the phone call from her friend Corinne, the tears. Erika remembered the betting; even Pam (who must have been in fourth grade during that episode) remembered how she always liked Scott, how the episode was so different from the rest, how "you would never suspect it." The community was forged with other viewers and with the characters. And the story of Scott's death was interwoven with the viewer's own self-narrative and sense of her past— of who she was.

One viewer expressly said that talk about the show gave her ways to attend to her past. College student Casey told an anecdote about her favorite episode, when school authorities threatened to withhold Donna's high school diploma:

CASEY: This is, this is my reasoning. I remember sitting in here watching it last year and my best friend was at home and she called me up. My friend [Tom] wasn't allowed to graduate with us (giggle). I swear to God when I went home that weekend, we were all talking about it. I don't know why, how it came up. We were just like sitting around drinking, all of a sudden, we saw a preview or something on TV, something brought it up, and we started talking about like what they did. And [Tom] came over to [Jeri's] house, 'cause we were at her house, her—he's like, "You guys didn't do that for me." And it was just kind of symbolic, like I could see my—the people in my class doing this.
G: Yeah.
CASEY: Like if we would have seen this show before and then this situation would have happened, they probably would have done it. It sounds

sick, but they would have. (Laughter) So to me, that's my favorite one, because I could just relate to it at home.

As she imagined retrospectively how the show's script might have been followed by her class, Casey (1) drew a connection between her life and the show; (2) attended to the show's narrative based on her own background; (3) attended to her self-narrative in terms of the show; and (4) spoke with authority and agency ("they probably would have done it"). (As discussed in the next chapter, in Casey's disclaimer—"It sounds sick"—we hear the oft-repeated refrain that only "sick" people copy the behavior of television characters.)

As members of their community went on skiing trips, had sex or didn't have sex, as a group member shot himself and another marched in a demonstration, these narratives gave viewers a way to interpret, measure, and value various aspects of their own experience. And the intensity with which viewers attended to these plots, the efforts they made to become skilled in their intricacies, suggested that these narratives had great importance for them. Without arguing that the show "made" viewers behave a certain way, I would suggest that it offered them a subject position from which to view the world, a yardstick with which to measure their own behavior and identities. And as viewers linked fictional and self-narratives, they discursively positioned themselves as authors of the blended narrative, concealing the role of the television text in structuring the normal and real.

This interweaving of narratives while positioning the self as the author of the process is another way that enculturation works; it is one of the microprocesses of hegemony. And as I have said throughout this study, one could see this active enculturation process as adaptive. If you are a teenager, it behooves you to understand your culture's construction of same (vacationing, having sex, demonstrating). However, in the previous two chapters, I also have argued that this process can be implicated in the reproduction of our patriarchal and capitalist culture. While the learning, analyzing, and recounting of plots has an active component, this process can work hegemonically to win consent to dominant notions of female identity.

90210 Narrative and Dominant Notions of Female Identity

Provocative and suggestive as all of these interweavings of self-narrative and *90210* narrative are, among the most intriguing is the way recitations of the show's plots and relationships blended with real-life narratives to reproduce and reinstantiate dominant notions of female identity.

Consider, for example, the way blending of fictional and self-narrative played out for college student Marion, who described how her boyfriend sometimes referred to an episode when Brenda locked the keys in Stuart's car: "It's like now like, [Dan] will say, 'Don't pull a Brenda,' you know, he'll say stuff like that." Dan's blended narrative foregrounded the typical impractical woman who would in an airhead move lock the keys in the car. That female identity was indeed offered in the text, and Dan recycled it into a real-life context.

The way that talking about narratives pleasurably won consent to the status quo can be seen most clearly in conversations about the characters' and actors' romances. A frequent topic of conversation ("Did they have sex this episode? Do they have sex the next episode? They still haven't had sex, have they?"), romantic relationships were recounted with avid interest. As one viewer said, "It's the only show that I know that I could tell you almost every [actor's] name, like, their marital status, you know." A few viewers said they purposefully ignored information about the actors, but most could effortlessly reel off information about the actors' private lives, as in this genealogy about actress Shannen Doherty, who plays Brenda: "She married a guy after only knowing him two weeks, [. . .] and he's really cute, but he's only 19 and [. . .] George Hamilton's son." Or as another viewer said, in talking about Brian Austin Green, who plays David, "I just think this is interesting. I don't know why I'm thinking of this, but I was just thinking—Brian Austin Green is dating Tiffani-Amber from *Saved by the Bell*, and Tori Spelling [Green's on-screen romance] use to BE on *Saved by the Bell*."

How pleased a schoolteacher might be with such a succinct notation of an irony, rattling off three names, three relationships, and a title! And how concerned the teacher might be that the most frequent topic of these recitations was the dating/marriage relationship—in terms set by the *90210* text and the rambunctious actors! As discussed in Chapter 4, I would argue that, while romance and dating are certainly important in life, this type of recitation naturalized them as of key importance. A constant subtext of the endless recitations was that a woman's identity is incomplete without a man, and that her primary task is to attract and keep him. And, as with talk about hairstyles and eyebrows, relationship talk gave these young viewers a certain way to attend to their own lives.

For example, consider the following quite similar reactions, from a college student, and then two eighth-graders, to a Valentine's Day subplot about Brenda and Stuart:

JOAN: It was Valentine's Day and he [Stuart] came and he brought her [Brenda] roses and candy. She was complaining around how she didn't get a Valentine, and he's standing behind her the whole time. But it was funny.

* * *

M: Um, um, my favorite part? I don't know. It was—must've been when Brenda was sitting there yelling. [. . .] It was funny part when Brenda—Brenda was sitting there.
G: Mm-hmm.
M: She's like all angry and everything. It was funny.

"She's complaining around"; "she's like all angry and everything"; "it was funny." College student Joan and eighth-graders Marissa and Melanie reconstructed the scene the same way and expressed the same pleasurable reaction: Brenda complained that she did not have a boyfriend to bring her presents on Valentine's Day, while Stuart, his arms full of flowers, stood behind her listening, and this was humorous.

A complex moment, this little scenario typified the way *90210* worked to perpetuate dominant notions of female identity. It touched a nerve in these viewers by opening up a relatively unusual and somewhat tempting subject position. Brenda makes an open and unabashed demand for love, something we all have felt the desire to do. And she is not pretty and nice about it; instead, she openly expresses confrontive emotions—she is "like all angry"; she is "complaining around." And indeed she gets what she wants—Stuart, in a re-enactment of traditional gender roles, has arrived with gifts and candy.

But even as Brenda's need is fulfilled, the text discredits her confrontive emotions. Stuart was "standing behind her the whole time"—her anger is reproved, shown to be unnecessary. The audience laughs at, not with, her. She gets what she wanted, but she looks like a fool. The notion that a woman might honestly and confrontively express her need is explored, presented as a possibility—then closed off, while the gender roles relative to Valentine's Day—active male, passive female—are reinstantiated. And this resolution, this comfortable return to the status quo, was faithfully reproduced in talk by viewers.

As discussed in Chapter 2, *90210* narratives of necessity are imbued with concealed hierarchies, value systems, and silences; built into their narrative structure is the necessity for discrediting identities that challenge the status quo. And I found that exploration of alternate identities for women, followed by ultimate rejection of them, were faithfully reproduced in viewers' pleasurable talk about the show's narratives. As with the talk about appearance and characterizations, talk about *90210* plots pleasurably won viewer consent to a status quo in which a key component of female identity is her ability to attract and keep a man.

Because of the volume of data in this area, and the importance it possesses in my eyes, I have accorded it a full chapter, the one on dating.

Summary

Talk about the plots and relationships created community; it invited an empowered, expert voice. Viewers actively "played pundit" as they memorized, critiqued, and analyzed plot twists. Indeed, they took this task very seriously, one-upping each other and arguing over their interpretations of producers' intentions. In so doing, however, they handed complete authority to the television text—even as they positioned themselves as authors of their opinions. They blended self and fictional narratives in ways that constructed themselves as expert and concealed the ways the television text structured ways they attended to their self-narratives.

A key subtext for those narratives was the notion that a major component of a woman's identity is her ability to attract and keep a man. While talk about narratives sometimes worked to open up alternate possibilities, it ultimately bowed to the authority of the text and closed those options down.

Theory suggests that narratives function to structure our reality, to naturalize socially constructed values, and to open some possibilities while closing off others. In memorizing and reproducing *90210* narratives, and in discursively weaving them into their self-narratives, viewers organized and prioritized life options that, I would suggest, worked hegemonically to win pleasurable consent to a world of limited potential for females. Thus, I would argue that talk about *90210* plots did not count as real discursive agency in the feminist sense, since it did not interrogate the naturalness of the narratives. These ideas will be explored in depth in the chapter on dating.

As I have mentioned before, one could argue that the memorization of narratives was an efficient and adaptive way to join one's culture, to prepare oneself to take one's place within it. But it is disquieting to recognize that the television industry is setting the terms by which viewers "learned" their culture—and that viewer talk concealed this fact. This insistence on the self as independent of the text, and the discursive concealing of ways in which the text exerted authority ("I don't know why I'm thinking this"), are examined in the next chapter.

Chapter 8
Talk About TV Effects: Enculturation

On my list of questions I prepared before doing the interviews, I included the simple inquiry, "Do you think TV affects you?" My intent was not to make a claim about *90210* in comparison or contrast to other types of viewing, or about "television effects" per se, but rather to elucidate a discourse that underlay viewer experience of *90210*, highlighting certain aspects of the viewing process and concealing others. While the responses turned out to be tangential to the theme of female identity, they speak directly to the ways the themes of community and expertise interlock with Western thinking about enculturation. To my mind, these conversations sent up some red flags that media literacy proponents may wish to attend to. I also hope this chapter might prove thought-provoking for viewers and readers in general in our media encounters.

The last several chapters have shown how viewers analyzed, critiqued, and memorized aspects of *90210*; as reported in Chapter 2, they also said they arranged shower and homework time, turned down jobs or left night classes early, switched off their phone bells or even recorded temporary new messages ("You know what I'm doing. Why are you calling?") to protect their *90210* viewing time. And all the while, these viewers denied that television affected them. To me, this way of constructing the notion of "television effects" suggested a complicated relationship between behaving, thinking, and "being affected" that called for exploration.

As background, I want to give a brief nod to the effects literature that has importantly influenced the way our culture—and the viewers I listened to—conceptualize television. And I will also use this forum to air the somewhat unorthodox belief that the history of television research is much more unified than generally indicated by our academic arguments about methods and models. It seems to me that both quantitative and qualitative researchers have carefully and fruitfully pursued that slippery and elusive question of what happens when people watch television. Though each research paradigm feels bound to critique the others for not taking its particular interests into account, it seems to me that we are all looking at different aspects of the same important issue. Indeed, as has been seen, even within cultural studies we have different ways of expressing the problem, different ideas about what counts as data, and different interpretations of our results.

But our concerns remain the same. Frankly, we worry: can the very large, very powerful, and very self-interested media industry manipulate us in ways that disadvantage us or are just plain bad for us? In fact, it was fear of the brainwashing power of media that inspired early American mass media research, which studied World War I propaganda. These researchers feared that malevolent senders could inject messages into helpless receivers with a "hypodermic needle" or "magic bullet" (for an overview, cf. Littlejohn 1989, Wimmer and Dominick 1983; for an overview of models, cf. Ruben 1988). Later research agendas through the 1950s included an increased interest in advertising, public information, and journalism, particularly political messages (e.g., Schramm 1954; Katz and Lazarsfeld 1955). Throughout, researchers feared that persuasive and controlling media could deliver a unitary, unidirectional message to an essentially passive and undifferentiated public.

This context provided a background as television became a focus of study: Mass media were seen as potent persuaders, suspected to possess the power to make people both passive and violent. The viewer was at first suspected to be malleable, a passive *tabula rasa*, and television a leveler, producing uniform effects on all viewers.

This position was abandoned several decades ago, as described by Klapper (1960), who concluded that research had invalidated the "magic bullet." In its place had come the theory of limited effects: mass communication can reinforce beliefs, but it cannot convert; moreover, neither violent nor passive behavior can be attributed directly to exposure to mass media. Social and psychological factors play an intervening role in the ways in which mass media messages are received, Klapper said.

Klapper outlined lines of inquiry that predicted, if not prescribed, mass media research agendas in the next decades—research that has become theoretically divergent: emphasis on powerful media vs. studies of a resistant public; emphasis on unilateral vs. limited vs. multifaceted message; emphasis on the individual vs. social effects of television; emphasis on qualitative vs. quantitative data. In part, this divergence can be traced to the fact that during the 1960s, before the consolidation in this country of communications departments, much media research originated within sociology and psychology, with a consequent divergence of research questions (Wimmer and Dominick 1983).

It is revealing to note here was that limited-effects theories were based on the psychological notion of the unified, stable self described in the chapter on social construction. And in my observation, both limited effects and the notion of the unified self have considerable cultural currency today, particularly around the issue of violence in the media. The discourse of television effects focuses on the power (or lack thereof) of the autonomous individual to resist media, which can reinforce but not convert.

This position has colored the findings of one of the most important schools of quantitative television research today, the cultivation theorists. This school has argued for decades that long-time exposure to television results in a shift in one's perception of reality (for an overview of research, cf. Morgan and Signorielli 1990; Rosengren and Windahl 1989). TV can both convince and reinforce, as Morgan and Signorielli (1990) put it: "Cultivation thus means the steady entrenchment of mainstream orientations in most cases and the systematic but almost imperceptible modification of previous orientations in others; in other words, affirmation for the believers and indoctrination for the deviants" (p. 19).

Cultivation theory has built up a considerable body of work that has had an important voice in political debates over media effects. Gerbner's annual television violence profiles, widely cited in the popular press, have become cemented in the nation's consciousness (cf., for example, Gerbner et al. 1980). However, in my opinion, American culture's entrenched devotion to the rugged individualist ideal has effectively counterbalanced its findings. Although many parents continue to object to television, just as they strove to censor comic books and then radio, most of us as adults simply do not want to believe that we are not in control of our viewing experiences.

And direct proof that television can change our behavior is frustratingly difficult to find. Moreover, this research is hampered by the wealthy and powerful media industry, which has gained an important voice in this debate. It was for this reason that, in this study, I turned to the social constructionists, who bring the argument to the discursive level, treating talk as action.

During the time of my study, these issues of individualism and agency vis-a-vis television were very live for viewers, especially the younger ones. My interviews occurred shortly after a much-publicized case in which a boy, in alleged imitation of the defiantly raunchy MTV cartoon *Beavis and Butt-head* set his house afire (e.g., "Mother blames a deadly fire," October 1993). Almost all of the viewers had followed to some extent the ensuing flap, which followed the familiar, if diluted, lines of the television effects literature: Concerned parents called for restrictions on television violence, while the media industry responded by arguing that television cannot make viewers do anything. These responses were echoed in talk by *90210* viewers; their often self-contradictory opinions were also somewhat self-interested because, for some younger viewers, viewing privileges could be at stake.

The Core Self as Separate from Talk and Behavior

Virtually all viewers maintained that television either did not affect them, or that they had the power to keep it from affecting them. Only a few suggested that television could affect them without their knowledge. In general, when asked directly, viewers' first reaction was to deny television effects:

G: Do you think it [TV] affects you?
AMANDA: I don't, I don't think so. I don't really think so.
G: (to Danielle) What do you think?
DANIELLE: I don't think it really does, no.

* * *

G: Do you think that television, watching television affects you?
JACKIE: Not really.
[. . .]
G: Not really?
JACKIE: I think I'd still be doing my life the way I'm doing it if there wasn't any TV.

What struck me at first were the repeated denials; on later examination of the transcripts, I was impressed by the repeated use of the qualifier "really." Television does not "really" affect you. In the second example above, I probed by repeating the qualifier, and ninth-grader Jackie responded, "I'd still be doing my life the way I'm doing it if there wasn't any TV." These viewers constructed a complicated division of self among their "real" selves, their behavior, and what they thought. Behind their actions sat the homunculus of Enlightenment thinking: We have a core, unitary self that guides our external behaviors and keeps us empowered and autonomous. Jackie spoke with authority, positioning herself as in control of the way she was "doing" her life, constructing an inner Jackie that guided this outward "doing."

This inner, core self bore a complex, difficult-to-untangle relationship with what viewers said they thought and did. For example, Esther, as quoted in the chapter on appearance, said she changed her haircut when Donna did—a move that, as explored earlier, has key links to identity. However, in a later conversation about television effects, Esther suggested that this change did not "really" affect her "self." She drew a distinction between changing her appearance and changing her thoughts and behaviors:

ESTHER: It does not. Shows do not affect people, really.
G: But wait, I thought you just said that—
ESTHER: Only if you want to change your appearance.
G: Uh huh.
ESTHER: Are we talking about in your mind?
G: Uh huh.
ESTHER: Or how you act?
G: Uh huh.
ESTHER: Not really.

"Not really." Although appearance might be changed, the core self was not. And Esther drew what was to be a recurring distinction between "in your mind" and "how you act" when talking about television effects. For example, viewers separated individual instances of behavior from the core self, exemplified by broader worldviews:

G: Do you think that television affects you?
KYLE: Not really. I mean, I don't watch enough to, like—I mean, aside from the fact that I suppose it affects, like, my conversations the next day at like lunch or dinner, whatever. But as far as like really how I view the world, things like that, not really.

Kyle distinguished between her conversations and "how I view the world." When you talk about a television show, it is not "really" affecting you, because such conversations do not affect your global world-view. Talk is just talk; who I am is much more reflected in "how I view the world," which is an internal attribute only tangentially related to anything I say or do.

This is an important point. Viewers saw talk about *90210*—which served as primary data for this study—as unimportant. This approach both gave viewers free rein to indulge in such talk, since it didn't really count for anything, and concealed from them the kinds of explorations and reinstantiations that this study seeks to show such talk accomplished.

Ritual Aspects of Viewing *90210*

This emphasis on the self as the origin of meaning also worked to conceal from viewers the ramifications of other ways in which the show quite obviously impacted their lives, particularly in the community-building ritual of the viewing itself. As mentioned in Chapter 2, younger viewers often watched the show with friends via the telephone; college students tended to gather in dormitory rooms or lounges. "It's such like a gathering," one college student said, and her friends called out agreement: "Yeah. Yeah. It's a ritual." This phenomenon has been observed in connection with other shows by researchers as diverse as Liebes and Katz (1989/91) and Brown (1994).

This ritual assumed large proportions in one sorority I observed, where students playfully put aside homework and extra-curricular activities to pile into their friends' rooms for two hours of delighted viewing. It soon emerged that this was a full-blown culture, with conventions, history, and protocols:

NICKY: Nobody goes out until after it's over with—
ALL: Yeah, right
NICKY: And then we turn on *Melrose.*
SHERRY: The showers are clogged here at 10—like after *Melrose*—
NICKY: Like you can hear a pin drop in the hall [while the shows are on]—it is so quiet—everybody's in their rooms—
PENNI: —and then like a good scene happens—everyone screams and you can hear it—
NICKY: It's like, "Oh my God!"

Knowing when to talk during viewing was an important issue for those who watched the show in groups:

MARION: I have more fun watching it with people as long as they know not to talk during it. Like if you're going to talk, know *when* to talk. You know what I mean?
KAREY: Know the etiquette of watching *Beverly Hills*—
MARION: Yeah. Like (garbled) you can say something like, "Oh my God I can't be—I hate her"—you can say something like that, but don't—
KAREY: Yeah, right.
MARION: —like in the middle of a crucial scene don't like, don't say, you, you know—
KAREY: —"Guess what I bought." (Laughter)
MARION: You know, things like that.

Like women Radway (1984/91) interviewed who closed their doors and protected their reading time, viewers made careful preparations, setting up the videotape and turning off the telephone bell. And like Radway's women, these viewers positioned themselves as in firm control of their behavior when they were making arrangements to protect their viewing time. Radway argued that this behavior worked to reinstantiate more firmly the patriarchal culture surrounding the women she studied. The point I want to make here is that viewers clearly constructed a difference between "being affected" by the show and exhibiting various overt behaviors as a direct result of it. The ritual did not, they insisted, affect their "selves."

Copycatting

It seemed that most viewers saw television as affecting them only if imitating a television character were to make them do something morally wrong, like the boy whose mother accused him of copying *Beavis and Butt-head* when he set the house on fire. Most viewers vehemently repudiated this position for themselves:

M: Like if I saw somebody having sex on TV, it wouldn't make me go out and have sex. You know.
G: Yeah.
M: So—that's what my mom thinks. My mom thinks, "Oh, this is so bad, you're gonna go out and do this." But, like, no, I'm not gonna do it just because it's on TV and some dipstick does it.

The voices rang with confidence. These girls knew right from wrong, and television was not going to lead them astray. This is a slightly different emphasis from the notion that television doesn't "really" affect you. On probing, most viewers impeached *others* as affected by television, and the examples they cited (highly influenced by the *Beavis and Butt-head* anecdote) consisted of direct imitation of morally reprehensible behaviors. In fact, after their statement just quoted, Marissa and Melanie added, "But actually, it doesn't like make me do anything. But some people it would, but not me."

The theme that *others* imitate television, but *I* don't, arose frequently:

G: Do you think they, sometimes your friends kind of act like the characters or try to imitate them at all?
PAM: Yeah.
G: Do they? In what way?
PAM: Well, it seems like most of them try and be like cool and snobby and, like, sort of like Kelly, they act like.

Often, viewers said that children younger than they were affected by TV. This approach held true, no matter how old the viewer was. "It's when you're younger, of course, things like that are going to affect you," said a college-age viewer. "Young kids get influenced," said an eighth-grader; a seventh-grader said, "Well it's not bad when you're older, but for little kids."

In particular, younger boys were seen as affected by *Beavis and Butt-head*. In addition to the publicized fire incident, some viewers cited first-hand experience, as in this interview:

JANE: I know my brothers like talk—you know how Beavis and Butt-head laugh. My brother was like acting like that, and drives me crazy. [. . .] But he, like, acts like Beavis and Butt-head. And he needed a mask so he borrowed a kid's. My mom's like, "Get this out of my house. I don't want this in my house." The mask. He just like acts like him all the time.

In the same way, sisters Sandy and Colleen, with her Colleen's friend Maddy, talked about a younger cousin who watched *Batman*:

SANDY: Like my cousin [Steven] he likes [. . .] he watches *Batman* so he thinks he's Batman. [. . .] He's got these capes his mom buys for him.
G: How old is he?
SANDY: Five.
[. . .]
COLLEEN: I like Bat—I like *Batman.*
SANDY: (garbled)—like that too. Well, like, littler kids are like that. [Ginny] doesn't—
COLLEEN: He's been Batman like for Halloween since he was like 3.
G: Really.
SANDY: Like two years in a row he was like Batman.
MADDY: Who?
COLLEEN: My cousin [Steven]. He's been Batman for like his whole life, he's been pretending he's like Batman. Like, "Batman, Batman can fly," he like—
SANDY: Every word that comes out of his mouth is like "Batman"—
COLLEEN: "Batman."
SANDY: "Batman."

A college student described similar behavior in boys she encountered in her student teaching who watched the show *Cops*.

G: So you don't think that it's [TV] affecting you?
JOAN: No, not at all. I don't think it has. I do believe it does affect some kids. I really do. I think more so boys.
[. . .]
G: You said, you think it affects boys more?
JOAN: Yeah, I think so. I think they get more aggressive. I mean, seeing the kids that I worked with and I dealt with at school, it definitely affected them. Like that show *Cops*. I mean, I got pretty upset when they came in saying—and they can sing the song to the show. I mean I know it's a pretty popular song and was on the radio and stuff, but—
MEETRA: If it means, the (inaudible)—kids watch that.
JOAN: Exactly, and that—
G: And how old are these kids?

JOAN: These kids are only 4 or 5 years old. And that got me really up-set. And the girls didn't know it [the song], just the boys. The girls had no idea what this song was. But these boys would come in sing the song for me.

MEETRA: 'Cause these kids are more affected by—at that age, affected by what's on TV.

The unspoken frame for this discussion is that television effects are bad. To be affected by television, viewers said, means to do something morally wrong in imitation of a television character. Underlying this statement was the implied notion that to be affected by television vio-lates the individuality of the self. So of course, younger children were more likely to be affected in this way because older children, like eighth-grade twins Marissa and Melanie, are more likely to know better:

M: It's OK to listen to some things that are, like you know—you might think are bad, or like watching things that you may think are bad, but, you know, 'cause they—I mean, they might be like bad for like young kids, you know, 'cause young kids get influenced (inaudible).

G: Mm-hmm.

M: But when you get past a certain age, you like, you know that you're not going to go out and do this just because some stupid character does it.

G: Yeah. How old do you think you have to be before you—

[. . .]

M: Twelve is like mature enough to know that you're not supposed to do this and, you know [. . .] like 12 is like very mature. You know, you know, you know—

M: Some people—

M: —what's right and wrong.

The key here is knowing right from wrong, sometimes that comes with age and maturity (not from the culture, parents, or teachers). Clearly, television effects had been a topic of discussion in the younger chil-dren's households (as quoted earlier, Marissa and Melanie commented, "My mom thinks, 'Oh, this is so bad, you're gonna go out and do this' "). The children I interviewed had been taught (understandably!) that they are not to imitate the behaviors of television characters—that they are to control their own behavior. As a high-school viewer put it:

KRISTEN: But I think it [TV] can affect you if you let it affect you?

G: Uh-huh.

KRISTEN: You know, but if—'cause if you don't make the connection between like reality and TV, then it could affect you.

G: Uh-huh.

KRISTEN: But, if you know the difference, then you know it's like not gonna like affect you in any way, then it won't.

TV will affect you "if *you* let it affect you." Viewers "knew" that they *shouldn't* let television affect them—and they were in control of their viewing experience. As a college student said, "Like, it's more like, like I use my own views to like critique the television. You know, like I don't, like, let the things the television does like change my own views. You know?" She emphasized that *she* wouldn't "let" TV change her. Another college student was quick to react to what she perceived as an implication that television might have affected her:

G: In the time that, since the show has been on, let's see, you were a junior in high school and now you're a freshman in college. Do you think that you've changed during that time?

REBECCAH: Well, I know I've changed. I don't think the show had anything to do with it, though.

Rebeccah prickled at the thought that watching the show had in some way changed her. Indeed, this defensiveness may stem from an unspoken assumption, articulated by a few viewers, that there was something wrong with people who were affected by television:

M: And like some people kill themselves because of something they saw on TV or heard on a record and stuff. But, those people are like way too—you know.

M: They're messed up. Like you know those people who like listen to the records and like they hang themselves or something and—

G: Yeah.

M: Do whatever they say on the records? That's like, yeah, right. You know, like—

M: Not—

M: No normal people would ever do that. You know?

M: Yeah.

[. . .]

M: You know? If they know it's not right and they go and do it anyway, they're obviously disturbed. OK? You know?

To me, this conversation has a slight overtone of whistling in the dark, as the twins toyed with the notion of doing something they knew was wrong ("If they know it's not right and they go and do it anyway, they're obviously disturbed"). In any case, this construction echoed through much viewer talk. Conclusions drawn from media-literacy units in school and from press or textbook accounts of TV violence studies were common, as in this conversation with two communication majors, who knew about limited effects:

ERIKA: Um—I don't, I don't think that if you're saying like, the whole thing about TV inducing violence—
G: Yeah, right.
ERIKA: Mmmm, I don't know about that. I think you already have to have some, some problems previously to that—
CASEY: Yeah. TV does not induce violence. I did a paper on it—(laughter)—when I was a freshman. It does not. It's the child, the way they were raised, the family they live in, the environment—there's too many factors to pinpoint it to TV. [. . .] It's all someone's mentality.

"It's all in someone's mentality." "You have to have some problems previously." Bad behavior in imitation of a television show is "not TV's fault [. . .] you can't blame TV," Marissa and Melanie said. They carefully constructed television as a possible motivator only for those who are "mentally disturbed," "very insane":

M: If you like listen to something on TV or radio or music, I mean, you're obviously like either mentally disturbed or like not very smart.
G: Mm-hmm.
M: You know? 'Cause like, if you go out and do drugs just because somebody's doing drugs on TV, then, you know, you're very stupid or like very insane, 'cause like that's not like the real reason that you would want to do something, you know.

"That's not like the real reason that you would want to do something." The twins touched on a central issue: The "real reason" for behavior comes from inside the individual. You would never "want" to change your behavior simply because of external or social forces: People who imitate bad behavior on TV do so because they haven't "really" thought about what they were doing.

Good Behavior as the Product of Thought, Not Imitation

The more I studied these opinions, the more I realized these viewers were caught in a tautology of circular reasoning: If you imitate bad behavior from television, they said, it's because you haven't thought about what you are doing—or your thought process is impaired, you are "very stupid or very insane." If you thought about it sanely, you wouldn't do it. On the other hand, viewers accepted the notion of imitating something good on television—but only because they could then hypothesize an intervening thought process. If you *do* imitate behavior you saw on

TV, it's because you *have* thought about it, and thus you, not television, are in control of the process. One's inner, autonomous self—the self that knows right from wrong, reality from unreality—also can pick and choose its television effects by interposing a rational thought process between viewing and behavior. Take, for example, the issue of abortion:

M: They wouldn't say, "I'm not gonna have an abortion because Andrea didn't." You know?
G: Yeah. Yeah.
M: You know, like they might see that like—
M: But—
M: —a baby, she like knows that the baby is like a living thing, like if they didn't realize it themselves but they saw that it was on TV, then that would change their minds.

"That would change their minds"—which is constructed as something different from changing their behavior, even if different behavior resulted. The key point is that they didn't just blindly imitate Andrea, but Andrea sparked them to think about things for themselves.

Most viewers said that television could in fact make them think about things with positive results. This process, however, was not initially constructed as a television effect but rather fell into the category of helpful information, as described in the chapter on fictional narrative and self-narrative. Indeed, to reiterate an exchange already quoted, two seventh-graders articulated that process:

G.: Do you think that TV affects you?
PAM: Yeah. I guess.
G.: Yeah, in what way?
PAT: 'Cause you kind of learn stuff on TV.
G.: Mm-hmm?
PAT: Like how certain people act and do you want to act like them and stuff.

Here, I will put the emphasis on "do you *want* to act like them." These viewers constructed an interior process that made all the difference between direct imitation of bad behaviors, which implicitly is mindless, and you yourself *wanting* to do something after thinking about it. Below, a college student constructed for herself this identity as an autonomous thinker whose ideas were sparked by the television show *911*, which concerns people who are rescued by emergency squads:

JOAN: Um, well I just know the only thing that really affects me is if I watch *911* or something like that. I mean that really affects me. 'Cause the things that happen on there, that makes me think.

MEETRA: Yeah, 'cause it's real.

JOAN: And it kind of scares you. I mean that's what really affects me. That's the only show that really kind of changed my life. 'Cause when I go to do things, I think twice. Yeah, 'cause things that happen on there. I mean they're such stupid things but, I mean people really get hurt. Like this one girl was standing on the stool in front of the window and she fell right through it. And it showed everything, and I was just like, "You know, I would do that, I would stand on stools," and I was like, when I went to stand on the stool I was like (inaudible) — 'Cause I didn't want to fall into that window.

"The things that happen on there, that makes me think." Television making one think was not constructed as an effect, even though the result of this thought process was a behavior that imitated something seen on television. It was Joan, guided by her core self, who would be careful the next time she stood on a stool.

TV did not "affect" viewers, but it could make them think about things and teach them things. If viewers decided to change their behavior after watching TV, they weren't affected because they had thought about it. The emphasis here has to be that "TV makes *me* think." It is still the core self that does the thinking, that is in control of the thought process. Television might launch the process, but the thinking viewer is autonomous.

Producers as Manipulators

In a few isolated instances, viewers from better-educated backgrounds hesitantly suggested that they were not quite so in control of the viewing experience. This voice contrasted with the empowered self constructed by those who took their showers early, told their friends not to call, and gathered for a ritual experience with its own rules and regulations, meanwhile claiming to be unaffected. Only a few viewers suggested that television soap operas in general, and *90210* in particular, could manipulate.

Some viewers said they watched *90210* because they were tricked by the producers and writers. They spoke of this process half-delightedly, half-resentfully. As one Princeton University viewer said, "Well, like, they, they do enough emotional wrenching that they make you want to watch the next time. Like you're going to stick around and see what happens the next, and you'll have to see the next episode just because they've gotten, gotten you into it." Another Princeton student said, "They completely entice you like that, and the (inaudible) shows next week, and you watch it next week. [. . .] I mean, you live for like [. . .] the cheesy plot twists." Or, as a group of high school students, all of whose parents have advanced degrees, vividly described both the seductive process and their delight in it:

CHRYSE: And also, like, they trick you. It's like any soap opera. Like if I sit down in the afternoon with my snack and I turn on the TV, I'm like, "Uh oh, it's a soap." But then I start watching it. Even if I don't know who the characters are or anything—
KAITLIN: Yeah.
CHRYSE: Like, once so-and-so starts to murder somebody else, and then these two people are running off together even though they're both married to each other's siblings—
ALL: Hysterical laughter.
CHRYSE: You get really interested. Like, you—
MARY: Yeah, it's ridiculous.

While they celebrated the pleasure they derived from the show, and by and large consented to its beguiling terms, there were moments when the viewers said they were also victimized by this process. As Kaitlin said, "I'm always saying, 'No, I need to do my homework,' and then I see *90210*, and then I start watching it, and I can't stop. And then I'm like, 'Oh, I'll just watch this one show.' And then, this [*Melrose*] comes on right after it. Then how could you not watch it? It's like once you start, you can't stop."

These viewers discursively constructed themselves, not as in control of their viewing experience, but rather as at the mercy of the writers and producers. An undertone even hinted at addiction: "Once you start, you can't stop." However, this voice existed parallel to the empowered one that celebrated the ritual, unplugged the phone, or called in sick to tedious meetings. The Princeton students and the prep-school students spoke of their viewing experience in contradictory ways: It made them feel powerful but at the same time it sapped their self-control. Is the parallel with drugs too obvious to be underlined?

Indeed, self-control was not always the issue—these same viewers also suggested that television could affect them without their being aware of it. The prep school students, while making the inevitable references to studies of television violence, suggested that television violence could indeed desensitize them.

G: Do you think television affects you?
KAITLIN: Hmm, yeah. Yeah. I mean—
MARY: I'm sure in some ways.
KAITLIN: Yeah, like, number one like the violence on TV, that affects like everybody. You know. Like there was like a study or something on shows like—

MARY: I think it really does desensitive you for real. For a while I didn't think it did, but it does.
KAITLIN: Yeah, like—
MARY: It does. Like—
KAITLIN: —watch the news. Like when there are like murders every night, you're just like, "Oh, another one."
MARY: Yeah, you know, I'm sure if I saw one in real life I'd be like, "Aahh," yeah, and it would freak me out a whole lot. But not as much as it would if I didn't see it on TV like every day.

"For a while I didn't think it did, but it does," Mary said, citing television news. This double discourse—it doesn't, but it does—was articulated by the Princeton students also. Once again, the first response was "no," followed by more reflexivity.

G: Do you think that TV affects you?
COURTNEY: No.
RUTH: Like these shows?
G: Well, any kind of TV.
COURTNEY: Yeah, I would say some—what—
RUTH: I don't, I don't really think it does that much. But, I mean, it probably does, I just don't know it.

At first, the empowered voice answered firmly no, or reiterated the claim that television doesn't "really" affect you. This tone segued into one much less assured: "It probably does, I just don't know it." The voice is much less certain than the self-confident immunity of the viewers who said firmly, "TV does not affect you." However, it is also much less contradictory.

   Interestingly, in a different interview, another Princeton woman made a sophisticated connection between television effects and identity:

G: Do you think that television affects you?
REBECCAH: Well, I—I'm really quick to say no, but I'm sure it does in some ways. I mean I wouldn't think I'd purposely go out and try to do something that one of the characters on the show did, but I'm sure that you do pick up on things that you, you like. There are certain characteristics that you like about a person, and so you do maybe try to pattern yourself.
G: Hmm.
REBECCAH: But I wouldn't say I'd try, do I think about, "Well, I like her so I'm going to try to do this more often." I think I just kind of—

Typically, the voice trails off, not finding the language to suggest that there are ways in which a show can affect our discursive identity construction—can offer us ways of attending to our lives, can add value and meaning to certain things, and silence or close down others—and that these structures can cycle into who we think, and say, we are.

Summary

All these viewers distinguished between their identities—who they *were* —and what they *did.* However, that distinction led to the contradictory claims that (1) constructed *others'* identity on the basis of what these others did, and said that this behavior was affected by television; (2) said there was something wrong with people who "let" themselves be affected by television, and constructed themselves as knowing better than to be affected by television; and (3) said when they did change their behavior as a result of television, it was because television "made them think" and that therefore *they* were in control of the process, and it was not a television effect.

Moreover, if they occasionally hinted that they were manipulated by television, their voices sounded uncertain and confused, in great contrast to the decisive strength of the denial. As these viewers separated and essentialized thinking, behavior, and identity, they ended up with a contradictory discourse that concealed or trivialized aspects of their viewing experience that I argue in this book are indeed of central importance. In shrugging off their talk about the show, in separating their community rituals from their core selves, and above all, in speaking the language of limited effects and the autonomous self that shuts down other notions of identity formation, these viewers bracketed ways I would argue television intersects importantly with our sense of who we are.

At the risk of driving home my point with a sledge hammer, I would suggest that this pleasurable consenting to a television-created sense of empowerment and community allowed viewers for the most part to silence the contradictory voice that suggests we do not control our viewing experience. As admittedly subtle television "effects" are discursively concealed, the hegemonic reproduction of culture proceeds unremarked. Viewers positioned themselves as authors and sources of television-centered behaviors; in the process, cultural norms could be naturalized and uncritically perpetuated. As I have mentioned elsewhere, enculturation is not necessarily bad; culture is what makes us human. What I object to is the discursive concealing of ways in which this perpetuation of the status quo is carried out on the terms of the consumerist, patriarchal, self-interested television industry.

Clearly, many issues are at stake here. In this study, I have focused on the way talk about *90210* is implicated in the pleasurable winning of consent to a particular female identity that feminists have argued disadvantages women. It seems to me, however, that this approach could yield fruitful insights in many other areas—and perhaps suggest to media literacy theorists ways to denaturalize this process.

Chapter 9
Issues: Closing Down the Moral Voice

An up side of arguing that *90210* is implicated in reproducing culture might reasonably be cogent viewer discussion of the issues it addresses. As mentioned in the chapter on the show, *90210* has been touted in the media as important because of its treatment of topics such as pregnancy, abortion, and drug abuse. Following this hype, I thought that much of the spontaneous talk would explore new positions and identities in relation to the show's treatment of these themes. I went into the study expecting to hear considerable debate over the issues around which plots were constructed.

During the time of the study, about every third episode delved into some new topical issue. The others either were reruns or focused primarily on the dating relationships that are analyzed in the next chapter. The issues foregrounded by the show during my interviews dealt with drug addiction (David uses cocaine, then breaks the habit); animal rights (Andrea works in an animal research lab while Brenda joins an animal activist group); and diversity (David dates a blind woman, Donna dates a black man, Steve finds out the president of his fraternity is gay). Just before the study started, there was an episode about teen pregnancy (finding herself pregnant, Andrea wrestles with the idea of having an abortion, ultimately deciding to marry the father instead). Intertextuality added complexity to this last issue because, as mentioned in the chapter on the show, the actress who plays Andrea was pregnant in real life, and all of the viewers reported knowing that fact.

Episodes approached the chosen issue from multiple angles. With David's drug addiction, we see his struggles, his excuses to take drugs (he has to stay up late to study), and his fear of getting caught. We also see some consequences: His girlfriend Donna is confused and hurt by his erratic and sometimes cruel behavior; he passes out on a park bench when he is supposed to be babysitting his little half-sister, who disappears and is the object of a frantic search (she is found unharmed). We see both enabling and tough-love responses from his friends. In the animal rights episode, the pregnant Andrea defends research animals by saying her lab's findings on Sudden Infant Death Syndrome "could help save my baby's life"; however, a dog on which experiments have been done dies of cancer, breaking Donna's heart (temporarily), and Brenda's activism is punished by an arrest. In the diversity episode, we see that black people, blind people, and gay people are "just like us" in many ways. Naturally, however, many aspects of issues were avoided.

This chapter begins by asking whether the producers' hopes for the show's treatment of issues were reflected in viewer talk, both in their weekly construction of the show's issues, and through varied reactions to a single issue, David's friends' "tough love" reaction to his drug addiction. This analysis is illuminated by three of the central themes of this book, the concepts of the "expert" voice, the community with the characters, and the cycle between viewer background and television text. Talk about issues also exemplifies the polysemy explored in earlier chapters. Moreover, in comparing the construction of a "tough love" message by different groups, and asking how they interpreted it, I explore the data in part through the lens of Gilligan's (1982, 1989, 1992) treatment of female morality, as outlined in Chapter 4.

In the final section, the other themes that have proven important—pleasure, agency, and narrative—are brought into a look at moral issues in the construction of gay identity.

Issues and Realism

Viewers generally agreed they liked *90210*'s treatment of topical issues. As one viewer said, "*90210* actually deals with you know, issues that day-to-day people can relate to," and her friend added, "That's why it's more interesting." Moreover, viewers tended to say the issues were "realistic"—or at least, "not unrealistic":

COURTNEY: I think they really made an honest effort to try and deal realistically with issues.
RUTH: Like what, such as?
COURTNEY: Such as like the pregnancy thing and (inaudible).
RUTH: Oh, like the friend getting shot?
COURTNEY: [. . .] Yeah, the friend getting shot, stuff like that.
* * *
CASEY: They do portray situations, like, right, like do you know what I mean? Like when David was in drugs and stuff?
G: Uh huh.
CASEY: Like that's not unrealistic. That's a problem that happens.
* * *

DANIELLE: I think Donna and David are realistic, like [. . .] how he did drugs and, like, he got off and then he got—he went back on and like—a lot of people probably do that.

At first, I expected that this construction of the issues as "realistic" might work in the same way as the construction of characters as "real"—to provide a pathway toward engagement, permitting the real exploration producers hoped would happen. However, I quickly came up against the curious and misleading meaning of television "realism." As Fiske (1987) has pointed out, television is perceived as realistic, not because it literally reproduces reality, but because it reproduces the dominant sense of reality: "Realism is not a matter of any fidelity to an empirical reality, but of the discursive conventions by which and for which a sense of reality is constructed" (p. 21).

In discussing the realism of issues with younger viewers, I found that they saw the issues as unconnected with their lives. They had no direct experience with drug addicts and suicides (thankfully!), and in addition they expressed the belief that they never would be exposed to such problems. As one seventh-grader said, "Well, it's not like it's gonna happen to us, so." In another interview, an eighth-grader echoed that sentiment: "Like, you know, it's interesting. 'Cause, it's like, never happens to you. So." For these viewers, the realism of the topics seemed to be part of a cultural narrative (drawn in part, no doubt, from the media!) in which drug abuse, suicide, and pregnancy have been much publicized as teen issues. Thus they called the issues "realistic," although they said they hadn't encountered them and never expected to. I wondered what this meant.

The opposite was true for older viewers. They called the issues "realistic" when they could draw a real-life parallel:

JOAN: 'Cause like when he shot himself accidentally makes me think about when I was in high school and things like that. Or like if one of the girls thinks she's pregnant. I mean that happens a lot, you know what I mean. Have that good old fear sometimes. (Laughter)
[. . .]
MEETRA: It's like even with, well, the drugs. I mean, it's like you—everyone's had friends that are like, you know had problems with that and—and then you try to help them out but you can't, you know.

These reactions gave extreme support to Morley's (1980) finding that direct experience with an event or issue had a powerful effect on viewer read: older viewers said they wouldn't even engage with the issues unless a connection with real life could be drawn. For example, when questioned about the rights and wrongs of a character's behavior in relation to David's addiction, one viewer said, "I don't know. I can't really relate to that situation, so I don't really know."

A comparison of two sets of reactions to the animal rights episode illustrates this intertwining of polysemy and viewer background in judgments of "realistic." In watching Donna and Brenda demonstrate in favor of animal rights, seventh-grader Pam was skeptical:

Protesters: "Animal rights, now!"
PAM: I didn't like this because, like, who would actually protest in real life?
G: Who would actually what?
PAM: (sarcastically) Like teenagers protest in real life like that!
G: Really? You think that is not very realistic?
PAM: Yeah.

"Who would actually protest in real life?" Pam presented herself as an expert in protest protocol, although her opinion of this stock stereotype of entertainment television was limited her to idiosyncratic experience — and who can question that? Two older viewers, one a senior in college, the other a recent graduate, reacted differently:

Protesters: "Animal rights, now!"
KAREY: [Marion], maybe we should have gotten more involved in a cause in college, do you think?
MARION: I know. Why did you graduate? We could go protest that hate speech the other night.

This study is not equipped to delve into Pam's specific experiences that led her to "know" that protesting was "unrealistic." The point here is that, as with Donna's hat (discussed in Chapter 5) and Lucinda's sexuality (Chapter 6), a viewer's background importantly guided the way she attended to the show's treatment of issues. Whether they dismissed it as a possibility, as Pam did, or playfully explored it, linking it to a real-life event, as Marion did, viewers constructed their reads with reference to their backgrounds.

Thus, viewers went through a two-step process as they judged whether and how to explore issues raised by the show. Some viewers, usually the younger ones, drew on cultural narratives about what issues *should* be salient to teens; if there was a match, these girls then attended to them. Older viewers drew on their own backgrounds to "relate" to issues; here, if there was a match, they found the issues "interesting."

The ways in which age seemed to intersect with consideration of the issues (although I can't make causal claims) was succinctly summed up by a group of high school students, who looked back to the time when they started watching *90210* in eighth grade:

MARY: I don't know. I didn't really deal with any—
KAITLIN: No, we didn't deal with any issues.
MARY: —like real issues.
KAITLIN: We were all just like, "Ha, ha, ha, we're going to high school, woo hoo."
MARY: (Inaudible) Yeah, like, "Nothing ever happens—"
KAITLIN: "—happens to us, no."
G: Uh-huh. And now things do? Or—
KAITLIN: Now, like, yeah. Now, like you're in kind of like the situations they do, only you don't really do what they do, since they're on TV and we're not. Yeah.
G: Can you, can you give an example?
KAITLIN: Um, I don't know. Like, you have friends who get like pregnant and—like people do drugs and stuff around you, and like all that kind of stuff. And you know, you deal with it. And when you're in eighth grade, you know, you're in eighth grade—
MARY: —you don't think about it. It's not gonna happen to you.

In eighth grade, they thought, "Nothing ever happens to us." In high school, this naivete was shattered as friends got pregnant and people did drugs.

Thus, I found the producers faced important constraints in presenting issues for viewer consideration: For some viewers, the issues had to match cultural narratives of what is "realistic" for teens; others demanded that issues bear directly on real-life experiences. And on probing further, I found that each of these mandates structured viewer "read" of the episode's "solution" in such a way as to close down any real, thoughtful exploration.

Choking Off Discussion: Playing Pundit Versus Political Correctness

As I generated talk about issues, I found that some viewers, usually the youngest ones, seemed to embrace the moral message, particularly concerning the episodes about David and drugs. As mentioned in the last chapter, these youngest viewers consistently suggested that they could learn things from television; in response to my questions about issues, they said they could learn important moral lessons. As eighth-grade twins Melanie and Marissa said, TV "teaches you lessons and stuff, not to do this, not to do that." They added:

M: And like the drug thing, you know, like, if somebody sees, like, if somebody would want to like, thinking about trying drugs—
G: Uh huh.

M: —they would see like how the police came in and everything—
G: Uh huh. Yeah.
M: —they would like know not to do that.

"They would like know not to do that." Whether or not this response was an artifact of my questions, clearly these girls deemed it an appropriate statement. For example, in this next exchange, I asked two seventh-graders whether they thought about the show when they weren't watching it. I thought they would say something about the plots, the clothing, etc. Instead, they spontaneously brought up how David's drug addiction served as a model of how not to behave:

KATEY: Well like, I would think like, if I was in a position, and I lost my little sister, I would be like in a lot of trouble.
JANE: I think about him [David] and drugs. 'Cause like—then I know I wouldn't do 'em 'cause how he is now. Like I would never do drugs and get put away in jail. So that's how I sorta think about it.

"Then I know I wouldn't do 'em 'cause how he is now"—a provocative sentence. It seemed that the show's "messages" were getting through to these viewers.

However, the ramifications of this kind of talk are unclear. These girls emphasized that they wanted to see these issues portrayed, but the reason seemed to be, so they would know the "right" answers. As explored in the chapter on narrative, one important aspect of their viewing was "playing pundit." All the younger viewers said such things would never happen to them. They needed to "know" not to do drugs, but they never thought they would be tempted to get high. Thus, there is a sense in which statements such as "I would never do drugs" can be seen as similar to plot recitation for these girls. Learning these lessons—whatever else it accomplished—gave these viewers the now-familiar forum in which to construct themselves as expert, knowing the answers. Talking about David's drug addiction did indeed intersect with the futures these girls discursively constructed for themselves, but this talk suspiciously resembles Danielle's comment in the chapter on narrative about going to college in California. Just as when Danielle gets close to college age, the importance of going to college in California might fade, so might the force of David's example, were the girls to come into contact with peers who do drugs.

Nevertheless, in talking about the issues as realistic but as unlikely to touch their own lives, these girls did accomplish identity work similar to that accomplished in other talk about the show: They blended narratives drawn from the show ("he got off and then he went back on"), cultural narratives of which they presented themselves as authors ("it's realistic"), and self-narratives ("it's not gonna happen to us"). Talk about the show gave them ways to attend to themselves, and vice versa. What these viewers did *not* do was enter into a discussion of the nature of drug addiction, its temptations and repercussions. They simply learned the answers ("Like I would never do drugs and get put away in jail").

For other viewers, perception of the moral messages behind the issues served to choke off discussion in a slightly different way. As twins Melanie and Marissa said about "the abortion thing": "When they said she was gonna have an abortion, I'm like, 'No way.' They never make you [allow you to] have an abortion on TV because they're trying to tell you that abortion is wrong." The sense that the way problems were solved was motivated by a socially correct message closed off any discussion of hard choices or the ethics of the situation. Melanie and Marissa did not discuss whether Andrea should or should not have an abortion; in talking about Andrea's ultimate decision, they were concerned to "play pundit," in the words of Chapter 7, to pinpoint the motivations of the producers.

Many viewers explicitly called the show's approach politically correct or PC, a label that bracketed the issues as just not worth discussing. As one viewer said, "I think they're realistic, it's just I don't think the show did them justice at all. I think they're just there to, you know, promote the idea, so that they can seem like a PC program. They [the issues] just didn't seem to have any strength behind them." For another viewer, just the notion that the issues were "produced" was enough to keep her from exploring them:

G: What, um, what do you think of those classes, those Lucinda classes? and that whole subplot?
ERIKA: I think, again, that's one of their little like plotlines, like you know, how the strong feminist thing is, is around now—
G: Uh huh.
ERIKA: —that's just something else they have to bring into the show. I don't think it necessarily means anything. I think it's just a popular thing right now.

"I don't think it necessarily means anything." The feminist dogma preached (not very clearly) by Lucinda was not even worth considering, because Erika saw it as a move on the producers' part to plug into "the popular thing right now."

In still other cases, discussion of issues also was closed down by intertextual knowledge, which could constrain and direct discussion. As mentioned earlier, the actress Carteris's pregnancy, something all viewers said they knew about, complicated the possibility that Andrea might have an abortion: "Yeah, like with Andrea getting pregnant. Which she's pregnant in real life and that's why they did it. And I knew ahead of time before they even put it on, because I read it somewhere, so." Indeed, Carteris was already singled out in viewers' minds as the oldest actress on the show—she was 33 when she had the baby—so it is doubtful if viewers really saw it as a teen pregnancy issue. This knowledge colored their discussions of abortion:

COURTNEY: I don't think it was intentional. I think it just happens 'cause—
RUTH: I think she's gonna have to have the baby, since she's pregnant in real life.
COURTNEY: She's—I know. Well—
RUTH: Exactly, yeah.
COURTNEY: I doubt they planned it, like, when they were plotting the story line or whatever. Make her pregnant. They'd never do that.

Courtney and Ruth talked about Andrea's pregnancy, but only in the context of the actress' life, the producers' intentions, and their own position as pundits, experts ("And I knew ahead of time before they even put it on"). They did not ask themselves if Andrea should get an abortion; neither did they explore that subject position for themselves.

Another frequent complaint was that problems were solved too quickly:

CHRYSE: And it all happens in an hour. [. . .] And then it's all—
KAITLIN: Yeah, and everything always gets resolved—
CHRYSE: —resolved in an hour.

Similar comments abounded: "When Steve had the drinking problem, that one was solved like really fast (G: Oh, really?) and that's why it seemed weird"; "And he [David] got addicted so fast to that stuff. [. . .] They—people don't really get addicted that fast, like, like in two days or something. But people do get addicted, though. That's what they were trying—they couldn't like make him stay on it for too long, like, [. . .] but um, so, they have to like make you scared of it on TV to make you like think, you know, 'Don't do this.'" On television, time has to be collapsed, and "they couldn't make him stay on it for too long" or viewers would get bored. But drug addiction *is* a real-life problem, the twins said, and it is important for television to convey the message, "Don't do this."

Viewers also commented on the speed with which issues come and go. Having a new issue every second or third episode put the producers into the typical soap-opera dilemma of giving their characters lives jam-packed with crises:

M: It's like, well, they, they probably wouldn't do that many things—
G: Yeah, right.
M: Like that's what I'm saying. But like a couple—like take about 500

people and just do everything that they do and put it against them, and then that's probably like it.
G: Right. OK. I see what you're saying. So in that way, it's only unrealistic that everything happens to these same people.
M: Yeah, yeah.

Many viewers pointed out that the show had begun to stretch issues over multiple episodes, and they spoke favorably of this trend:

CASEY: Because before it used to be one show, and they never connected it. And now it's all interlocked. And now it's all interlocked, I think people want to watch it more. To see—
G: That's interesting.
CASEY: —what's going to happen. [. . .] It used to be like show, show, show, show, show—now it's like all linked.

* * *

COURTNEY: Oh, I can remember everyone remarking how impressive it was that they actually continued David's drug abuse for five episodes—
G: Yeah.
COURTNEY: —as opposed to just having it be a one-episode thing, that they actually made—
RUTH: And I had thought it was going to go away, but like they made it go away and then it came back.
COURTNEY: Yeah.

However, even though the links between shows made the issues a little more realistic, viewers still complained about the predictable solutions.

KRISTEN: Well, I guess in the show, like, they show the problems, but, like, sometimes they don't really show, like, how it would really happen.
G: Mm-hmm.
KRISTEN: 'Cause, like, everything always turns out good in the end.
JEANNETTE: Yeah, there's always a happy ending, they always live happily ever after.

"There's always a happy ending." Repeatedly, the older viewers objected to the pat, predictable, and "happy" solutions. Perception of a moral behind the show, along with intertextual knowledge, cursory treatments, and happy endings, led viewers to dismiss the issues as just not worth talking about.

Again, this talk did serve to accomplish some of the identity work seen in earlier chapters, cementing the community and providing a forum for the expert voice. "They actually continued David's drug abuse for five episodes," Courtney said, in a tone that positioned her as authoritative. Viewers were experts on what producers would and wouldn't do:

"I doubt they planned it, make her pregnant. They'd never do that." An authority speaks. Moreover, the talk once again effected a blending of television narrative and life narrative ("If I was in a position, and I lost my little sister, I would be like in a lot of trouble"). What the talk did not do was explore the personal, ethical, and social dilemmas involved in getting an abortion or doing drugs.

Negotiating Realism: "No Consequences"

Once I stopped looking for meaningful discussions of drug addiction and teen pregnancy, I realized that the talk about issues could inter-twine with self-narratives in a way that increased the text's hegemonic implications: As viewers complained that the consequences of wrong behavior on the show were minimized, they also felt resentful that their own problems could not be solved so neatly. Unlike their discussions of characterizations, in which they negotiated ways to see the characters as real, in talking about issues, viewers wished life could be more like art.

Viewers did express dissatisfaction that characters seemed to es-cape real consequences. For example, our conversation about the show sparked a discussion among two college-age viewers about the time one of them got her driver's license. "We were gone," she remembered. "We went everywhere, did everything. And we never got in trouble, but still, some of the things we did. We could have gotten in like some really bad trouble." Her friend added: "And it's like now, I wouldn't even think about doing stuff like that. But we were very, very lucky though." Appar-ently, the real-life consequences were favorable—"We could have gotten in trouble," "but we were very lucky." Nevertheless, these viewers ob-jected when similar behavior by Brandon went unpunished:

JOAN: Well I remember Brandon got in a car accident, he was drunk which—that was OK. But it just seemed like, didn't seem real. Like if that happened in real life there would be more consequences than what he went through. I know it's TV but, with that, I—you know, I just thought that they should have did it a little bit more. I mean he just got in that car accident because he was drinking and then it's like, bam, he's out of jail. And—
MEETRA: It's like they say things on that show are supposed to be like real life. I mean they are but like to a certain point. It's like well like, if I got caught drinking and went out and got thrown in jail I'd be sitting there. (laughter).
JOAN: Yeah, exactly.

"I just thought that they should have did it a little bit more." "If I got caught drinking and went out and got thrown in jail, I'd [still] be sitting there." The criticism was voiced almost resentfully that these viewers wanted to see Brandon languish in jail, at least for a while. As Joan said later about the show, "And it's like no consequences. There's none."

Beyond the mimetic criticism, however, ran an undercurrent that seemed to want to deny the consequences. "I didn't want him to get caught"; "she doesn't deserve that" resonated through the talk about issues. If only *I* weren't subject to such consequences, these viewers seemed to say. Taken from this viewpoint, one could make the case that, if anything, talk about *90210*'s issues undermined conventional morality with its characters who are exempt from the consequences of bad behavior. Watching this could make viewers wonder how to manipulate the system so that they, too, could be exempt.

Thus, contradictory drives—it "should" be like real life, but you don't "want" to see negative consequences applied to these characters —fueled these discussions. The talk these interviews generated about issues came in basically two forms: (1) deliberately elicited by interviews, resulting in a mix of "right" answers, references to real-life experiences, all in the "expert" voice; and (2) spontaneous talk, especially during viewing, which was almost overwhelmingly dominated by a sense of community with the characters that sometimes urged exoneration even to the point of blindness.

Elicited Talk and Female Morality

Throughout the interviews, I deliberately explored reactions to David's drug addiction by directing viewer attention to a scene that occurs after David tells his friends he has quit, but secretly continues to use drugs. This clip was one of three that I showed most viewers. (Another drug-related scene, which to my surprise turned out to be "about" Donna's hat, was explored in Chapter 5; the third scene, about date rape, generated redundant data that in the interests of brevity I chose not to detail in this analysis.)

In what I dubbed to myself the "tough love" scene, David oversleeps as a result of his habit. His roommates—Kelly, his stepsister, and Donna, who is his girlfriend although they don't sleep together—come in to wake him up. Kelly discovers drugs in his drawer and immediately takes a tough stance. She accuses David of being both "a drug addict and a liar." Donna is reluctant to be so confrontive and apologizes to David for nosing through his things. Kelly demands angrily, "What are you apologizing to him for?" She then announces, "If this is the way you're going to live your life, then I am moving out—*we* are moving out." David retaliates angrily, "Fine. Move out. I'm tired of living with you two high priestesses of sobriety anyway."

The text is rich. (1) It presents Kelly as confrontive, both to David and to Donna, but possessing a kind of negative agency, in which she withdraws from the situation, rather than kicking David out of the apartment the three of them share; (2) it makes available the position that confronting is a way of helping; in a later scene, the characters explicitly call it "tough love" (Kelly: "We're not deserting him. You've got to get that through your head." Donna: "Tough love." Kelly: "Right. And it works. Believe me, I have first-hand experience"); and (3) it also makes available the position that confrontations can painfully rupture a relationship, in this case for Donna, who continues to want to be "nice" and to try to patch things up with David. Completely backgrounded are any concerns that David is breaking the law and harming his health by doing drugs (needless to say, his perfect physique shows no ill effects). Nor did the text suggest that outside help was needed—never were counseling, support groups, or treatment specifically mentioned, and there was of course no thought of informing his parents. And for the most part, viewer talk unproblematically reproduced this approach.

After showing the clip, I specifically directed the discussion to an ethical level, asking if Kelly was "right" to move out. The wonderfully various responses I heard illustrate a number of points. As mentioned above, viewer background intersected importantly with comprehension of the text's moral messages, supporting Morley's (1980) findings. For example, viewers who reported no experience with drug addiction, either in real life or in school drug-education classes, were much less likely to talk about ways to help David. However, those who had learned about drug addiction in school, or reported first-hand experience with "tough love," applied this knowledge to the text by speculating on ways that David might or might not be helped. Moreover, prompted by my questions, viewers did address the morality of the characters' behavior, and most of the viewers saw the clip in relational terms, either as conflict between the two women, or as conflict between the women and David. Thus their talk reflected and illustrated Gilligan's (1982, 1989, 1992) findings (described in Chapter 4) concerning the dual voices of justice and care in girls' and women's moral judgments, the conflict between caring for self and caring for others, and the tension between being "nice" and initiating necessary conflict. The progression Brown and Gilligan (1992) traced of decreasing relational morality and an increase in abstract judgments as education increased also appeared.

I will start with the reactions of the younger girls. Two seventh-graders focused on the women's moral responsibility to look out for themselves and to punish behavior for which they themselves presumably had been penalized, such as lying. Reporting no background experience with drugs, they attended to David's problem only when questions prompted them to this point of view. These viewers focused on Kelly's and Donna's responsibility to save themselves from possible harm inflicted by David, and to get back at him. This conversation—drawn from the first interview I conducted—occurred right after we had watched the episode from which I later took the clip (and this interview was instrumental in my selection of it as a discussion-starter to show other viewers):

G: What was your favorite part of the show tonight?
JANE: When they walked out on David.
KATEY: Yeah.
ALL: Laughter
G: Oh, tell me, why did you like that?
JANE: Because he deserves it, because he has been doing drugs and lying to 'em.

The girls celebrated the women's power to punish David, to give him what he had coming. David has been doing drugs and lying to Kelly and Donna about it, so he "deserved" to be penalized. I cannot emphasize enough that, from first to last in these discussions, there was no mention of the fact that doing drugs is illegal and unhealthful. Other discussions emphasized David's fear of getting caught, following the television text. But the facts that David is both breaking the law and potentially harming his health was not something these viewers talked about.

At first I wondered if this lack of emphasis on the illegal nature of drug use was in part a result of a dominant cultural message in the Nancy Reagan vein that puts the onus on the individual to resist, rather than on the justice system to punish: "Just say no." However, the Reagan approach certainly is culturally counterbalanced by a societal preference for increasing jail sentences for drug offenders. In any case, emphasizing personal responsibility for wrong-doing may be a self-serving move for the television industry, not only because it advances the American metanarrative of individualism, but also because it suggests that television is not implicated in copycat crimes. Whatever the reason, the pressing issue for these viewers in talking about this text resided in the relationship among David, Kelly, and Donna.

After emphasizing punishment for David, Katey and Jane focused on self-protection for Donna and Kelly:

G: So you think it was good that they walked out for them—because for them, it was better for them to—
BOTH: Uh huh.
KATEY: 'Cause I wouldn't want to live with a druggie.
JANE: Because he used to be so mean to them. And they might get hurt from him.

For these viewers, female morality meant punishing wrong-doing and preserving the self through physical self-protection, that is, putting the self first. There was no speculation about whether walking out on David might be an emotional struggle, especially for Donna, although that position is available in the text (and was taken for granted by me). Nor did they suggest that the women might have a moral responsibility to help David (Kelly is his stepsister and Donna is his long-time girlfriend). These viewers cheerfully sacrificed David, applauding the women's decision to leave someone who was mean to them and might hurt them.

In these early interviews I was a little blinded because the "tough love" aspect dominated my "read" of the scene, and I thought it would do the same for viewers. So (as can be seen by my question below) I kept trying to elicit the notion that Kelly and Donna were motivated by concern for David. However, these young viewers—fueled by a preview that suggested David would be caught with drugs and "locked up"—suggested the opposite: that the women had been "keeping on top of him," holding his habit in check, and that in their absence he would do drugs "a whole lot more":

G: Oh, yeah. So, you think by doing this they really helped David? By moving out?
JANE: Yeah.
G: (to Katey) You look doubtful.
KATEY: Not really, because now he's on drugs a whole lot more.
[. . .]
G: So you liked it when they walked out, but you think it's not going to help David?
KATEY: I think he's going to get worse.
JANE: And kicked out of school. 'Cause he's probably in jail. 'Cause when they said he was locked up [in the preview]. Because they were keeping on top of him the whole time and then when they're trying—I don't know. I just don't think they'll—I think he's going to get worse.

Two points need to be made here. These girls articulated a strong moral responsibility to care for self, a voice that Gilligan celebrated in young girls, even as she described ways it is stifled by formal education. (Indeed, as described in Chapter 4, this loss happened to the girls she interviewed before they reached seventh grade.) The talk I heard from these girls might suggest that Gilligan was right in attributing the loss of this voice to the combination of increased education and age. More interesting to me is the fact that the "tough love" read of Donna and Kelly's departure completely escaped Katey and Jane, despite the way I inadvertently put it into their mouths at first ("So, you think by doing this they really helped David? By moving out?"). They spontaneously identified the moment when Kelly and Donna moved out as their favorite, but not because of any positive effects on David. Rather, they applauded Kelly and Donna's move to protect themselves.

Twin eighth-graders Melanie and Marissa grappled a little more with Kelly and Donna's responsibility to maintain connection with David. They said immediately, "I don't want to be like living with a person who's doing drugs, you know, but I wouldn't like stop being their friend because of it, 'cause it's like, that's like, kind of being mean to them." Interestingly, this move to maintain connection with David, also encountered by Gilligan, translated into at least a partial exoneration of David's behavior, a struggle over whether to condemn drug users: "And it's, like—well, it *is* their fault, but it's not like [. . .] some people, some people might be doing it [drugs] for like certain reasons and (G: Yeah) you just like—some people, it's just like having a bad time, and they don't know what's going to happen to them. You know?" Doing drugs here was interpreted as "having a bad time," a behavior the user might have avoided if s/he had known "what's going to happen to them." The twins added:

M: It's like, if they're not hurting you and they're not pressuring you into doing it [drugs], so—
G: So you think Kelly shouldn't have acted so—
M: No—
M: No, I mean—
M: I think she acted like kind of mean to him because, you know, like—
M: It's like that—that won't help anybody. You have to be like nice and help him through it, but—
M: You have to like try to like, you know, go, don't—you know like, like, you know, be there. Like dump all the stuff in the toilet. Like, don't let him do it. Gotta be tough when you're around him.
G: Yeah.
M: It's like but, you know, like you don't want to just like dump him. Because like how's he going to work out his own problems? He can't do it by himself.
G: Yeah.
M: Like all he's gonna do is get money and buy drugs. You know?

"If they're not hurting you and they're not pressuring you into doing it"; "You have to be nice and help him through it"; "Gotta be tough when you're around him"; "He can't do it by himself." It is complicated to unpack these statements. The sense of self-preservation remained, but these girls emphasized that David wasn't hurting Donna and Kelly, or pressuring them to do drugs. The desire to exonerate David resonated strongly in their talk; the women's job was to be "nice and help him through it." As Brown and Gilligan (1992) found, Marissa and Melanie focused much more strongly on the importance of being "nice." Moreover, these girls later said they had learned in school that addiction is a problem with which one could be helped. Once again, the show sparked no new exploration of ways to handle drug addiction; rather, these girls regurgitated what they already knew about the topic, mixing in with their preoccupation with being "nice."

High school students Jeannette and Kristen focused on the relationship between Donna and Kelly, finessing the whole problem of David's addiction:

David: *"Fine. Move out. I'm tired of living with you two high priestesses of sobriety anyway."*
JEANNETTE: Donna gives in too easily.
KRISTEN: Yeah.
G: Does she?
KRISTEN: Yeah. Definitely.
G: What—tell me what you mean by that.
JEANNETTE: She, like, she didn't do anything to fight it. 'Cause she doesn't want to move out, and she's just letting Kelly do it.
G: Ah.
JEANNETTE: She gave in too easily.
G: So you think they shouldn't have moved out?
JEANNETTE: Well, I think they should—Kelly was right because they need to help David with that. But Donna really didn't want to move out. She should have stuck up for herself.
KRISTEN: Yeah, she should have had the choice.

The importance of helping David received lip service in response to probing ("Kelly was right because they need to help David with that"). But Jeannette's whole focus (with Kristen as chorus) was on the relationship between the two female characters. Her community did not include David; rather, her moral judgment focused on the relationship between the two females, and on the importance of standing up for yourself when your female friend tries to make you do something you don't want to do.

Interestingly, these girls did not wrestle with the conflict between caring for self and caring for others. They spoke in the voice Gilligan (1992) maintained has generally disappeared from girls this age—instead of focusing on being "nice" and avoiding conflict, Jeannette said a girl has a moral imperative to stand up for herself among her female friends. This voice resembles the one that praised the cocky, aggressive female heard in Chapter 6. For these girls, the scene was about Donna's and Kelly's relationship.

Interestingly, these viewers completely ignored the dilemma of how to handle David's addiction. Unlike Melissa and Melanie, Jeannette and Kristen reported no background experience with drugs—they said they had never encountered users, nor had they been taught in school about how to handle a drug abuser. And they did not discuss Kelly's choice of how to handle David's drug addiction.

Even college students did not uniformly access the "tough love" read, although to me it seemed a stock-in-trade television treatment of drug addiction. Only those who reported having had experiences with helping a drug abuser in the family mentioned it. In the conversation about the clip below, college student Alison completely missed the "tough love" aspect, so her friend Casey drew on her own experiences to elucidate and validate it:

CASEY: They were worried about him.
ALISON: They didn't seem worried about him, I don't know.
G: They *didn't* seem worried about him?
ALISON: Like she, what's her name—
CASEY: Kelly?
ALISON: The one you guys like. (Laughter) Kelly, was all worried about, "I don't want to deal with this," you know?
CASEY: It's not that she didn't want to deal with it, it's that she's handled the situation before. And I don't know how like you guys are, but like I know how drugs are around my house, and like I've seen people, and my cousin was in drugs before, and the only way to get someone to realize what they're doing is to let them see how alone they will be? 'Cause like if you sit there and cover up for someone and you do this, they're gonna think that the habit's OK, know what I mean? And there—someone's always going to be there to help them? The only thing to let them do is fall on their face on their own so that they'll realize it. So like I can understand why they moved out, and that's what she called it, tough love. That's what it is. They love him enough to do this to him. They don't want to see him do it, but the only way he'll realize is that he knew how alone he was. And he finally did call Dylan, 'cause no one else was there.
G: But—
CASEY: At first it didn't work, but it takes time.
G: Yeah, but you think they made the right decision?
CASEY: I do. I guess it's maybe just more situational in my life. I've seen it before.

The "tough love" move was not accessible to Alison. And Casey's explanation of it provides a clean example of the way in which a background experience, a television text, and a self-narrative can intersect and reinforce each other.

Following Gilligan (as discussed in Chapter 4), in this conversation female morality was firmly focused on doing what is best for another, even though it may not be pleasant for the self ("They don't want to see him do it, but the only way he'll realize is that he knew how alone he was"). And Casey instantly accessed the "message" of the clip with all its nuances—and said that she has already wrestled with the issue of "tough love" in precisely the same way ("My cousin was in drugs before, and the only way to get someone to realize what they're doing is to let them see how alone they will be"). She had seen drug abuse in action in a close family setting, and she knew that tough love is a painful but accepted solution. And this background led her to expand on the television text, exploring Kelly's feelings ("They love him enough to do this to him"), and even attributed them to Donna, even though this position is subtly contradicted in the text as Donna apologizes to David. Casey recalled the later scene in which tough love was explicitly discussed ("that's what she called it, tough love. That's what it is"). The text then cycled back to reinterpret and reinforce her own experience, giving her an additional way to attend to herself, constructing for her a unique, expert identity ("I guess it's maybe just more situational in my life. I've seen it before"). Her experience with her cousin gave Casey a way to attend to the show; talk about the show gave her a way of attending to her life and her identity—if only to proclaim herself expert.

Princeton University student Courtney had a similar reaction to the clip, whose tough love message escaped her friend Ruth, in an echo of the interaction between Casey and Alison. By the time these two viewers watched this clip, David's drug problem has been resolved, so they had the additional knowledge that the "tough love" approach worked. This excerpt begins with the voice examined in the chapter on appearance, as viewers commented on exteriors and appearance, ignoring on-screen developments:

Exterior of apartment.
COURTNEY: That apartment is so lush, I can't get over it.
Donna: "David, get up!"
COURTNEY: He's got a nice body, too.
RUTH: Even though he's doing drugs.
Kelly: (to Donna) "What are you apologizing to him for?"
RUTH: Really!
Clip ends.
G: Should they have done that?
COURTNEY: Definitely. Well, it ended up working. Well, not (inaudible), but—I mean if you, if you, I mean co-dependence or facilitators or whatever. I don't know. My dad's—my dad is—my dad is the child of an alcoholic so he's very much into all the lingo and—

G: OK, so he knows all that—

COURTNEY: Yes.

G: Does he do AA and stuff and talk about tough love?

COURTNEY: Well, he—my, my grandfather was like—it was kind of funny—a brief family history: He was a heart surgeon, yet he smoked and drank.

RUTH: Ohh.

COURTNEY: And tried (inaudible) case and he al—I mean, he was like, it was like in the '50s and '60s when like, you know, when people would, people would drink too much and they would be alcoholics, but, you know, it was like socially—

RUTH: Right.

G: Yeah. Right.

COURTNEY: (inaudible)—drink a little too much, so that it was all denied and under the—whatever. And so, he kind of grew up with him like that and then my grandf—I never knew my grandfather, he died before I was born. But, um, my dad's was very like, tough love stance, sort of like, you know, you confront them and, I don't know.

RUTH: Yeah, I mean, but also they're kind of like walking out, like they're letting him, they're going to let him go on, I guess. I mean, it works out making him like realize that he has to (inaudible), but they're leaving him (inaudible) and kind of deserting him also.

G: Yeah. I kind of was surprised at that too, but. What would you do in that situation?

RUTH: I guess, I mean, try to get the person help. I mean, sometimes they won't accept it, but, I guess if it's dangerous for you, you have to get away.

COURTNEY: Yeah.

RUTH: So—

COURTNEY: I mean, I've been lucky enough not to have any friends with like drugs or alcohol problems, really, but I mean, it would be such a helpless feeling, 'cause, I mean, you, no one is going to be helped unless they want to be helped. And so, to try to make them understand that, I mean, I guess that, that was Kelly's way of doing it. 'Cause I guess her mother had been like an alcoholic and—

G: Yeah, I guess so.

COURTNEY: And she was just like, "No more, I'm not going to deal with this. And you're—I'm not gonna help you, I'm not going to cover for you, you're going to have to deal with it." You know? "And whether it takes you realizing that you're messing your life up or whether someone else, it takes someone else telling you that you're messing your life up, i.e., handcuffs or body bag, you know, I'm not going to be there to clean up the messes any more." Which I think is a pretty legitimate way of dealing with it.

Like Casey, Courtney combined the "tough love" ideology with references to real-life experiences in an expert voice. Paradoxically, her sympathetic portrayal of her grandfather ("it was like socially drink a little too much") bordered on supportive enabling, the opposite of tough love. But she had learned the dogma of tough love, and her overall exploration of that subject position was remarkably like Casey's:

CASEY: If you sit there and cover up for someone and you do this, they're gonna think that the habit's OK, know what I mean? And there— someone's always going to be there to help them?

* * *

COURTNEY: "I'm not gonna help you, I'm not going to cover for you, you're going to have to deal with it. [. . .] I'm not going to be there to clean up the messes any more."

However, Casey, a student at Rider University and from a less educated background, interjected some care into the decision: "They love him enough to do this to him. They don't want to see him do it," while Princeton student Courtney, from a well-educated background, concluded with a distanced justice voice: "Which I think is a pretty legitimate way of dealing with it." For Casey, morality had to do with inner motivations and emotions; for Courtney, with external judgments. This contrast seems to illustrate Gilligan's case that increased formal education mutes the relational voice.

Ruth, meanwhile, struggled with the notion that Kelly in a way was abnegating her responsibility to David, "kind of deserting him." She said she would "try to get the person help" but she also confronted the self-preservation issue, "I guess if it's dangerous for you, you have to get away." Once again, in an echo of Gilligan, female morality is caught between caring for others and caring for self.

While this study does not set out to make claims about relationships between education, age, and morality, patterns did emerge that seemed to support Gilligan's points (as described in Chapter 4). In this type of talk, the viewers were indeed wrestling with the dominant notion of female identity in terms defined by patriarchy.

This talk also illustrated another, perhaps less-expected point: Real-life experience drove talk about how ethical issues should be handled. The way the characters handled the issues was tangential. If viewers had not already encountered the issue in their lives, they simply did not grapple with it. As one ninth-grader said flatly, when asked for her reaction to the clip, "I don't know. I don't understand it, actually"; a seventh-grader echoed that sentiment about the drug plotline in general:

G: Have you been watching it recently when David was on drugs?
BOTH: Mm.
G: Yeah. What do you think about those shows?
PAM: I think they're like, kind of way over my head.

For all but a few viewers, the "message" of tough love was obscured, transformed, or buried. If the viewer had previous experience with the tough love approach, she accessed the message; otherwise, she did not. Younger viewers might memorize or regurgitate televised solutions, but (in this case, at least) if viewers did not have previous experience with the issue—if it didn't "remind" them of their lives—the message did not seem to get through.

This finding suggests something relatively heretical: Talk about a show like *90210* can recirculate, reinforce, and perpetuate dominant notions of what it takes to be a white, middle-class member of our late-20th-century consumerist, patriarchal culture, but *90210*'s ability to teach moral lessons could be much more limited. These findings seem to reflect the limited-effects model that television reinforces but doesn't convert—or, in the language of this study, those with no prior experience learned the "right" answers; those with experience bolstered their positions as "expert." But in neither case did they engage with the issues in a thoughtful and reflective way.

Spontaneous Talk: Community and "Us-Them" Morality

Another way to look at these data is to understand that viewers did not see the show as really "about" the topical issues the text apparently addresses. Viewers simply did not spontaneously talk about ethical decisions made by characters in the face of drug abuse, suicide, or teen pregnancy. Such talk was generated only by my questions. Whether it was because they knew all problems would be solved (even if it took "five episodes"); or because they saw the show's preaching as irrelevant to their lives, or as unworthy of their attention; or because the happy ending would of itself close off any real exploration; or because they were concerned only to memorize rules of behavior, these viewers simply did not talk creatively or in depth about moral dilemmas posed by the show or about the solutions presented—either in reference to their own lives or for the characters.

Instead, when they spoke spontaneously about the issues, what viewers emphasized was their sense of community with the characters and their emotional involvement with them in terms of the consequences of behavior. They sometimes said the show "should" be like real life—that the exigencies of television production shouldn't get in the way of a real exploration of the consequences of doing drugs or getting pregnant— yet overwhelmingly viewers didn't "want" to see these negative consequences applied to these characters. This approach offers a new way to interpret Katey and Joan's emphasis on the women characters' need to protect themselves from David, and Jeannette's emphasis on Donna and Kelly's relationship. For these viewers, *90210* was "about" the relationship among the characters—and the viewer's own community with the characters. Survival of the ensemble depicted in the group snapshot in the opening credits represents the show's metanarrative, into which viewers willingly thrust themselves.

In earlier chapters, I have argued that this community can work hegemonically to reinforce and perpetuate patriarchal and capitalist values, an argument that gains ammunition here. In the ethical realm, the community worked to foster an "us-them" read of the issues that glossed over any serious consideration of right and wrong. The text the show seemed to be preaching was that those in our community are right.

In the episode following the one about tough love, David's drug dealer gets busted and hands a drug stash to David to guard. David hides the stash in his apartment and agonizes about what he should do. Finally— in the turning point of his recovery—David calls Dylan for advice. Dylan makes him flush the entirety down the toilet. David thus narrowly misses being arrested, as the police storm his apartment moments later. For the rest of the season, he stays off drugs for good.

Fueled by the previews, which showed police breaking into David's apartment and the drugs spilling into the toilet, viewers followed these details with avid interest and conflicting concerns—that David go unpunished but also that he kick the habit. As sixth-grader Colleen said, "I didn't want him to get caught but I didn't want him to still do drugs." The glimpses of the coming drug bust had raised viewer anxiety quite successfully. Talk about previews will be examined more closely in the chapter on guessing; here let me note that the television text was an important player in the way viewers constructed the problem.

Initially, viewers condemned David's foolishness in accepting the dealer's drug stash. Knowing that the police would overrun David's apartment, they frantically speculated on ways he could get rid of this incriminating evidence, unproblematically working in the preview-suggested idea of flushing them down the toilet. During viewing, twins Melanie and Marissa energetically condemned David's acceptance of the stash and offered excited solutions:

Dealer: "The whole dorm's going to be busted."
M: So stupid.
M: He's gonna get busted.
M: Idiot! Idiot! I would never do that.
[. . .]
M: That was stupid to take it. I'd be like, "Here, *you* get in trouble, go away." I'd burn it. I would like just throw it down the toilet.

Again, neither viewer confronted the legal issue. It was an "us-them" situation, and if someone has to "get in trouble," it had better be the drug dealer, not David. The situation was translated into, Who will get caught? ("Here, *you* get in trouble"). Suddenly, there was no discussion of David's weeks of wrongdoing, which under my questioning had generated the sometimes uncertain, always varied reactions described above. "He deserved it," "they have to be nice and help him," and even "it's his fault" were nowhere to be heard. Rather, the viewers were now in a wagon-circling community with David against the dealer and the cops. David is "stupid," not essentially, but in the sense that a friend might be called "stupid" if he or she made an error in judgment. These viewers manifested an easy and eager assumption of David's position, exploring what they would do under those circumstances: "I'd be like, 'Here, *you* get in trouble, go away.' I'd burn it. I would just throw it down the toilet."

A few days after that episode aired, sixth-grader Colleen spontaneously began to talk about what David should have done with the stash (to my puzzlement at first). Like Melanie and Marissa, she put herself in David's shoes, her grammar deteriorating as, with increasing vehemence, she made her point:

COLLEEN: I don't think he [David] should have taken the drugs, even if the guy said to, anyway.
G: You mean the—?
COLLEEN: The guy who was selling them. I don't think he [David] should of took the bag of drugs anyway.
G: Oh! When he was in there and they were giving them, he took the bag into his apartment, yeah. Well—
COLLEEN: I wouldn't have tooken them into my, into my apartment.
G: Yeah?
COLLEEN: I would have put them somewhere else.

Knowing the police will raid the apartment, Colleen urgently suggested that David should have taken the drugs elsewhere, saying *she* would have "put them somewhere else." This fascinating blend of preview narrative, show narrative, and self-narrative, spoken with authority and intensity, was importantly fueled by a value for the viewer's community, of which David was a part.

These viewers focused on fears that David would get caught. As they watched David agonize, then Dylan come to the rescue, then the amusing montage as a remarkably sizable collection of pills is flushed down the toilet, they speculated, in voices filled with concern for David, on how the preview would fit in:

SANDY: I thought, I wasn't sure what the cops were going to do, I thought they were going to find like drugs in the toilet or something.
COLLEEN & MADDY: Yeah.
MADDY: And after they showed it on a commercial [preview].
COLLEEN: 'Cause he was like dumping it all over the place, like he was missing it [the toilet].
MADDY: Right.
G: Oh, yeah, you mean when he was putting them in the toilet.
COLLEEN: 'Cause he was missing it all over.
SANDY: I thought the toilet's going to clog or something—
G: Yeah, I did too.
MADDY: Are they going to bring some dogs in or—
G: Yeah.
MADDY: —they're going to need the toilet or something?

Viewers never suggested that David was breaking the law or that Dylan was protecting a felon, truths that were backgrounded by the text as well. Moreover, viewers did not talk about David's struggle with the addiction and his decision finally to call for help, positions easily available in the text. Rather, they focused on the community. Concern for our crowd took overriding precedence. The drug dealer deserves to go to jail—no one wastes a second thought on *him*—but it was overwhelmingly important that *David* not be punished:

SANDY: I'm glad he didn't get caught because that's—just the police coming scared him enough.
G: Yeah.
SANDY: He was so scared. So that scared him enough.
MADDY: He really freaked out with the cops—
SANDY: I think he's going to stay off them for just at least for a while.

For these viewers, the show did indeed serve as a resource for discussions about (1) drug-taking as wrong, (2) what some effects of addiction might be, and (3) how it should be dealt with. However, this type of relational morality was collapsed into an ethos that emphasized restoration of equilibrium in the community over an abstract sense of right and wrong—an "us-them" mentality.

And, as with other talk, pleasure comprised an important component of participating in this community. The viewers enjoyed the safety of the group, and the positions of agency they could construct for themselves as they defended it. They felt active and empowered in this process— even as they avoided really dealing with the issue, and as they worked to excuse characters from deserved consequences.

This attitude recurred in viewer talk during the episode in which Brenda gets arrested for helping the animal-rights activists break into a research lab. In this episode, the dog Donna has adopted dies, and the group learns he had cancer as a result of some tests done on him at the lab. An angry Brenda joins a group that has been protesting the lab's experiments. She is invited to participate in a plan to break into the lab and set the animals free. Her assignment is to act as lookout because she can pass as "just another student roaming the halls." When the pro-testers arrive, Brenda realizes that the first lab to be disrupted is the one where Andrea works, which is doing research on Sudden Infant Death Syndrome. The pregnant Andrea has defended this research to Brenda as having the potential to save her baby's life. Brenda tries to protest but is silenced. Moments later, the police arrive, catch the activists red-handed, and arrest them, including Brenda.

The following episode begins with Brenda going to jail, and the view-ers with whom I watched focused on denying Brenda's guilt:

Brenda being booked.
JEANNETTE: I feel bad for her. She doesn't deserve to be in jail.
JACKIE: Yeah, she didn't really know what was going on, they just told her to come up.
[. . .]
Brenda led to jail cell.
JACKIE: Oh, I'd be so scared in there.
JEANNETTE: Uh huh.
[. . .]
At the hearing. Warden: "Bail was preset at $50,000."
ALL: Ohhh! No way!!
Warden reads formal charges.
JACKIE: She didn't do that!

While there is no doubt that Brenda *did* go with the animal activists to break into a research lab, these viewers maintained that she didn't de-serve to be punished. Not only did they enter into her feelings ("I feel bad for her"; "I'd be so scared in there") but they also vociferously de-fended her innocence ("She didn't really know what was going on"; "*they* told her" and she did what she was told, so she is not responsible for her actions). It is true that Brenda did not know that Andrea's lab was to be trashed, and she did try to protest that decision at the last minute. However, even if the viewers were responding to this change of heart, they painlessly avoided the fact that Brenda definitely participated in the overall planning of the attack, and went to the lab intending to disrupt the research. Instead, these girls expressed a strong sense that Brenda should not be penalized. Jackie even went so far as to object to the formal charges, not asking whether they were legalese for breaking into a lab, but flatly denying Brenda's guilt ("No way! She didn't do that!").

Further, as with talk about characterizations, in talk about issues the males were constructed as active, while females were active with each other but passive towards males and authority figures. These findings echo the talk about characterizations. For example, Brenda's arrest was constructed a little differently from David's brush with the law. In both cases, viewers said the character should not be punished, and in both cases talk explored the character's options as viewers put themselves in the character's shoes. Marissa and Melanie imagined being given an awkward bag of booty; Jeannette and Jackie imagined being booked into jail. However, for David, viewers invented a myriad of alternate behaviors ("I'd be like, 'Here, *you* get in trouble, go away.' I'd burn it. I would like just throw it down the toilet"). But with Brenda, they concentrated on how bad she must feel and her ignorance of the situation. Brenda, the female, took on the character of the victim. No one said, "I'd run away. I'd bribe the guard. I'd tell the other activists, 'Here, *you* go to jail.'" And this construction of the female cycled into talk about self as passive ("I'd be so scared in there") rather than self as active ("I'd burn it. I would like just throw it down the toilet").

This pattern of passive female in the face of males and/or authority figures was so noticeable I have devoted the next chapter to it, the one on dating.

Community, Morality, Narrative, and Pleasure: "The Gay Guy"

A rich example of the way the themes of this book combined in talk about moral issues was the viewing session with the three prep school students. We happened to watch the diversity episode, in which Steve "outs" the gay president of his fraternity, Mike Ryan. Talk during this episode is especially interesting because it was more equivocal and layered than the talk about David's drug use. Here, community definitions were less clear-cut and the television moral was less palatable to these viewers. For this reason it affords an excellent look at these pro-

cesses of community, agency, and pleasure as they worked hegemonically in talk about the show and about the self. And because the plot
was contained in a single episode, it allows me to bring into the analysis the problems of the "pat" endings and the ways that the traditional
narrative form structures and values events.

The show's moral is embedded in Steve's discovery that he has more
in common with a gay man than he previously thought—a premise that
right away positions gays as "other" and accepts discomfort with them
as "normal." The episode opens with Steve entering a strange coffee
house and gradually perceiving that something is "wrong." The viewers
derived intense pleasure from realizing ahead of Steve that the all-male
clientele is homosexual ("They're in a gay bar, oh, God!"). This situation was greeted with hilarious delight, as well as some ambivalence and
discomfort. At this point, the girls were in community with Steve, who
manifests horror at his surroundings. Their talk expanded on the text,
relating it to their own lives and negotiating a complicated relationship
between the show and reality:

KAITLIN: Yeah. They're in a gay coffeehouse.
MARY: Is there such a thing?
KAITLIN: Guess so.
MARY: That was a good call, though.
KAITLIN: What about Zadar in New Hope?
MARY: Oh, I didn't realize that was a coffeehouse.
KAITLIN: That's what it is.

In "verifying" the show, the girls seemed to be asking themselves,
"Could this happen to me? Might I inadvertently find myself in a gay
coffeehouse, just as Steve has done? Is the gay identity something that
could touch my life?" They explored with each other ways in which they
might encounter gays in their own lives (inaccurately, as it happens,
since Zadar's is not a gay coffeehouse but a heterosexual night-club,
although it is located in a nearby town with a large gay population). As
the viewers confirmed that, indeed, they could encounter a situation
similar to the fictional one, this possibility cycled into the meaning they
made of the show—and, conversely, the show added new meaning to
their own lives.

This process occurred within the context of feelings that paralleled
Steve's growing discomfort:

Steve looks around, horrified.
ALL: (screaming and laughing) Yes!
MARY: See his face.
KAITLIN: See, this is truly funny that Steve is in—(all scream and laugh)

The girls enjoyed the moment intensely. Steve, the macho frat rat, is the perfect lightning rod for exploration of this encounter with a community outside the viewers' own. Steve is a member of "our" community; gays are "other." Indeed, the viewers leapfrogged off that experience in a way not anticipated by the script, which simply states, "A SERIES OF SHOTS establishes that all the customers are men":

CHRYSE: It's also really funny how everyone in there is like a minority.
KAITLIN: It is.
CHRYSE: He's [Steve] like the only blond person in there, like everybody who's gay—
KAITLIN: —is like dark-haired.
CHRYSE: —is Latino or Italian.

In their talk, the girls foregrounded, perhaps even interrogated, but certainly reified, the "otherness" of the gay community they were observing. While the commentary was ironic, it nonetheless underscored the marginalization of the gay population.

This position persisted as Ryan approaches Steve at the fraternity. Ryan has wrongly inferred from Steve's accidental presence at the coffeehouse that Steve, too, is gay. Steve is anxious to correct this impression, and the conversation is loaded with innuendo that these viewers thoroughly enjoyed:

Ryan asks Steve if he can get him a cappuccino.
ALL: (hysterical laughter)
KAITLIN: That was awesome.
Ryan: "I thought I saw you yesterday having a cappuccino."
MARY: He's [Steve] like, "Shut up, shut up."

The viewers took Steve's side, entering into his experience, and speaking for him ("He's like, 'Shut up, shut up' "). They sounded like Melanie and Marissa entering into David's experience of being handed a bag of drugs ("I'd be like, 'Here, *you* get in trouble, go away' ") and Jackie sympathizing with Brenda's jail experience ("I would be so scared in there"). Activity and pleasure resounded as these viewers worked to solidify community with the characters and normalize the text's treatment of the situation, in this case, constructing Ryan as "other."

However, when the consequences of Steve's homophobia began to dawn on them, the girls questioned their allegiance to Steve, focusing on relational issues:

Steve: "I have NEVER had a cappuccino."
ALL: (hysterical laughter)
MARY: Oh the poor guy [Ryan], he's [Steve] just gonna be all mean to him.

The immediate reaction was that Steve was wrong to "be all mean to him." As Brown and Gilligan (1992) suggested, those in our community are "nice," not mean. However, during the next commercial, these viewers began to construct, if not a defense of Steve's behavior, another way of looking at it that helped make him less culpable:

KAITLIN: To me that's so stupid because why would anybody, like why would that guy want to go be in that fraternity—
MARY: If he was gay?
KAITLIN: Yeah, like obviously—
MARY: I have no idea.
CHRYSE: Maybe he's trying to deny his sexuality. Who knows.

This excerpt provides is a clear example of the way that talk about *90210*'s liberal, tolerant values, as described in the chapter on the show, can work to perpetuate the status quo. The girls refrained from condemning Ryan because he is gay. But, paradoxically motivated by a concern for Ryan, they perpetuated, even defended the fraternity system that marginalizes him. The viewers did not suggest that exclusionary institutions are wrong; their tolerance extended to fraternities as well as to gay bars. They reinstantiated the status quo, the class system, and right of dominant groups to marginalize less powerful ones. They never questioned the logic of the show by, for example, suggesting that Ryan was in the fraternity to provide maximum narrative impact. Instead, Mary searched for solutions that continued to naturalize the situation (Ryan is "trying to deny his sexuality"). The girls pleasurably consented to the status quo, and used the expert voice to naturalize it.

During a commercial break, the girls continued to speculate about what would happen. In their shifting patterns of talk, they began to suggest that Steve, although he was "mean," would in the end do the right thing. Although they expressed a liberal dose of skepticism toward the message, they nevertheless focused on repairing the relationship rather than changing the system:

CHRYSE: Or maybe Steve defends him, or—
KAITLIN: Yeah, Steve's gonna have to defend him or else the show wouldn't be PC enough—
ALL: Yeah, yeah, Steve's gonna have to—

The girls emphasized that the show has to be politically correct. But also, they worked to redeem Steve. Mary suggested, "He could still have a change of heart though." She began to excuse Steve's "mean" behavior as transient, not the "real" Steve:

MARY: Like, right now he's [Steve] feeling a little bit homophobic, but then like he's gonna—
KAITLIN: Right. [. . .] They're gonna like, somebody's gonna say that he's gay or something. Steve—like, Steve's gonna get like his image blasted by, I don't know, somebody. And then he's gonna be like, "But wait a minute guys, what if I *was* gay?"

As these acute viewers predicted, someone *does* accuse Steve of being gay. But instead of defending Ryan, Steve "outs" him. The viewers fully participated in the scene's artfully suspenseful treatment of the revelation and vehemently censured Steve's behavior (in language that convinced me these polite and well-educated young women had momentarily forgotten my presence):

Artie (about Steve): "Doesn't she look fruity." Steve: "Artie, if you're so busy looking for fruits, why don't you look at a market a little closer to home?"
ALL: (gasps)
KAITLIN: Ahhh, you jerk!
MARY: Oh, no!
KAITLIN: Don't do it! You're an asshole!
Fade out. New scene. The brothers shoot looks of repulsion at Ryan.
KAITLIN: You told him! Ahhh!
MARY: Oh, no!

In the heat of the moment, the girls ruthlessly castigated Steve ("You're an asshole!"). However, in the ensuing commercial, they worked to soften this position. First they tried to avert or soften the soubriquet "bigot" as applied to Steve, then they negotiated ways to diminish his culpability in a reprise of their earlier position:

Steve: "Why in the hell are you still in the closet anyway?" Ryan: "Because of bigots like you."
Commercial.
MARY: Man.
STACEY: I don't think that's [bigot] the right word, is it?
MARY: Yeah.
CHRYSE: Yeah, it is.
MARY: I guess so.
KAITLIN: Oh, God!
CHRYSE: You see, I don't understand if he's gay why he wants to be in a house full of—
KAITLIN: Yeah, people who—
CHRYSE: —bigots.
KAITLIN: Yeah.

The girls expanded their ways of attending to both show and life by exploring the meaning of the word "bigot" and then applying it. However, their active negotiation of this meaning also narrowed their ways of attending to both life and show, because it focused the discussion and limited the subject positions available. Anyone who objects to homosexuality now has a convenient label and pigeonhole. But that process also reifies and naturalizes the bigots. No longer are they the ones to be criticized or interrogated; rather, the viewers returned to the puzzle of why Ryan doesn't accept his marginal position ("You see, I don't understand if he's gay why he wants to be in a house full of bigots").

This excerpt provides a microcosm of a process I found particularly distressing. For a moment, these girls truly explored an alternate subjectivity; they connected on a deep level with Mike Ryan's marginalized position. They strongly critiqued Steve and worked to interrogate the notion of bigotry. Their backgrounds gave them ways of attending to the show, and the show's meanings cycled into, and expanded, the meanings they made of their lives.

But during the break their usual way of thinking about Steve, and about gays, reasserted itself. From then on, the girls' "activity" was harnessed in an effort to patch the community back together, to re-establish equilibrium—to perpetuate the status quo.

In the next few scenes, the girls struggled with their relationship with Steve, a relationship that has become uncomfortable because Steve is now a member of a community of bigots. They attempted to soften this situation by continuing to construct Ryan as other, as the destabilizing factor that must be "clawed back" into the mainstream.

Steve: "Did she and Ryan work things out?" Artie: "Why don't you go ask him yourself?"
STACEY: Did they throw him out or beat him up or something?
KAITLIN: He's gonna be like tied up in the bathroom or something.
STACEY: Or like beat up. Or moving out.
CHRYSE: Oh, they (inaudible) it.
Ryan is moving out.
MARY: Yup, moving out. Good call.
STACEY: Oh, no.
Steve: "What are you doing?"
MARY (answering): "Moving out."

When the text invites viewers to guess what has happened to Ryan, the viewers constructed images of violence. "He's gonna be like tied up in the bathroom or something." "Or like beat up." Now marginalized, Ryan will be punished.

The feelings were mixed. Steve is in the wrong—Mary's answer, "Moving out," had an undertone of blame. She seemed to imply, "And it's your fault." But then, Ryan also is not blameless. The girls' next exchange continued to construct Steve's efforts to repair the situation as laughable, but that the overall situation remains basically Ryan's fault. And at least Steve is not as insensitive as his fraternity brothers, who were presumed capable of violence:

Steve: "Come on, Mike. It was a stupid prank. I'm sure the guys didn't mean anything by it anyway."
MARY: Yeah, sure.
Steve: "I would never do anything to hurt you, bro."
ALL: (Laughing)
Ryan: "Somewhere where I don't have to apologize for being who I am."
STACEY: Whoo hoo!
CHRYSE: You should have done that before.

Steve has begun to lose credibility, but Mike Ryan continues to be culpable. "You should have done that before." Bigots are not to blame when they are deliberately provoked.

Vacillation in the construction of community—with community members defended, and those outside the community challenged—characterized the girls' talk throughout the remainder of this storyline. In the next scene of this subplot, Steve does attempt to make amends to Ryan by seeking him out at the coffeehouse. In an inspired moment, Chryse suggests that the way to include Ryan in the community is for *Steve* to change:

Scene changes to coffeehouse.
CHRYSE: Oh, now we're back at the coffee house. [. . .] Is Steve going to come out of the closet? What's going on?
KAITLIN: That would be so cool.
CHRYSE: That *would* be so cool. I would watch this show forever and ever if Steve was gay. That would be great.
MARY: Steve's not gay.

For a moment, Chryse struggled against the inevitable marginalizing of Ryan inherent in narrative closure, and with renewed vigor worked to explore gay identity. If Steve were to move from outside the gay community to a position as part of it, Chryse might also have an entree. And Steve's *faux pas* with the "outing" would be amply repaid—perhaps even explained. Mary, perhaps defending her original community with Steve, perhaps in a more down-to-earth read of the genre, closed off that possibility, refusing to explore further ("Steve's not gay").

Steve and Ryan then have a conversation about the people they are dating, a conversation that immediately constructed them both as male in the eyes of the viewers, who suddenly lost their connection with Steve:

Ryan: "Did you keep her separate from the rest of your life?" Steve: "That was a big part of it."
CHRYSE: I don't remember Celeste.
STACEY: They're bonding.
MARY: They're finding a connection.
Ryan: "I guess we're more alike than we realize."
MARY: Hmm.
STACEY: Fancy that.
KAITLIN: Why did he keep Celeste separate from the rest of his life?
CHRYSE: He wanted to date other girls. He loved her, but he screwed up.
Steve: "I'll stand up with you."
ALL: (Laughter) Da-da-da-dah!

"They're bonding." "They're finding a connection." The viewers' exclusion from the male community—along with the reminder that Steve "screwed up" with regard to Celeste—combined with a skeptical response to the pat ending to inject a note of derision into the conclusion. And this mockery worked to re-establish the community of viewers. The intense anguish when Steve "outed" Ryan ("Ahhh, you jerk!" "Oh, no!" "Don't do it! You're an asshole!") evaporated. And the real exploration, which was hinted at when Chryse suggested Steve might be gay, disappeared also. The happy ending, and the values imparted in the traditional narrative structure, served to diminish the community with Steve to pre-episode levels. And as narrative closure re-established Ryan as "other," the community of viewers reasserted itself as superior, expert, authors of their viewing experience—hiding ways their consent had been cheerfully won to this position.

In the final montage, Ryan is shown posing for a photograph with a scarf around his neck:

ALL: (Laughing hysterically)
KAITLIN: They were, like, let's put a scarf around the gay guy's neck.
CHRYSE: The gay guy with the scarf.
MARY: Oh, that looks funny.
ALL: (Laughing)

Once more, Ryan was simply "the gay guy," and all the girls' discomfort with that identity had returned. Gone was the sympathy, even empathy, heard earlier in the episode. And the return to the status quo was voiced with pleasure and empowerment.

This interview uncovers the complexity of the hegemonic process vis-a-vis *90210*. The marginalized voice was present, and the viewers explored it in a real expression of agency. But when the issue turned moral, the solution first was relational ("Oh the poor guy [Ryan], he's [Steve] just gonna be all mean to him"), then degenerated into "us-them" ("You should have done that [moved out] before"). And as the narrative structure "clawed back" the marginalized voice, the viewers pleasurably consented to the return to the status quo. This read is especially distressing because, if anyone can be expected to reject marginalization of gay identity, it is these middle-class, liberal white girls.

Summary

In their talk about the issues raised on the show, viewers used a multitude of voices. They fluctuated between two epistemological positions, distanced vs. immersed, and these shifts were at least in part because of discursive context. When a critical tone was introduced, usually by me, the group tended to adopt it. But their more natural tone, while often critical, came from a position of immersion.

As I asked viewers their opinions of the show's issues, patterns emerged across ages, and the answers I got contained both good news and bad news for producers. In what may be an encouraging sign, the younger viewers memorized the text's treatment of issues—right along with the characters' appearance, characterizations, and romantic relationships, making it difficult to assess the meaning of this process. The older viewers, however, complained that the pat solutions kept them from exploring the issues in depth. Indeed, they said that if they did not already have experience with an issue, it held no interest for them. Here, viewer background seemed key—my analysis suggests that a viewer needed to have encountered a predicament such as drug addiction in real life to understand the show's treatment of it. Lack of previous experience with an issue could mean the text's "message" was missed. Moreover, the viewers who "got" the message did not explore the show's treatment of the issue; rather they applied their own knowledge, expanding their real-life position as expert.

My questioning about the ethics of characters' behavior was carefully answered with talk that ran the gamut described by Gilligan (1982, 1989, 1992)—abstract to relational, justice to care. Moral judgments about female behavior varied: Sometimes viewers said females should stand up for themselves, at least to other women, but often they said females should be nice and helpful to males, illustrating Gilligan's (1982, 1989, 1992) points and perpetuating this dominant notion of female identity.

But this sort of discussion did not typify viewer talk about the show. Because of the way they saw the show as "produced," the older viewers in particular did not see serious talk about ethics as appropriate, although the issues did offer them opportunities to construct themselves as expert and superior. Instead, when watching or thinking about the issues and the ways in which they were handled, viewers worked to construct a community with each other and with the characters.

This community operated on a variety of levels, but its ethics were relatively uncomplicated. Viewers did not want anything bad to happen to members of the community; when the main characters in the community behaved wrongly, viewers worked to exonerate them, citing outside circumstances, or shifting the blame to more expendable characters. They constructed narratives that worked in a number of ways: to excuse character behavior, to solidify the community of viewers, or to present the viewer as an expert within that community. In a pattern that will be systematically explored in the next chapter, one of the narratives constructed the male as active (David should burn the drugs, flush them down the toilet), while another constructed the female as a victim (the lab break-in wasn't Brenda's fault). All judgments were voiced with pleasure and empowerment.

In short, the moral code is simple: Those in my group are privileged. And conversely, I wish I were as privileged as my television community. While viewers sometimes did explore alternate subjectivities, most of their talk intersected pleasurably with the show's text to close off explorations that might seriously challenge the status quo as portrayed by the television text. The idea that one might really accept gays as a member of her community was pleasurably opened, then just as pleasurably closed, by the viewers with whom I watched.

This pattern is explored further in the next two chapters with regard to gender identity.

Chapter 10
Dating: The Passive Female

If talk about the moral implications of drug addiction and animal rights was academic and dispassionate, conversation about characters' romantic relationships was the opposite. This type of talk resonated with the intensity and excitement that conversations about issues lacked. Here sounded the passionate and enthusiastic voices that had attracted my attention to *90210* in the first place.

Certainly, the text frequently did foreground dating as an important business of high school and college students. And the viewers I listened to delightedly acquiesced in this read. As high-school student Jeannette said, "We try to predict what's going to happen [. . .] like who's going to break up with who and who's gonna get together with who." Her spontaneous description of last week's episode brims with this gleeful catalogue of trysts and tribulations:

JEANNETTE: Yeah. Like, this Wednesday what happened was—
G: Oh, yes, tell us what happened.
JEANNETTE: Now, Kelly and Brandon are interested in each other, and—
G: What happened to [. . .] the wife of the professor?
JEANNETTE: Yeah. Dylan's with her now.
G: Now, wait. I thought Dylan and Brenda were supposed to be getting back together.
JEANNETTE: They are. And Dylan's losing Kelly to Brandon. And Brandon's losing whatever-her-name-is to Dylan.
G: Wow.
JEANNETTE: So everything is shifted around.

A dizzying sequence of events, cheerfully and confidently—if somewhat contradictorily—expounded!

As with other talk, this recitation worked to reinforce a pleasurable community in which the viewer could take a position of expertise and authority. Often, however, there was more. Viewers reported passionate feelings about who might date whom, who "should" date whom, who they "wanted" to date whom, and how the dating couples should behave. Intertwining with this talk was an absent totality—the notion of a lexicon of dating the rules and regulations—that was linked to powerful emotions.

Rules of Dating and Female Agency

As I examined conversations about dating and relationships, I became convinced that the primary function of this talk about *90210* was to negotiate and instantiate cultural rules of dating. The complex intertwining of self-narrative and fictional narrative worked to infer and articulate this code that regulated female behavior in the dating situation. For example, in the following conversation, I was probing for talk about issues, but what I heard was talk about the "rules" of dating:

G: Um, you said that sometimes you would imagine if you were them, what you would do?
MADDY: Yeah, like the other choices.
COLLEEN: Oh, yeah, like—
MADDY: —like—
COLLEEN: —like you wouldn't cheat on your boyfriend or something.
MADDY: Yeah.

A primary rule: Don't cheat on your boyfriend. Another entry in the lexicon had to do with dating people your friends have dated:

CASEY: And then like she goes and like pulls a move on her best friend.
ERIKA: Her best friend's boyfriend.
CASEY: I mean that's just so wrong.

* * *

KATEY: Because if my best friend went out with my boyfriend, even though we weren't going out anymore, I'd still be mad.

* * *

M: I mean, like, like best friends don't keep switching boyfriends and everything. [. . .] They're kind of like messed up.

On an intertextual note, a concurrent article in a teen magazine dealt with this issue of whom to date. On the forbidden list: your professor, your friend's boyfriend, your doctor, your boss. This list is noteworthy in itself for the ways in which it resonates with cultural and media stereotypes—and for the way in which to an extent it was echoed in viewer talk (the doctor and the boss were irrelevant here):

MEETRA: No, it's like, you can't date your professor.

* * *

CASEY: I just couldn't do that. I will never kiss the same guy that my best friend's ever kissed.

The way this lexicon resonates with our culture is provocative, but here I want to examine its ramifications for female agency and identity. This was the type of talk I had expected, but didn't hear, about issues. Viewers took sides, arguing vehemently and excitedly; they painstakingly analyzed the characters' dating behavior (as the examples already cited make clear, often disagreeing with a character's choice); and they extracted rules that they discussed in reference to their own lives. This talk frustratingly danced around the topic of female agency, ambiguously constructing it first one way, then another; flirting with but rejecting alternate subject positions and ultimately suggesting that women should be passive in interactions with boyfriends. Although viewers grappled intensely with the issue of female agency in a patriarchal society, their talk ultimately reinstantiated and perpetuated the notion that males are active and females are passive when it comes to a romantic interaction. At the risk of repeating a tired refrain, this process, to my mind, pinpoints the way hegemony works—the delighted articulation of multiple voices in which any deviant ones are "clawed back" and the dominant ones pleasurably instantiated and perpetuated.

Indeed, the prevalence of the word "just"—like the word "really" in the television effects chapter—provides an important signpost. "You just don't do that" suggested an unexamined principle, a premise "out there" that the viewers were eager to codify and master. The word "just" signaled the closing down of the possibility: Intriguing as it may seem to flout these rules, you just don't.

In talk about dating issues, a catalyst was the Brenda-Kelly-Dylan triangle, which in some ways is the prototypical test case for relational morality: Brenda and Kelly are best friends, but rivals for Dylan's affection. When Dylan is first introduced as a character (interestingly, he was not part of the original lineup), sparks fly between him and Kelly. Then Dylan and Brenda begin to date in a charismatic romance that feels like the stuff of legend; they remain together for about two years, real time, breaking up in the fall of the third season. During the summer vacation before the breakup, Brenda and Donna go to France, where Brenda is attracted to Rick, another American traveling abroad. Meanwhile, back home, Dylan and Kelly get briefly involved; he breaks that affair off on Brenda's return. Brenda agonizes over whether to tell Dylan about Rick and finally does so. Dylan does not return the openness but keeps his entanglement with Kelly secret.

Rick then turns up in Beverly Hills and wants to date Brenda. She is tempted. Finally she has a conversation with Dylan about dating other people. He breaks the news about his involvement with Kelly over the summer, and she leaves, clearly with mixed feelings. Hurt and angry, she tells her friends that "Dylan can date anybody he wants," and proceeds herself to date Rick. Dylan and Kelly have a romantic dinner at a restaurant and depart with the clear intention of sleeping together. (Let us not forget, these are supposed to be two kids in high school!) At the door of the restaurant, they encounter Brenda and Rick, who are just arriving. Sparks fly as it becomes clear that the relationship between Brenda and Dylan really is over, and Dylan will stay with Kelly (this notable confrontation is examined in detail later in this chapter). Brenda quickly becomes disenchanted with Rick, and subsequent episodes make it clear that she is still attracted to Dylan, leaving open the possibility in viewers' minds that the couple might reunite.

In their talk about this love triangle, some viewers emphasized the importance of the friendship between Kelly and Brenda, which they saw as violated by Kelly's willingness to date Dylan. This view—that the situation is "about" Brenda and Kelly's relationship—is available in the text. But so are other interpretations, picked up by viewers who said they "wanted" Kelly and Dylan together, or Brenda and Dylan together. Especially interesting in this talk was the way viewers vacillated between presenting the women as active, or at least in the powerful position of ownership—Kelly "has" Dylan—and as passive—Dylan "picked" Kelly. Whatever stand viewers took, they clearly found dating a more compelling topic than drugs, animal rights, or diversity.

"I Really Want Her to Be with Dylan"

In the first place, viewers emphasized that a key aspect of a woman's identity is for her to "have" a boyfriend—the subtext being that a woman is defined in part through her relationship with a man. Indeed, I think it is no accident that Brenda's breakup with Dylan and subsequent failure to "land" another long-term boyfriend preceded her disappearance from the show. Many viewers expressed a passionate desire that Brenda and Dylan get back together:

JOAN: And, I feel, I really want her to be with Dylan. It's like God, I just feel like those two belong.

* * *

KATEY: And they like made a perfect couple.
G: Why, why do you say that?
KATEY: I don't know. I just think that they did.

* * *

KAREY: I feel like really stupid that I'm talking about them like they're real people. But I want Dylan and Brenda to get back together.

As with talk about television effects, this construction contradictorily both situates the locus of control outside the speaker, and positions her as the author of her feelings. As mentioned earlier, the word "just" is a laden one: "I *just* feel like those two belong," "I *just* think that they made a perfect couple" closes down interrogation of the source of these meanings. At the same time, the construction "*I* just feel like those two belong," "*I* want Dylan and Brenda to get back together" reasserts the speaker's authorship of the feeling. Viewers never suggested that producers, writers, or actors had done anything to provoke such responses. Viewers took ownership of their desire for Brenda and Dylan to reunite.

In so doing, they also took ownership of the necessity of a boyfriend to a woman's identity. "I really want her to be with Dylan" positions the self as the author of the notion that Brenda on her own is unsatisfying. Without Dylan, Brenda is deficient, partial, wanting. This attitude was articulated in a conversation among three Princeton University students about scholarly Andrea, now married and pregnant:

TERRY: I'm glad they gave her a life, though. I mean, maybe they went a little bit excessive, but she never used to date.
KYLE: Yeah, she did.
TERRY: Well, not really.
KYLE: She dated Brandon in high school.
TERRY: Yeah—
KYLE: She never dated—
TERRY: (inaudible)—but after—
REBECCAH: That was the first girl Brandon went out with, I think.
TERRY: I thought they never did.

"I'm glad they gave her a life though." A loaded statement! Even to these ambitious young women in a top educational institution, Andrea's intellectual pursuits, editorship of the school paper, etc., did not qualify as "a life." But a husband and prospective baby did, although Terry did qualify her statement, suggesting that "maybe they went a little bit excessive" in suddenly landing the studious Andrea with both.

This excerpt is also interesting for the way Kyle, who said her favorite character was Andrea, staunchly and confrontively rebutted Terry's attacks on Andrea's "femininity" ("Yeah, she did. She dated Brandon in high school"). As discussed, for example, in the chapter on appearance, arguments on other subjects were rare. But in discussing characters and plots, viewers firmly situated themselves in the community of characters. Kyle had indicated in a previous interview that her self-narrative and community were tied up with Andrea's history, and in this conversation she firmly rejected the notion that Andrea didn't have a life. Tellingly, however, Kyle did not suggest that Andrea's scholastic and leadership achievements constituted "a life," but instead refuted her friend's charge by correcting memories of Andrea's dating history.

Often, viewer talk objectified the boyfriend and externalized him as an accoutrement of the woman, as when Marion said she lived vicariously through the show, wanting to "have what Kelly has, like Dylan" (quoted in the chapter on characterizations). Many viewers emphasized the importance of having a "cute" boyfriend, in language that would be deemed sexist coming from males talking about women. Considerations like common interests, mutual support, or even income and job prospects were not considered. In this conversation with sixth-grader Colleen, I (stubbornly and futilely) struggled to channel the talk into issues against a flood of talk about dating:

G: Were there any other times when you thought something else different should have happened? Than really did?
COLLEEN: I thought Andrea should have kept her old boyfriend.
G: Oh, which one?
COLLEEN: The, uh, the one she (garbled)
G: The R.A. [Dan]?
MADDY: Yeah.
G: In the beginning?
SANDY: He's like, he's cuter.
G: Yeah?
MADDY: The guy now [Jesse] is ugly.
[. . .]
COLLEEN: His head is like smaller than his body. (Laughter)

"He's cuter." "The guy now is ugly." An attractive boyfriend is an important attribute for females, viewers said, even though opinions on attractiveness may vary:

COURTNEY: I like Andrea's boyfriend [Jesse] too. He's a cutie.
G: Yeah, he's very cute, isn't he? Did you see when they first met? I didn't see that.
COURTNEY: Yeah, he was a bartender.
G: Bartender.
RUTH: Oh, yeah.
G: Yeah.
RUTH: She was with like her other boyfriend [Dan].
COURTNEY: Her other boyfriend was a dork.

Whichever of Andrea's boyfriends a viewer preferred, it was important that the boyfriend be cute—a term that may also refer to wholesome personality, but undeniably emphasizes appearance. Though Courtney recalled that Jesse was bartending when Andrea first met him, she felt no need to mention that his primary occupation was as a law student. Rather, she placed primary emphasis was his cuteness. This notion held true for real-life dating relationships as well, as in this comment about actress Jennie Garth, who plays Kelly:

JOAN: I just seen a couple of pictures of Kelly [actress Jennie Garth] and the guy that she's with. I just think he's (inaudible)—I know, he looks like a—I don't know. He looks gross or something.
G: Does he have like long hair or something?
MEETRA: He has that look like, she shouldn't be with him.
JOAN: He's got this scruffy face and he's like—doesn't look like a blond.

"He has that look like, she shouldn't be with him." At first, it is hard to distinguish if Meetra was talking about appearance or a "look" seen to signify a negative character trait. But Joan's next comment focuses on superficials: "He's got this scruffy face and he's like—doesn't look like a blond." This way of attending to people was foregrounded in the show, reiterated in talk about the show, and cycled back into ways in which viewers attended to their lives: Your boyfriend is less a person you relate to than a key identity marker. As feminists since de Beauvoir have pointed out, a woman is defined referentially, a construction that was reified and perpetuated in talk about *90210* dating relationships.

"Why in the Hell Are You Going To Tell Him?"

In this context, it is important to revisit the constructions of strong woman characters overviewed in the chapter on characterizations. As mentioned there, the behavior of a woman who says what she means and goes after what she wants won praise in as long as she did it with her female friends or her parents. It was good for Kelly to tell her female friends how she feels, and for Brenda to confront her parents. I have already suggested that even this non-passive construction of female identity still perpetuates the hierarchical, patriarchal dualism. That dualism was preserved in talk about dating.

Moreover, in such talk, aggressive behavior was uniformly criticized when it was directed at a man. For example, in one episode, Brandon asks Kelly to be his "date" on a retreat, because a powerful administrative figure has told him that he needs a good wife if he is to succeed as a politician (no comment!). We know that Brandon has always been attracted to Kelly, and at the retreat they kiss. Kelly tells him she will remain faithful to Dylan; indeed, when they return, Kelly announces she will tell Dylan that she kissed Brandon. Two sets of viewers ardently objected to this plan:

Kelly: "I'm going to have to tell him what happened between you and me at the retreat."
MARION: Are you stupid? Why in the hell are you going to tell him?
KAREY: I know.
BOTH: (Laughter).
KAREY: Quickest way to ruin a friendship and a relationship.

* * *

Kelly: "I'm going to have to tell him what happened between you and me at the retreat."
PENNI: Bad idea!
NICKY: What he doesn't know—
ALL: —won't hurt him. (Laughter)
SHERRY: Never put anything in writing.
PENNI: No way. Exactly.

When it comes to a dating relationship, viewers declared, speaking out is dangerous; honesty is seldom the best policy. These comments have the ring of maxims: "Quickest way to ruin a friendship and a relationship"; "What he doesn't know won't hurt him"; "Never put anything in writing." The important thing is to know the rules and apply them. And clearly the community knows the rules and agrees on their application; Nicky has only to begin the aphorism ("What he doesn't know—") to generate a chorus of support. But more importantly, each one of these rules works to give the female a kind of negative agency. When with a man, a woman shouldn't say what she thinks or do what she wants. She must restrain herself, choke back her voice. Not only does this mandate contrast with the positive construction of the female who does what she wants and says what she thinks vis-a-vis female friends and parents, but it also focuses attention on negative agency, of closing down and shutting off the self, something that resonated through all of the talk about dating.

And I heard an undertone reminiscent of viewers' conflicting desires for David and drugs, quoted in Chapter 9 ("I didn't want him to get caught, but I didn't want him to still do drugs"). Viewers wanted the woman to be strong and cocky, but they also wanted her to have a boyfriend. And the key point is, for these viewers, these two possibilities didn't mix, particularly in Brenda's case. This attitude, incidentally, echoed through media coverage of actress Shannen Doherty, who has been branded repeatedly on magazine covers as "a bitch" and "out of control," beating up on her boyfriends and getting a divorce after a few weeks of marriage.

"Dylan Picked Kelly"

In part, it was inappropriate for a woman to say what she means to men because it was often constructed that it is males who "pick" their girlfriends, not vice versa. This position was complexly available in the text. For example, consider the famous breakup scene between Brenda and Dylan (shown in Figure 1). The dialog constructs Brenda as relatively active. As the scene opens, she energetically confronts Kelly, and it ends with her bitterly calling Kelly a "bimbo." Moreover, Dylan reminds Brenda that she was responsible for their breakup because she wanted to date Rick—another position of agency for Brenda.

However, Brenda as victim also is an available read. There are more closeups of her than of any of the other characters, as she struggles with the pain of the situation. Kelly gets the last word ("Go to hell"), and the final shot lingers on Brenda's battle with tears. As Kelly and Dylan exit, Kelly aggressively bumps Brenda and Dylan gives her an intense look that could be read as aggressive. Much of the scene is over Dylan's shoulder, from his point of view, subtly putting him in control of the situation. Though both Kelly and Brenda voice hostility to each other, neither confronts Dylan; his role is to sit in judgment, and his verdicts about Brenda are harsh: "Hey, give it a rest"; "You're the one who broke up with me, all right? Don't you ever forget it." He also gets off a sarcastic shot at his successor: "Bren tells me you're a hell of a tour guide, Rick." The male rules the scene (Dylan "picks" Kelly) as Brenda dissolves.

And it was this latter read that almost uniformly was reconstructed in viewer talk. The choice was Dylan's:

M: I mean, especially when, like during the whole face-off thing when like Brenda and—I thought he was gonna pick Brenda—
G: Mm-hmm.
M: But he picked Kelly, and I was like really upset.
* * *
JACKIE: Dylan had decided between Kelly and Brenda, and they, he chose Kelly. [. . .] I thought that was really emotional (giggle). Almost made me cry.
G: Ooh, cause of Brenda being upset?
JACKIE: I really wanted him to pick Brenda.
* * *
JOAN: I remember the show when he told her he was going to be seeing Kelly and that like hurt me too. 'Cause I was like, I felt so bad for her.

Figure 1. Confrontation scene: Dylan, Brenda, Kelly.

2 shot, Rick and Brenda, over Dylan's shoulder. Rick is closest to camera.	(ENTER BRENDA AND RICK)
2 shot, Dylan and Kelly reacting. Dylan is closest to camera.	
CU Brenda	**BRENDA** Oh my God.
CU Kelly	**KELLY** Brenda!
CU Dylan	
2 shot, Rick and Brenda over Dylan's shoulder. Rick is closest to camera.	**BRENDA** I can't believe this. I can't believe you would do this to me.
2 shot, Dylan and Kelly	**KELLY** You said Dylan could go out with whoever he wanted.
2 shot over Dylan's shoulder	**BRENDA** And you said you were my best friend. What a joke.
2 shot, Dylan and Kelly CU Brenda	**DYLAN** Hey, give it a rest, Bren, all right? **BRENDA** You know, if you're trying to make me jealous, Dylan, it won't work.
CU Dylan CU Kelly, looking at Dylan	**DYLAN** Hey, you're the one who broke up with me, all right? Don't you ever forget it.

Kelly slow blink, looks at Brenda	
	BRENDA So how
2 shot over Dylan's shoulder	long has this been going on with you two?
	DYLAN
2 shot, Dylan and Kelly	Since about 6:30.
	BRENDA
2 shot over Dylan's shoulder	You know, Kelly, if you're trying to lose your bimbo image, I honestly don't think this will help.
	KELLY
2 shot, Dylan and Kelly	Look, Brenda!
	RICK Listen, I've got to say something here.
2 shot over Dylan's shoulder	Obviously there's a lot of history between all of you, but hurting each other is not going to accomplish a thing.
2 shot, Dylan and Kelly 2 shot over Dylan's shoulder	By the way, I'm Rick.
	DYLAN I'm Dylan.
2 shot, Dylan and Kelly	Bren tells me you're a hell of a tour guide, Rick.
	BRENDA
CU Brenda	Can we go please?
	RICK Wait. Why don't we all just sit down and
CU Dylan	try to talk this thing out. I mean, I know it's going to be a little bit uncomfortable,
	but you guys have known each other for
CU Rick	too long to just blow it off like this.
	KELLY
CU Kelly	I am not a bimbo.

CU Brenda	OK?
	BRENDA Whatever you say, Kelly.
Bring up music	BRENDA But I was always taught that if it looks like a duck, and it walks like a duck . . .
CU Kelly	KELLY Go to hell.
CU Brenda. Kelly passes her, bumping her; Dylan and she exchange looks as he passes her. She rubs her forehead, close to tears. Music. Fade out.	

Though Brenda the "bitch" cuttingly labels Kelly as "bimbo," Brenda is constructed as the victim in this scene. The notion that Dylan picked Kelly, and that Brenda didn't have much agency in the matter, held even among viewers critical of Brenda:

G: Well, you know, I've discovered a lot of people have very strong feelings about Brenda and Dylan breaking up. A lot, a lot of people. Is, is that what you're saying a little bit, or no?
COURTNEY: Breaking—well, we just like to see bad things happen to Brenda—
RUTH: —to Brenda.

"Bad things happen to Brenda." Brenda—though constructed as aggressive and outspoken—is a victim when it comes to men, punished for her aggressive bitchiness. Indeed, one group of viewers even constructed Brenda's infidelity to Dylan in Paris, which was one of the factors that precipitated the breakup, as something Brenda could not control:

SHERRY: Yeah, but look what Brenda was doing over in Paris.
ALL: Yeah, right.
NICKY: I like Brenda still.
PENNI: She's in Paris, what do you expect her to do?
NICKY: You go to Europe—
ALL: (garbled) Kelly—
NICKY: —you go to the land of love and see if you're faithful.

ALL: Exactly. The land of amour.
NICKY: (garbled)—with a man, looking at the stars, of course you're going to kiss him.

You're "with a man, looking at the stars, of course you're going to kiss him." You are not really in control over that situation. Brenda is the one who was called "cocky," who says what she thinks—but she is helpless when it comes to whether or not she should kiss Rick under the Parisian stars. In a lighthearted and almost flippant voice, viewers constructed this position for Brenda. Their jesting tone did not belie the way their words reified and perpetuated the female as passive when it comes to men.

This mixed attitude towards Brenda's aggressiveness is reflected even in something as simple as a narrative about the adoption of the dog:

G: So now they have a dog.
JOAN: Because Donna wanted it. Yeah.
G: So Donna's keeping it.
JOAN: Yeah, her and Brenda were kind of like fighting over it in a nice way. You know, Brenda's like "Well, I want it." But, and Donna won out and Donna took it. 'Cause the dog liked Donna. So. Andrea's like, "Well I guess the dog picked who he wants to be with."

As Joan constructed this situation, at first, Brenda is actively fighting ("in a nice way," of course, as befits a female) with Donna for possession of the dog. Here, Brenda and Donna are constructed as in a contest, and, as usual, Brenda knows what she wants and goes after it ("Well, I want it"). However, that wasn't the end of the story. At first, Donna's victory is constructed as quite aggressive: "Donna won out, and Donna took it." Then suddenly there was a shift. A key aspect of this "winning" is Donna's ability to win the affection of the dog (who is male). In this identity, Donna is in the passive, "object" position—it was the *dog* who liked and picked *her*. The situation has become a rivalry for affection, and Donna's winning is subtle enough to need validation by a third party, Andrea, who sums up the situation. Ultimately, what Donna wins is not so much an active fight with another woman but a more passive attraction of love: "Well I guess the dog picked who he wants to be with."

A complex and laden discursive negotiation of identities is going on here: active/passive, aggressive/nurturing, male/female. These issues are of real political importance, and viewers wrestled with them. But the television text ultimately framed this talk to close off the possibility that an aggressive female can be loved by a male—that the dog would "pick" a pushy Brenda who said, "Well, I want it"—in the same way that any real discussion of homophobia was closed down in the talk about the gay fraternity president. The strong female subject position is available in, but not privileged by, the narrative. Viewer discussion fought and re-fought this battle—and faithfully perpetuated this resolution. The talk demonstrated the ongoing struggle by which the hegemonic process wins and rewins consent to the status quo.

"I Knew It Was Going To Be Over Between Her and Her Boyfriend"

Moreover, if a woman has to be pretty and nice to be picked by a man, she must remain non-confrontational to avoid a breakup. In one epi-sode, Brenda accompanies her fiance, Stuart, on an abortive camping trip. They pause in the desert to watch the sunset, and Brenda acci-dentally locks Stuart's keys in the car. Stuart becomes extremely angry; Brenda is apologetic but game. At her suggestion, they hitchhike to a motel. Stuart insists on not returning to get the car until the next day, and spends the night moping in an armchair instead of in bed with a determinedly cheerful, plucky Brenda. The next day, they return to the scene to discover that the car has been vandalized. Upon arrival at Stuart's father's house in Palm Springs, Stuart relates the incident to his father, giving Brenda the full brunt of the blame. Brenda loses her tem-per, throws his ring down, and stamps out.

During viewing, Brenda's outburst evoked only one comment, and it was critical of her:

Brenda: *"I can't believe I thought this weekend would be the beginning of any-thing. I don't even want your damn ring. Here, take it!"*
ERIKA: What is her problem?

Erika focused on the fact that Brenda lost her temper—a female taboo. The provocation was not explored; Erika simply reinstantiated the notion that women who lose their temper at their boyfriends have a "problem."

High-school student Jeannette highlighted the conflict also, but gave equal agency to Stuart and Brenda:

JEANNETTE: They were supposed to go camping, ah, she locked Stuart's keys in the car.
G: Mm-hmm.
JEANNETTE: He got really upset and started throwing this really big tantrum. They went to a hotel for the night.
G: Oh.
JEANNETTE: And the day they got back, the car was broken into and—
G: Oh, wow.

JEANNETTE: Yeah. And, like, so, Brenda was trying so hard to make it up to Stuart.

G: Mm-hmm.

JEANNETTE: He wouldn't listen, so she, she dumped him in front of his father.

Stuart "got really upset and started throwing this really big tantrum." Brenda, in typical female fashion, "was trying so hard to make it up to Stuart," but "he wouldn't listen," so she retaliated by dumping him. Brenda has a negative agency—when Stuart doesn't listen, she can withdraw from the situation—but she is now once again without a boyfriend.

Sixth-grader Maddy focused solely on the destructive power of Stuart's anger:

G: What did you think about that when she went to the desert and locked the keys in the car?

MADDY: I knew then it was going to be over between her and her boyfriend.

G: Did you?

MADDY: Yeah, because he had like, um, a freak attack, and he started like, um, swearing and all.

I am not in a position to make claims about the relationship of age to these different constructions. My point is that any anger between boyfriend and girlfriend was seen as highly problematic; indeed, these viewers said, such conflict probably signals that the relationship will "be over between her and her boyfriend." In a direct echo of Brown and Gilligan's (1992) findings (as discussed in Chapter 4), these girls and young women said that anger is an emotion that inevitably ruptures a relationship. This explosive and devastating quality of confrontation holds, even when anger is seen to be justified, as in this next example. Consider this detailed retelling of the same incident—Brenda locking the keys in the car—by two college-age viewers:

JOAN: Yeah, I thought that was cruel. He acted so cruel towards her. I mean, it was a mistake. And then I'm thinking, "Why don't you just break the window like she said?" I mean, then he ends up getting his car totally like stripped or whatever happened to it. I mean when he could of just broke the window and grabbed the keys. You know, got back in there.

MEETRA: He didn't have to break the window because (inaudible)—If he had lifted her up, she could have basically got her arm right in and opened the windows. It's like—

JOAN: That's why I thought that was stupid.

MEETRA: He didn't want to. It's like, he knew what he was doing.

JOAN: Yeah, he was like in control. And she was the stupid one 'cause she locked the keys in the car. And yeah, he like degraded her.

MEETRA: And I guess she tried to like, make things up to him in the motel, and he's just like, didn't even—didn't even care at all.

[. . .]

JOAN: And he blames it on her right in front of his father. Because he can't do anything wrong in the eyes of his father. It *was* her fault, you know, I mean like—

MEETRA: But I think I was cheering actually. She like told him and his father off.

JOAN: Yeah, I know. I don't believe she told the father off. But I was like, "GO!"

Stuart "degraded her," so Brenda is right to be aggressive; in fact, her agency was cautiously celebrated—although the target was reconstructed as the father, to whom it was acceptable to be aggressive ("I don't believe she told the father off"). Nevertheless, these viewers obviously had given much thought to ways in which the confrontation could have been avoided. Joan suggested they should have broken the window; Meetra said Brenda could have gotten her arm through the crack. The reality was that Brenda was right, but it was Stuart who was "in control," who refused to consider Brenda's suggestions, and "didn't even care" when she tried to "make things up to him." Brenda is justified in her angry reaction because Stuart is culpable. However, the cultural caveat remains: The bottom line is, Brenda is once again without a boyfriend—incomplete, partial. These conversations frequently were followed by a reiterated yearning for Brenda and Dylan to get back together.

In the chapter about characterizations, Joan was quoted as being glad that Brenda was portrayed as strong—"it's a really good character that she can be that way." At the same time, however, Joan did not suggest that this willful behavior is any advantage to Brenda. As pointed out in that chapter, talk about the show did explore this issue of the assertive female. But, when a male is involved, the talk inevitably ended by closing down the female who says what she means. The intersection of life and show led viewers to attend to Brenda's aggressive qualities—and to the way the television text shows them to be inappropriate when it comes to males.

"On the Loose"

The clearest condemnation of female aggressiveness appeared in talk about Lucinda, first introduced as a married woman who flirts with an unwilling Brandon, later as the divorced teacher of a feminist course

that Brenda, Kelly, Donna, and Andrea take. Although Brandon firmly
rejects her while she is married, he reinitiates contact with her once she
is divorced and they have a torrid affair. Despite the fact that Brandon
is at least as active as Lucinda in reinitiating the liaison, only Lucinda's
behavior was censured, and that relatively consistently:

MEETRA: I don't like her.
JOAN: Yeah, I don't like her character either.
G: Really. Why?
JOAN: She just seems that she's just out to get (inaudible).
MEETRA: She's too devious. I mean—it's like—
JOAN: —'cause she was married, and she gets divorced. And now all of
a sudden she's like on the loose or something.

Lucinda is "on the loose." What was fascinating to me was that no
one seemed to remember Brandon's persistence in pursuing Lucinda,
against her better judgment, after her divorce. As in the scene with
Dylan, Kelly, and Brenda, both reads are available in the text—Lucinda
as seducer and as seduced. Viewers, however, uniformly constructed
her as predatory, perhaps because of her power position as teacher
and as older than the students. This position, it must be emphasized,
was reinforced intertextually—I was surprised to read in *USA Today* that
Lucinda was "the woman who seduced Brandon" (Seller, 1995).

Moreover, Lucinda feels no compulsion to limit herself to Brandon. In
the episode confusingly recounted by Jeannette at the beginning of this
chapter, while Brandon and Kelly are at the retreat, Lucinda meets with
Dylan to discuss whether he will give her financial backing for her research project. During the course of the conversation, Lucinda attempts
unsuccessfully to seduce him. Joan and Meetra vehemently disapproved:

MEETRA: It's like she wants Brandon. But then, she dumps him. Then
she, like, you know makes a move on Dylan. When, I figured when I
saw the previews that, you know, when they showed those two getting
together, I thought it was Dylan's idea to make the moves on her. But
just watch it, I mean, you know the way she acted towards him. I mean
that just really turned me off to her character. I didn't like it at all.
[. . .]
JOAN: Yeah, she doesn't like care. She doesn't care.

Meetra had assumed that Dylan would take the "natural" role as aggressor, and she didn't censure that—even though it meant that Dylan was
cheating on Kelly. It might be acceptable for a man not to "care," but for
Lucinda to put the moves on Dylan broke an important rule of dating.
Lucinda's sexual forwardness generated considerable disapproval from

other viewers as well. Indeed, one group of viewers even condemned the sexuality that motivated her to attempt to seduce Dylan:

PENNI: Really, I think she's a nympho. I don't think she wanted his money so much. She's a nympho.
ALL: Yeah, I think so, too.
[. . .]
PENNI: She could have just kissed him if she wanted him to back her, but she *wanted* to sleep with him.
ALL: Yeah, seriously.

"She *wanted* to sleep with him"—which brands her a "nympho"—and therefore she was condemned. A complex process is at work here. First, in the above exchange, it was constructed as acceptable that Lucind should go after Dylan's money—indeed, that she should tease him sexually to accomplish that: "She could have just kissed him if she wanted him to back her." It was completely natural for a kiss to come with a price tag. It was Lucinda's sexuality that was threatening, that branded her as "on the loose." On the one hand, women were praised when they say what they think and go after what they want. But when what they want is a particular male, then this behavior was condemned. As college graduate Karey put it:

KAREY: I hated Kelly and Dylan. I did not want them together. [. . .] I guess I was so mad that she was getting, you know, that she was getting him. She was getting what she wanted.

"I was mad that she was getting what she wanted." Throughout these conversations, there was a powerful ambivalence about the woman who goes after a man. This is one of the key issues that made women's identity so difficult for these viewers—a woman is identified by the man she is with, but she is strongly constrained from going after the man she wants.

And even in the one instance when Lucinda's sexual aggressiveness was praised, it was clear that her behavior was being judged in relation to the "rule" that the man should be the aggressor in dating relationships. As quoted in the chapter on characterizations, one viewer commented: "She's very forward (G: Uh huh)—you know, it's like she knows what she wants and she doesn't—I can't say that she doesn't play games because she does play games, but she, like, she does it for herself." This viewer suggested that Lucinda was right to do it "for herself." Nevertheless, the point holds. Whether her forwardness was greeted with cheers or jeers, Lucinda was judged with reference to the yardstick that men should pursue, women attract; men are active, women passive or possessing only negative agency. The talk actively reified and perpetuated this dominant female identity.

And there was general forgiveness for a man who went after a woman. As mentioned above, when Meetra thought it was Dylan who initiated the contact with Lucinda, she didn't object. And consider her recitation of Brandon's attraction to Kelly:

MEETRA: And then Kelly and Brandon went on that retreat. And then, um, Brandon told her how he really felt about her, and he tried to make a move on her, and she was like, "No, no, no," she's like, "Back off."
G: Oh, really. Did she say, "I love Dylan, I love Dylan," or—?
MEETRA: She just like, I think she wanted to give in, but I guess she's still in love with Dylan.

A complicated negotiation of female agency! Brandon is not "on the loose" even if what he wants is to seduce Kelly. Instead, he simply "told her how he really felt about her." This stock phrase at once brackets Brandon in conventional romance terms, and forgives him, accepting him as sincere. In Meetra's retelling, it appears Kelly has the agency to end the interaction. Kelly has the final word—the decision about whether the romance would happen or not was hers ("No, no, no, back off"). However, Kelly's refusal was not explored, even in response to prompting, which generated a single-sentence reply ("She wanted to give in, but I guess she's still in love with Dylan"). Kelly's feelings are uncertain ("I *guess* she's still in love"); but her behavior is constrained by the rules of dating: you just don't cheat on your boyfriend. Whatever her motives, and no matter how she felt, it was Kelly's role to turn Brandon down, to remain faithful to Dylan. Kelly's agency is negative.

This retelling leaves no room for Kelly to be active with regard to Brandon. Her options were to push him away, tell him to back off—or to "give in." Following the rules (telling him to back off) gives negative agency, but breaking the rules wasn't active either, but rather a passive "giving in." The agency still lies with the man to say what he means and go after what he wants. The position so praised in the chapter on characterizations, that a woman can speak and act honestly, has vanished.

"Go, Kelly!"

In what is to me the most painful aspect of this construction, viewers also condoned conflict between women when a man is involved. Once a man has picked you, you are very justified in fighting other women to keep him, viewers said. In the excerpt below, viewers applauded Kelly and criticized Lucinda as they watched an in-class confrontation between the pair. Kelly has learned that Lucinda attempted to seduce Dylan, and she is filled with righteous anger:

Kelly: "We didn't finish Wednesday's discussion on fidelity."
NICKY: Oh, really!
Kelly: "I don't think we ever really explored the concept of betrayal."
ALL: Gasp.
Lucinda: "Kelly, we talked about how men and women aren't monogamous by nature."
ALL: Mmmm!
SHERRY: She is a piece of work.
Kelly: (sarcastically) "So, going after a friend's husband is actually a natural reflex?"
PENNI: Go, Kelly!

"Go, Kelly!" The situation was constructed as a contest between the two women with Kelly emerging victorious. Kelly was seen by these viewers to score the winning point when she mockingly says, "So, going after a friend's husband is actually a natural reflex?" In viewers' minds, the answer clearly was, "No, of course not." Only a "piece of work" would think such a thing. Lucinda's position as in control of her own sexuality effectively was closed down.

The shifting patterns of agency in this moment are fascinating. Kelly and Lucinda have considerable agency in one way—Lucinda to "go after" Dylan, Kelly to confront her and fight her off. Where is Dylan's agency to "pick" whom he wants? Apparently, it is in men's absence that female agency appears, and is directed at other females. And Kelly's battle with Lucinda to "have" and "keep" Dylan was applauded.

This episode and viewer reaction to it was particularly distressing to me. Once labeled the "bimbo," Kelly has numerous sexual adventures in early seasons of the show. And in 1994, for several episodes, Kelly has been Lucinda's greatest admirer, adopting some of her feminist talk and urging Dylan to back her research project. This confrontation episode between the two, however, ends with Kelly breaking completely from Lucinda. As she snuggles up to Dylan, Kelly promises she will abandon her feminist opinions; an approving Dylan characterizes himself as "old-fashioned" (an odd statement for a "rebel" James Dean-type to make, underlining perhaps that even rebels are sexist). The text firmly closes down Lucinda as a viable identity possibility, once one of our community, Kelly, rejects her.

I am not suggesting, incidentally, that it is wrong to feel pain in betrayal or to fight to preserve a relationship. I am simply pointing out that, in this talk, the forum for such a struggle was between women. Within the couple, the woman is silenced. And the text closes down the possibility that, in some contexts, a woman could be in control of her sexuality and be defined without reference to a male. Instead, the way the choice is presented discredits that voice, "clawing back" the female identity into the patriarchal status quo.

Attending to Show, Attending to Life

As they talked about the characters' dating relationships, extracting a lexicon of rules for females (they must be passively pretty and nice to attract a cute boyfriend; they can fight each other over him but they should avoid conflict within the relationship; and they should remain faithful to him), viewers hegemonically reified and perpetuated these dominant notions of female identity. Females can have agency with each other, but when it comes to males, power is gained through following the rules, avoiding confrontation, not saying what you think or doing what you want.

This way of attending to the show cycled back and was mirrored in ways viewers attended to their lives, as is fascinatingly illustrated in a serendipitous example of a talk during an interview about real-life dating relationship by women at Rider University:

CASEY: (Answers phone) Hello. No, she's not. Uh huh. Oh yeah, I did. Yeah, thank you. Right this minute? No. No, not right now, OK? All right. Bye. (Hangs up.) Three guesses.
ERIKA: Super [Sam].
ALISON: Oh no, really?
CASEY: Stop calling this room. (Giggles) This guy is hooked on my roommate, and he's so whacked, he was here a couple of weeks ago to watch TV with us—
G: Uh huh.
CASEY: —and he tells my roommate, he goes, "All right, I'll talk to you in a couple of days," and he's like, "Bye, I love you." And [Lily] goes, "Oh my God." (Giggles) She goes running in here 'cause I left her alone, she was really mad. I'm like, "What's wrong?" She goes, "He told me he loves me." I was like, "Oh God."
ERIKA: She's never given him any indication—
CASEY: Never.
ERIKA: —of anything.
CASEY: The funniest thing is—if you want to laugh, just read that one card, that one above the (garbled), oh, just rip it off the wall. It is so hysterical, no you gotta read the front of it.
G: (embarrassed) I did, I just—
ERIKA: Oh. (Laughs)
CASEY: They've never had a date, they've never kissed—nothing. And she doesn't like him. It's very sad, actually.

G: I think he's having a fantasy life here (laughter).
CASEY: He calls her, "Can we go out? Can we do this? I'm here, I'm there." He calls, he takes her skiing. That's the only thing they've ever done, is gone skiing, and she kind of used him. She's so stupid 'cause look what happened. I mean he calls from the 201 area code like seven times a day. I'm like, "[Samuel,] I'm on the phone. Can she call you back?" I mean, I feel bad but, and then he's like—
(garbled conversation)
[. . .]
CASEY: I remember one night he called, and I said that she was sleeping, and then the next day he was here, and we said we were up 'til two o'clock watching a movie. I'm like, "She fell asleep, and she woke up."
ALL: Laughter.

In their talk about "Super Sam," the young women marshaled a pleasurable community of deceit along gender lines that constructed them as empowered. Clearly, Sam's behavior was common knowledge—Erika guessed it was he on the phone, and Alison reacted knowingly ("Oh, no, really?"). To each other, they spoke from strong positions of agency —Lily "kind of used him" to go skiing. And yet, when it came to male-female interactions, this aggressiveness was diluted into passive-aggressive behavior. Although they indicated that his attentions were inappropriate and unwelcome, this had been communicated to Sam only through omission ("She's never given him any indication of anything"). The women avoided confrontation, offering no active discouragement except for lying ("I said that she was sleeping") and avoidance ("I'm like, 'Samuel, I'm on the phone. Can she call you back?' "). Where is the much-vaunted independent woman who will do what she wants and think how she wants? The agency disappeared with the appearance of the male—incidentally, one who may have been insistent but hardly domineering! Just his presence, however, necessitated that these women continue to be pretty and nice, and not say what they think.

And this passive position was concealed as these women discursively constructed themselves as agents, expertly following their rules of behavior with regard to males. They constructed a community in accordance with these rules, and their talk reinforced both community and rules. The agency is similar to that examined in connection with appearance, in which rules were codified, expert judgments made, and actions taken. Like Radway's (1984/91) women, who actively bought and read romances, these young women constructed themselves as agents—in ways that hegemonically reinforced the status quo.

They were not resisting the patriarchy any more than they resisted the commercialism of an emphasis on appearance. Unlike the women studied by Ang (1985) and Brown (1994), they did not mock the system or interrogate the rules. They were concerned to learn and follow them. And talk was key to this process. The ways in which they attended to the show cycled back into a way of attending to life: The talk about "Super Sam" bears a striking resemblance to talk about *90210*. One could almost fill in the blanks: "—and he tells Brenda, he's like, 'Bye, I love you.' And Brenda goes, 'Oh my God.' (Giggles) She goes running into her room 'cause Kelly left her alone, she was really mad. Kelly's like, 'What's wrong?' She goes, 'He told me he loves me.' Kelly was like, 'Oh God.' " One can hear the ring of "Brandon told her how he really felt about her, and he tried to make a move on her, and she was like, 'No, no, no,' she's like, 'Back off.' "

Only one group of viewers, women who attended Princeton University, deliberately constructed themselves as "above" this preoccupation with relationships; as superior to, and looking down on, the traditional female dependence on relationships and "the whole scene" of clothing, hairstyles, relationships, etc.—the terms that permeate talk about *90210*. In the excerpt below, they celebrated their strength and rejected those who conform with the traditional female identity or, as Ruth put it, of "selling herself" to the husband and 2.5 children. They contrasted this position to choices made by characters on the show:

COURTNEY: I mean, we like to think of ourselves as strong Princeton women. Which is sometimes more true than others, but, other times, but um—Well, just like, I mean, just like the fact that, you know, we, we feel like we're educated and intelligent and have a lot to offer and don't really have to conform to—
RUTH: —sell ourselves.
[. . .]
COURTNEY: We're our own—we are our own people.
G: Mm-hmm.
COURTNEY: Our own persons.
G: In terms of decisions that you make.
COURTNEY: Yeah. And, and, so what, if we don't have like—
RUTH: They're [the characters on *90210*] like so, I mean, they conform so much, it seems like to me.
COURTNEY: Yeah. Yeah. They're all, they're all very much alike.

"We like to think of ourselves as strong Princeton women." "We are our own people." "Don't really have to conform [or] sell ourselves." This voice rings with agency.

A great deal can be said here. The *90210* characters were criticized for conforming, both to dominant notions of female identity and to each other. Backgrounded is the way that the Princeton viewers were conforming to another model, the male standard of intelligence and autonomy ("we are our own persons"), the autonomous self identified as a cultural narrative by Bellah et al. (1985) and Gergen (1991). This is not the place to scrutinize all the ramifications of this narrative for these women, and the ways in which this narrative, too, can disadvantage them. What I want to highlight is the way in which (1) they concealed the patriarch dualism that forced the choice to be cocky and aggressive or pretty and nice, as seen in the chapter on characterizations; and (2) even as they rejected the emphasis on relationships, appearance, having a cute boyfriend, "the whole scene," a certain wistfulness resonated in their voices:

COURTNEY: I used to sort of fantasize about like having like the boyfriend like—you know, I've kind of gotten more skeptical about relationships and cynical.
RUTH: Definitely.
G: A little bit more cynical. Oh, really?
COURTNEY: Well, just like kind of realizing that it's OK to be you, and that you don't have to aspire to be—live the life—
RUTH: Right. Well, now you're more independent at college and—
G: Mm.
RUTH: —kind of look down more on their [the characters'] dependence on relationships and stuff like that.
G: Oh.
COURTNEY: And their dependence on just like the whole scene.

These women were attempting a discursive shift, but their language was tellingly self-contradictory: While they "look down" on the characters' depedendence on relationships, at the same time, they said they didn't have to "aspire" to live up to the demands of a dominant female identity. The woman who defines herself in relation to a man simultaneously was beneath their notice and above their reach—an untenable position.

This conflict was echoed in an interview with another Princeton student, who said the show was "obviously not realistic 'cause they, um, they obviously do focus all on their social lives and don't even pretend that they have any other things going on in their lives. [. . .] 'Cause we kind of discipline ourselves to think about our work, but what we *want* to think about is our personal lives." The show is "obviously not realistic" because the characters give precedence to their social life, but in the next breath, the viewer said she would *like* to live that way: "what we *want* to think about is our personal lives." They attended to the show in terms of the relationships it highlighted, and cycled that attention back to their lives—even as they defined themselves in contrast to the show.

Courtney and Ruth projected a future with an emphasis on education and career, not marriage and children:

G: So, what do you, what do you see yourselves doing at 25?
COURTNEY: Med school.
RUTH: Med—oh, yeah—
COURTNEY: (inaudible) dead bodies, I don't know.
RUTH: You know, working or—
G: Right, that's—
RUTH: We'll be out of med school or still be in it?
COURTNEY: I'll still be in it.
RUTH: For the rest of our lives.

These young women anticipated a high-powered educational career—but that anticipation had an undertone of resignation. In the next excerpt, both constructed themselves as rejecting the relational and superficial aspects of *90210* and the show that they saw as its natural sequel, *Melrose Place*. But their resistance came reluctantly, looking backward:

COURTNEY: I wish I were called to do like executive business-type work. I really wish I could just have like a normal life.
RUTH: And I kind of—I considered that, but then—
COURTNEY: 'Cause like, you know—
RUTH: —something—
COURTNEY: Get up in the morning, go work out, you know, live the life of the professional and get—go to work in spiffy outfits and hang out with our friends after work for drinks.
RUTH: (Inaudible) I feel like I'm doing something worthwhile.
COURTNEY: That's so true. And I was like, I really wish I were called to do that, I'm just not called to do that. You know, I have to do what I feel like I'm called to do.
G: Which is med school?
COURTNEY: Which is med school, yeah.

"I have to do what I feel like I'm called to do, which is med school." Courtney constructed herself as "called" by forces beyond her control—in almost an echo of the identity where Dylan "picks" Kelly. Ruth did throw in a positive sentiment, "I feel like I'm doing something worthwhile." Courtney, however, spoke of this key life decision not in terms of the people she could heal as a doctor, or the service she could provide, or even the financial independence it could provide. Rather, she spoke of her rejection of a "normal life," with its attendant emphasis on appearance and relationships.

This resistant voice sounds quite different from the statement, "If Donna and David have sex, I would feel like I'M having sex," a comment that joyously succumbed to the seduction of the show. The Princeton women were voicing and living their resistance to dominant notions of female identity. But what is distressing is the disempowerment with which this position was voiced. Courtney was "called," over and above her desire for what is "normal." Resistance to norms is hard to do; swimming against the tide has brought an undercurrent of fatigue into even these young voices. Contrast this tone with the confident, relational futures Rider student Joan, and her friend Meetra, predicted for themselves:

JOAN: Well, actually me and her are kind of thinking about things. 'Cause her parents kind of want her out of her house. We were talking about this before. And so um, I'm thinking about going to graduate school now. And, which I really didn't think about in the beginning of college. I really, I mean I just figured I'm going to college that's it. I get a job. I didn't think about that—[being] in graduate school. But now I'm really thinking about it 'cause my dad made me the offer. And he lives in North Carolina.

G: He said he would support it, you mean?

JOAN: Yeah, he would pay for it if I went to UNC. Because he desperately wants me to move down there so bad. [. . .] So I was thinking about going down there. And then if she [Meetra] wanted to she could move down there too.

G: So you can live in the same apartment?

JOAN: Yeah, we can share an apartment.

MEETRA: It's a good decision but, it's like. I would want her to move out. But it's like. It's just like um—I don't know if I'm ready to move that far, because I still have things up here that I'm still attached to and I don't know if I can bear to leave.

JOAN: Like guys.

(Laughter)

[. . .]

MEETRA: If she goes, I mean, it's like me and her are constantly together. So if she leaves, I basically wouldn't know what to do.

Joan's consideration for her future is purely relational. She had never considered going to graduate school until her father offered to pay her way, "because he desperately wants me to move down there so bad." But she also has to be concerned for Meetra, and Meetra is concerned about "things up here that I'm still attached to and I don't know if I can bear to leave—like guys." But, on the other hand, if Joan leaves, Meetra "basically wouldn't know what to do" because "me and her are constantly together." These women are weighing their futures in light of their relationships—and their voices have a ring of confidence absent from the talk of the destined-for-success Ivy Leaguers.

Whether they resisted the show's meanings or embraced them, however, these women identified a key discourse of *90210*—its foregrounding of the complex balance between a woman's agency to stand up to her female friends and "do what she wants," and her silence and her dependence when it came to relationships with men. Again, the way the talk reproduced the text, and the way the text cycled back through viewer talk, provides a close-up on the hegemonic inoculation to alternate subjectivities and cyclic rewinning of consent to the status quo.

Summary

As these women talked about dating in real life and dating as portrayed on the show, it became clear that such talk provided a key pleasure of *90210* viewing. Central to this talk were issues of female agency apart from, and around, men. Gender issues are real, life-long, and have enormous impact on one's future. And the show served to generate a community and a forum in which to grapple with them.

As they talked about the show, viewers vitally constructed rules and regulations for dating, and explored how they played out. As with other talk, they constructed a pleasurable community within which they could be experts, and positioned themselves as authors of the female identities they constructed. Key to this talk was the notion that, in the dating game, women are subject to important constraints: Don't date your best friend's boyfriend, don't cheat on your boyfriend, don't go after a man, don't want sex. It is the man's prerogative to do the "picking," and a man may "pick" where he pleases. These rules hedge a woman's identity into patriarchal territory.

Within these parameters, the woman can only exert a negative power: She can withhold her attention; she can lie by omission ("What he doesn't know won't hurt him"). And perhaps more importantly, she can be active and confrontive to other women, even though this activity privileges a constraining relationship with a man over an identity with other women in which she can say what she thinks and do what she wants. Within the community of females, one should stand up for oneself (cf., for example, Jeannette's criticism of Donna in discussing the tough love scene, quoted in the chapter on issues). When it comes to boyfriends, however, one should be passive. Around males, the community of females is divided against itself and subordinated.

In their talk, viewers painted a destructive cycle, then struggled to reconstruct it, exploring possibilities and taking on other subject positions. They built a world reminiscent of Ang's (1985) women grappling with the patriarchal cycle of *Dallas*, in which resistance was always futile. But there was a difference. Most of these girls and young women neither resisted nor interrogated the system; instead, as with appearance, they eagerly followed the rules they derived. And this process required endless and detailed activity—swimming with the tide is still swimming, keeping one's head above water.

Even when viewers resisted, they constructed themselves with reference to the dominant identity for females: The Princeton women weren't simply pursuing careers, as any male pre-med student would be; they were defined by their decision not to be dependent on relationships. I found it hard to argue, with Ang, that these viewers' imaginative experience with the show was simply an added dimension of their lives. To me, it seemed to comprise a central identity struggle.

And a satisfactory solution to this struggle seemed to hover just out of reach—just as the previews, week by week, promised renewed openings that, at the end of the episode, would inevitably close. New situations seemed eternally to open up new options, new ways of thinking about and exploring relationships with males; but as each episode wound down to its conclusion, as Brenda threw down the ring or Donna apologized to David, the dilemma came to rest—until next week, when it was reopened. The eternal dating possibilities, seductive and fascinating, were what attracted and held interest. Just out of reach was the tantalizing prospect that—maybe—a woman could say what she thinks, go for what she wants—and still, somehow, be pretty, nice, and have a cute boyfriend.

Chapter 11
Guessing: The Microprocesses of Hegemony

The previous chapter examined the way the hegemonic process works to win consent to the notion that females should be passive—pretty and nice—in their relationships with men, even as these relationships define them in key ways. An even more striking forum in which to see the hegemonic process at work was the viewers' pleasurable guessing about what was going to happen next on the show, both during the course of an episode and in other talk about it. Particularly clear in this type of talk is the way the narrative structure, described in Chapter 2, intersected with viewer constructions, and how the now-familiar construction of self as the author of reading concealed the hegemonic process.

As mentioned earlier, the writers and producers demonstrate extraordinary skill in building in moments of suspense to sustain viewer interest. Such techniques as close-ups with music at the end of scenes provide reverberating pauses that encourage speculation about plot twists. Events as minor as a doorbell ringing or knock prompt viewers to guess who is arriving; cliffhanging endings (will David get arrested?) tease the viewer's imagination. The scripting does the same: Almost every scene contains some surprise, but carefully planted clues allow viewers to surmise what is coming next—usually (and most pleasurably) just ahead of the characters.

Virtually all viewers tried to predict plot twists, and they often said guessing what was going to happen in the next episode buttressed their interest in the show:

MARION: To me, to me, I mean, that's the main thing [. . .] the curiosity, you know the cliffhanging.
G: Yeah.
KAREY: Yeah, it's not like a normal, like a sitcom, where it's [the plot is] different every week—
MARION: Right, right.

KAREY: —you actually anticipate what is going to happen.
MARION: I don't think I would continue to watch it if it were [like a sitcom].

Needless to say, suspense is a key ingredient of most dramatic genres, and I am not claiming any distinction for *90210* in that area. I am simply establishing that viewers of *90210* said whenever they watched, they guessed, and that I often observed this phenomenon in viewing sessions. During one episode, for example, viewers were prompted to guess who was arriving for the next confrontation:

Knock on the door.
KRISTEN & JACKIE: It's Brenda!
ALL: Laughter.
Dylan: "Who is it?" Brenda: "Brenda."
ALL: Laughter.

* * *

Doorbell rings.
KRISTEN: Lucinda!
It's Josh.
KRISTEN: It's worse than Lucinda! It's super-geek!
ALL: Laughter.

Guesses were greeted with and accompanied by delighted laughter, whether they were right or wrong. And viewers said, no matter how certain they were of their guesses, they were glued to the screen until they made sure they were right:

CASEY: I think a lot of the fun is being able to sit here and know what is going to happen.
ERIKA: Oh yeah, I always, I always—
CASEY: We can call it.
ERIKA: —say that I write this stuff, 'cause I know exactly what they're going to say before they say it.
G: Uh huh.
CASEY: But yet you'll still watch it to make sure that you're right.
ERIKA: Just making sure.

Conversations about what was going to happen, whether they occurred spontaneously during a scene, during commercials, or between episodes, provided another tie binding the community together. Whether they bet or merely speculated, viewers spoke with involvement and authority, rarely contradicting each other. Sometimes they injected an element of playfulness:

Kelly: "*It pays to have a mother with a fine taste in crystal and bone china.*"
MARION: Kelly's pulling out all the stops with those babydoll dresses, huh?
(Laughter)
KAREY: Yeah.
MARION: This is the fourth one she's had on this episode.
KAREY: Yeah, I wonder why. (Laughter) Maybe she's pregnant. (Laughter) It's Brandon's.

This prediction about Kelly being pregnant was lighthearted—fueled with laughter and building spunkily on itself. Karey was safe to propose far-fetched reasons behind Kelly's attire; there was no possibility that Marion would turn to her and say, "That's ridiculous, of course Kelly's not pregnant." Moreover, the prediction stemmed from a position of careful and specific expertise: "This is the *fourth one* she's had on this episode" (but who's counting?). And talk about pregnancy is completely relevant here, since Andrea—a member of this community—actually is pregnant. Repeatedly, predictions clung to pre-existing patterns. Guessing what would happen on the show created a safe, spunky, and imaginative community that drew pleasure from harnessing expertise and gained security from following unwritten rules of appropriateness.

In predicting what would happen in the next episode, viewers drew on several sources, including press coverage of the show and interviews with actors (as when viewers guessed Andrea would have her baby because the actress was pregnant). One important handbook was *TV Guide*, whose cryptic summaries evoked much speculation.

JOAN: It says, "Brenda takes radical action after hearing bad news about Rocky," which is the dog. And, "More people learn about Brandon and Lucinda." (Laughter) And, "Kelly's classroom queries of Lucinda take on a personal note." So that's really a cat fight.
MEETRA: Maybe she might have said something about Dylan.
JOAN: And, "Steve bears the brunt of it when Dylan and Brandon nearly come to blows." So that's why they're going to have an argument.
G: It will be a good one. We'll be yelling at the screen.
MEETRA: You know what I said, that maybe Dylan will say something about uh—'Cause Dylan doesn't know that he's [Brandon] going out with Lucinda, does he?
JOAN: No, it's like they kind of traded girlfriends. (Laughter).
MEETRA: "Before you get mad"—because Dylan might say, "Oh well, yeah. She tried to make a move on me." Not knowing that she's Brandon's girlfriend. And maybe Brandon may get mad and say, "Well, I tried to do the same thing to you—"

JOAN: Yeah, 'cause Dylan doesn't know about it.

[. . .]

JOAN: I just want to see when his [Brandon's] parents find out. I just want to like—'cause they're going to be so shocked. It's going to be funny.

This excerpt exemplifies the way the viewers' knowledge of the genre, cultural narratives, intertextual materials, and their own backgrounds intertwined in the guessing process. The idea that Dylan and Brandon "nearly come to blows" piqued considerable interest since, as mentioned in the last chapter, these viewers were intrigued with conflict, about which they had many mixed feelings. Conflict, for them, was an important hegemonic arena of struggle with cultural narrative. Here, the viewers constructed a complicated scenario that would account for the conflict, taking into account both the *TV Guide* summary that "More people learn about Brandon and Lucinda" (when actually the fight was about Brandon and Kelly), and adding in their own expertise about what Dylan does and doesn't know, to "prewrite" the episode in their talk. Joan, who earlier said that Brenda and Brandon's relationship with their parents was of special interest to her because it reminded her of her own life, inferred that "more people" learning Brandon's guilty secret included Jim and Cindy. She pleasurably anticipated vicariously participating in a clash that apparently was all-too-familiar in her household, but that, in the context of the show, would not break up the community or have real consequences.

Reading the Previews

Contributing importantly to the predictions were the previews, televised promos offering a few tantalizing glimpses of the next week's show. These previews aired at the end of each episode (unless the next week was going to be a rerun), and the network repeated them sporadically during the week. To a surprising extent, they guided what the viewers talked about during the week and how they watched the show. A provocative study could be done on viewer use of previews alone. These data can provide some hints.

All viewers said how much the previews fueled their interest.

MEETRA: You don't want to miss what's going to happen the week—the next week. So it's like, like last week when I saw the preview of Brandon and Kelly—it was like, "I gotta watch, I gotta watch it." You know, 'cause I was really looking forward to seeing those two get together.

JOAN: It's the previews that get you. When they show you that. It's like oh—

MEETRA: And then like, like next week when they show I guess—I don't, you know—when Bran—I guess Dylan finds out that Brandon tried to make the moves on her. I guess they get into a fight.
JOAN: Yeah, it's supposed to be a good one.(Laughter) Every week we say that.

"Every week we say that." This pleasure in anticipation is reliable enough to be commented on.

RUTH: After we see the previews for next week, we're just like, "(inaudible) if that happens," or like we [. . .] if it's like a car crash or—that was on the other show—but something—
COURTNEY: Right.
RUTH: —we're just like, "Who's it gonna be?"

The previews provided endless topics for conversation. "Who's it gonna be?" Ruth and her friends wondered. Before the episode in which David's friend shot himself, for example, mentioned in Chapter 7, the preview indicated that "someone" would die. As one viewer recalled, "When Scott, Scott got shot by playing with the gun or whatever? Like, that was, you know, oh, they made it like so big, like, oh, 'One of the gang's gonna die,' or whatever." As recounted in the earlier chapter, these previews fueled intense speculation, including bets as to who the victim would be.

Indeed, the previews were as valued as any individual episode. In one Wednesday night viewing session, we watched the episode on tape an hour after it aired because the viewers were involved in an activity that ended a half-hour after the show started. We arrived at Kristen's house about 20 minutes before the episode ended. Gallantly but impatiently, the obedient viewers waited without watching while the episode finished, then rewound and watched it. As it happened, Kristen was also a *Melrose Place* fan, and after viewing *90210* in less than an hour (since we fast-forwarded through commercials) she wanted to switch on the end of *Melrose* instead of watching the *90210* previews, which she argued had not been recorded. Her two friends went through prolonged begging to see the previews, with Kristen arguing that the previews didn't make it onto the tape anyway:

KRISTEN: We cut it too soon.
JEANNETTE: Yeah, yeah, yeah. Fast-forward!
KRISTEN: We cut it too soon, though, it's not going to show.
JACKIE: WHAT?? Let's see.
JEANNETTE: Please show. Please show. Please show.
KRISTEN: Wait. If I am missing *Melrose Place*, you guys can miss that.
J&J: [about *Melrose*] It's over!!

During the extended pleading that followed, I tried to repair the situation (which in some ways was my fault—I had suggested this viewing time, forgetting about *Melrose*) by saying that the guessing would be better because they hadn't seen the previews. This suggestion fell on deaf ears—except as it was sententiously repeated by Kristen (who was bolstering her position):

G: What's gonna happen next week?
JACKIE: (slowly) Next week—
JEANNETTE: We don't know!
JACKIE: (slowly) I think—that—
JEANNETTE: (teasing) Take your time. No rush.
JACKIE: Well, maybe if I seen the next commercial [preview] I would know!
KRISTEN: Oh right, but you should have your own idea of what's gonna happen. You shouldn't have to use the commercial advertising to tell you.
JACKIE: Yeah, but then I won't look forward to it!

Jackie suggested both that if she saw the previews, she would "know" what was going to happen, and also that then she could look forward to it. Moreover, the previews guided the viewing experience in important ways, as during this viewing session with twins Marissa and Melanie. They "knew" from the preview that the police raided David's apartment, and they had concluded from this that David would be arrested. In this exchange they went back and forth between what the preview seemed to say and what seemed to be happening on the show:

Dylan arrives at David's apartment.
M: David gets arrested, doesn't he?
M: Mm-hmm. Dylan does too.
G (who they know has seen the show): I'm not telling.
M: Dylan does too.
M: David gets arrested.
M: Saw the preview.
[. . .]
Dylan and David flushing drugs down toilet.
M: Well, I guess he *doesn't* get busted.
[. . .]
Police at the door.
M: I guess he *does* get arrested. They have, they *have* to get arrested.

"Saw the preview [. . .] they *have* to get arrested." In fact, David does not get arrested. However, this exchange illustrates how eagerly these viewers amassed and tried to reconcile information in order to make predictions, and how important it was to them to be "right."

Interestingly, viewers never suggested that the previews might be deliberately misleading. Instead, they said that *they* were wrong if things didn't turn out the way they thought they would. In this context, I will add that I originally tried to keep track of the episodes by clipping summaries from *TV Guide* and filing them. However, I found the summaries' emphasis so "off" that I sometimes had difficulty identifying episodes I had seen from them. Consider the summary of the episode in which Brandon told Kelly "how he really felt about her" (as the viewers constructed it, quoted in the previous chapter); Lucinda propositions Dylan; and Brenda locks the keys in the car:

A reporter seeks "the truth" about Brandon (Jason Priestley), who is complimented by Kelly at an important social function; Dylan becomes valuable to Lucinda (Dina Meyer); a small mistake leads to big complications between Brenda and Stuart (David Gail). (Feb. 12–18, 1994. The names of the other regular actors are listed below the summary.)

While the information is not invalid, it is intriguingly skewed and tantalizingly incomplete, requiring more than a bit of deciphering. Nevertheless, viewers never questioned those summaries or criticized the previews, even when they realized they had been misled.

For example, in this conversation after Brenda is arrested, Karey remembered the way she had interpreted the previews about Brenda's arrest and the dog's death, which made Donna cry:

KAREY: I thought it was gonna be like something much different that she was getting arrested for. Like I had no idea it would be animal rights.
G: Really?
KAREY: I, I don't know what I thought. I was thinking, "All right, in the previews they showed Donna crying." So I'm like, "OK, maybe David did drugs again and Donna's upset about that so—"
G: Oh, uh huh.
KAREY: "—so, Brenda was in the room and they arrested her too." You know, like, I didn't know.

"*I* didn't know." As they reasoned about the previews ("All right, in the previews they showed Donna crying") viewers constructed themselves as the author and source of their conclusion. They never said that a correct guess meant a truly skillful reading of producers' minds and television codes. Although their guesses were almost entirely guided by hints in the previews, by foreshadowing in the text, and by their knowledge of production processes (Andrea will keep her baby since the actress who plays her is pregnant), they often constructed some inner intuition as the origin of the guessing, saying, for example, "I don't know why I think this will happen." When their forecasts did not come true, they blamed themselves, and they experienced enormous gratification if they turned out to be right.

Whenever the next episode was a rerun, no promos were shown, forcing viewers to come up with their own forecasts. One time I had the opportunity to compare such predictions, as two groups of viewers drew on their own resources to speculate about what would happen after Brenda's arrest. Although one group was seventh-graders and one was college age, the projections turned out to be startlingly similar (and, I may add, not very accurate):

PAM: I think, um, what's her face, uh, Andrea, is going to be like —
G: Uh huh.
PAM: I think Andrea is going to do something.
G: Like what?
PAM: I don't know. I just, because she was like, she was the one who told them about the crib death, like that, so —
G: Uh huh, uh huh.
PAM: I think she'd be the most mad.
G: Oh, she's going to be mad?
PAM: Uh huh.
G: Do you think she'll be mad at Brenda?
PAM: Yeah.

* * *

MARION: I think Andrea will, I think Andrea too will be pissed off at Brenda for doing, you know, for being involved in that —
G: Oh. Yeah.
MARION: —and I think that maybe that kind of like animosity, like —
'cause Andrea's —
G: Ohhh.
MARION: —so supportive of the research from the biological stand-point —
G: Yeah.
MARION: —you know what I mean? And so, I think that she's gonna be —
G: Ohhh, yeah.
MARION: You know what I mean?
G: Yeah.
MARION: —hold Brenda kind of responsible for it, like —
G: Yeah.
MARION: —be mad about that.

Actually, the producers chose to emphasize Kelly's jealousy as Dylan rushes to bail Brenda out. Nevertheless, as we have seen elsewhere, viewers made their predictions in empowered voices. They constructed themselves as the source of the guesses, both taking and giving full credit when guesses were right ("Good call, Kaitlin!" her friends cried when she guessed Steve is in a gay bar, as quoted in Chapter 9). The power and pleasure evident in this process concealed the ways in which it worked to reify and reproduce the dominant aspects of the show. Once again, these viewers were playing a very sophisticated version of "pundit" or color commentator, in which they learned the rules in order to work the system. And in so doing, they constructed themselves as the authors of the rules, then reproduced and reified them—and pleasurably and hegemonically perpetuated them.

Case Study: "Blind Spot"

An excellent example of this process can be seen during viewing of the episode dealing with diversity, entitled "Blind Spot." One subplot dealing with gay identity was explored in Chapter 9. In another, Donna went on a date with D'Shawn in an exploration of cross-racial dating that was of little interest to the viewers with whom I watched it. The primary plot, as indicated by the title, dealt with a handicapped woman, and talk about that part of the episode is analyzed here to demonstrate (1) the ways the text—and the girls' knowledge of the genre—worked to open up, then close off exploration of different female subjectivities; (2) the resulting ways the talk reified dominant notions of female identity; and (3) the role guessing played in this process. The characters here are David, a regular, who in this episode begins taking piano lessons from Holly Marlow (guest star Sydney Brown). The theme is treated over four scenes.

I watched this episode with four high-school students attending prep school. All of them had at least one parent with an advanced degree; some had two.

In her first scene, Holly is discovered playing the piano in a practice room. From David's point of view, we hear passionate, tempestuous music and see her from the back, with her long, flowing, light-brown hair. David enters the practice room for his first lesson, ostentatiously holding the piece of music that he will play. When Holly asks him if he brought the music, there is a pregnant pause, then he realizes she is blind. However, the piece of music David has prepared is one Holly knows and can play from memory (this fact is taken for granted in the text). The lesson proceeds well, with David making great progress.

Reproduced below are some of the teenagers' reactions during viewing.

Holly in practice room, playing.
KAITLIN: Oh, no. The beautiful woman piano teacher.

A comment laden with meaning! In characterizing Holly as "the
beautiful woman piano teacher," Kaitlin invoked a complex series of
discourses that I will try to untangle. Perhaps most obviously, she was
reading a stock character. "*The* beautiful woman piano teacher" invoked
the notion that Holly's personality and behavior will be subject to genre
conventions and expectations. "The *beautiful woman* piano teacher" foregrounded a stereotype characterized by appearance ("beautiful") and
gender ("woman"); the profession came last, almost as an aside ("piano
teacher"). All of these qualities invoked both tantalizing possibilities
and implicit constraints—as indicated by Kaitlin's "Oh, no"—what will
this mean for the plot? For David? For her as a female viewer?

Interestingly, Kaitlin was not constructing the teacher as a potential
identity for herself. Guided by camera point of view and previous identification with regular characters, and perhaps her own identity as a
student, her comment prepared her to take David's position as studying
with an attractive teacher of the opposite sex.

David meets teacher. David's point of view shot as we see teacher's face for the first
time and hear her talk. She speaks with exaggerated mouth gestures, quite slowly,
with virtually no animation to her face or voice.
MARY: There's something wrong with her.
CHRYSE: She's weird already.
KAITLIN: Her teeth.
MARY: Maybe she's paralyzed.
KAITLIN: She's got definitely something weird—SHE'S BLIND!
MARY: Yeah. Good call, [Kaitlin]. (Laughter)
Holly: "If you really want to have fun with me, you can move the furniture
around."

Here, as elsewhere in this episode, the show obviously is constructed
to allow for "prediction" and guessing on the part of the viewers. But
for these viewers, the invitation to speculate fed directly into a limiting interpretation of the characters. Had Holly done something that
immediately indicated she was blind, such as pick up a cane or walk
with a seeing-eye dog, the pleasure of guessing would have been re-
moved. However, in order to invite guessing, the text must first convey
that something about Holly is different. This telegraphing is accomplished through Holly's lack of facial and vocal expressiveness, characteristics that suggested at first to the girls that something was impairing

her enunciation ("her teeth") or causing her wooden body language ("maybe she's paralyzed"). To my ear, her talk contrasts jarringly with the distinctive "valley girl" speech patterns of the other female characters. And it seems to me that if the producers were after realism in this portrayal of a blind musician, whose ear presumably is acute, speech patterns would be the last thing that they would vary.

With the pleasure of guessing came the built-in construction of Holly as other, "weird." The viewers delightedly participated in the closing down of Holly's identity. They worked to determine what is "wrong with her"—automatically turning the issue of physical handicap into an essentially "different" unified self. Reaching this conclusion was pleasurable both because of the reward of the "right" answer and because they guessed before David did, putting them in the superior position.

Once the girls established that Holly's most important trait is her blindness, they instantly could spin out a plot line:

KAITLIN: OK. I predict in future episodes, she like asks him out, he thinks about it, he kisses her, and then he decides he could never go out with a blind woman.

The beauty of this system is that it keeps the viewers "hooked" until they see whether their predictions are right or not. Meanwhile, it invites a read that perpetuates stock (patriarchal, capitalist) narratives—in this case a stereotypical and superficial reading of the handicapped identity ("he decides he could never go out with a blind woman"). In Kaitlin's narrative, all Holly's identity, including her blindness, is boiled down to her potential for a relationship with a male. First, she was constructed as needing a boyfriend. Following genre conventions, Kaitlin never speculated that Holly might already be involved with anybody in a way that might interfere with her potential to date David. Once Holly's blindness was essentialized, it was assumed that she could not have a full personal life. (It should be mentioned that the girls were not rejecting Holly because of her guest star status. Guest stars have been incorporated into permanent relationships—Andrea's husband, Jesse, began as a guest star and then became a regular.)

As it happens, I am a musician, and my first thoughts about Holly related to the difficulty of learning music when you are blind. Everything must be learned by ear (by listening to recordings), by rote (having someone else teach you the notes), or from Braille music (which cannot be felt and played simultaneously), and of course you always have to play from memory. To me, she represented an admirable subject position, a triumph over a handicap. However, this position was not explored by either the text or the girls.

Instead, they focused on her potential to relate to a male. Indeed, at first they positioned her as an important player within this limited field—the prediction is that *she* asks *him* out. Holly has a certain agency in this matter, perhaps because she has authority as a teacher; or perhaps Kaitlin was drawing on what she expected from cliche-dependent producers. But in any case, as when Marion suggested that Kelly (like Andrea) might be pregnant, the show has already put this subject position into discursive circulation: We already have seen a female teacher, Lucinda, pursuing a male student, Brandon. Talk about a female teacher pursuing a male student, then, is entirely appropriate with reference to the show, and a good example of the ways talk about the show circulates and reinstantiates meanings.

But as with Lucinda's "forwardness," that quickly defined her as "on the loose," a "nympho," Holly's sexuality is quickly closed down, this time because of her handicap: "He thinks about it, he kisses her, and then he decides he could never go out with a blind woman." The bottom line is, Holly is blind, "other." The text's presentation might have been that she is blind but attractive; in choosing attractive but blind, it closes off certain possibilities. And Kaitlin already anticipated in the first few minutes of the subplot that the show will not explore Holly's identity in any depth. Certainly she herself will not.

As soon as this "read" of Holly was established, the girls began to search the text for support for Holly's "weirdness":

David plays and Holly listens. At one point, she corrects his fingering, playing the passage to demonstrate her point. David plays on with growing success and confidence. Holly: "Let the music play you."
ALL: Laughter.
KAITLIN: OK, there's a cheesy line right there.

Aha, Kaitlin said, I told you she was odd. And there's proof, "right there."

The text, of course, is complicit in this read. On the one hand, Holly is portrayed as competent (although she is blind, she can instantly and faultlessly play the piece David has brought in) and an inspirational instructor (by the end of the lesson, David's playing is miraculously transformed). Throughout, however, the "markers" of otherness are preserved in Holly's face, voice, and dialog, inviting viewers to see her as "cheesy." As the pretentious and scripted-sounding line, "Let the music play you," suggests, the lesson in fact smacks more of Hollywood than of Juilliard. While she does correct David's fingering, Holly's primary emphasis is on imagining attractive images rather than on improving his technique. And the suggestion that *she* lets the music play *her* subtly undermines her skill by placing her in a passive position.

The text is both open and closed: While presenting the possibility that a primary characteristic for Holly could be her musical skill, it invites the viewer to see this skill from a distance, always linked to her "otherness." And this position was adroitly and pleasurably read by these viewers, who continued to work to bolster that identity for Holly:

Lesson continues
MARY: She's a cheeseball. I don't like her.
Holly tells David to imagine he is water-skiing as he plays: ". . . feel the spray in your face . . . the wind in your hair . . ."
KAITLIN: In your hair?
David playing much better.
MARY: (sarcastically) It's a miracle!

In a few minutes, the girls reached a comfortable conclusion that Holly is "a cheeseball." And I agree that her lines were silly; in 15 years of keyboard lessons, I have never had a teacher say, "Let the music play you," much less, "feel the spray in your face, the wind in your hair." On the other hand, I feel reasonably certain that if Holly had said, "Using mental images helps me because I'm blind; learning music has been a struggle for me," her subject position might have remained available, at least for a little while longer.

Instead, the girls segued smoothly from their "read" of Holly as blind — and as such, unable to keep a boyfriend—to the decision that Holly is *essentially* unlikable, a "cheeseball." Mary said, "I don't like *her*" (something she probably wouldn't have felt free to say had Holly's struggles with her handicap been more foregrounded) and this quickly became the group "take" on Holly.

Holly: "Let it discover itself . . ."
KAITLIN: I really don't like her.
CHRYSE: I know, she's kind of scary.

In a few moments, the discussion had moved from "She's blind" to "I don't like her." Further, the girls constructed Holly as *essentially* unlikable; it was this move that closed down possibility of exploring her subject position was closed off. The viewers segued from Holly as other, to Holly as unworthy of our community. In so doing, they cemented closed the door that might have given entree to an exploration of her point of view. From now on, viewers concentrated on David's dilemma.

The possibility of an intimate relationship with someone "other" was one that had resonance for these girls. It is a way of being in the world that they could potentially experience. However, both threat and potential were defused, and the possible exploration rerouted onto familiar ground.

In later talk, they moved seamlessly from their firmly negative construction of Holly's character to a glib "read" of the show's intentions:

STACEY: (who came in late) What's going on?
MARY: Oh, that's David's new piano teacher; she's blind. It bothered him at first, but now he's coming to grips with it.
ALL: (Laughter).
CHRYSE: Seems to be a theme for the night.
MARY: Yes, accepting people.

"Accepting people." Not exploring their subjectivities, but observing their "otherness" and accepting it, as in the subplots about gay Mike Ryan (see Chapter 9). As discussed in Chapter 2, the viewers adopted the ironic, expertly pejorative voice of those who label the show "politically correct."

In the next scene, Holly is giving David a lesson in David's apartment, and Donna walks in. She makes her presence known by applauding after David stops playing. The incipient love triangle was commented on immediately:

David: "I didn't realize I had an audience."
CHRYSE: What? He didn't realize? Is *he* going blind?
Holly: "He's coming along beautifully."
CHRYSE: Donna seemed all jealous, did you see that look she [Donna] gave her [Holly]?
MARY: [Chryse,] good call.
CHRYSE: Did he just kiss her [Holly]?
MARY: No, but he's like—
KAITLIN: He's like trying to hide Donna from her.
MARY: Yeah.

In a witty and condensed verbal construction, Chryse linked Holly and David ("is *he* going blind?") and referenced David's "blindness" towards Donna's jealousy. Continuing to close off an exploration of Holly's position, this statement foregrounded not only Holly's handicap but also the way David's association with, and attraction for, her groups him in her community as "other." Because of Holly, David has become *emotionally* blind—to Chryse's disapproval.

On Holly's prompting, David introduces her to a hurt and suspicious Donna. Interestingly, this cued an exchange in which Chryse expressed sympathy for Holly and criticized Donna. This passage initially puzzled me a good deal:

Holly: "Nice to meet you, Donna." Donna: "Yeah . . . you too."
MARY: Ouch.

CHRYSE: Oh, [Donna,] don't be a bitch to her [Holly], it wasn't her fault.
MARY: No, what was happening was she [Donna] came in—
KAITLIN: No, she just didn't introduce her—he just didn't introduce her.
MARY: Oh. Oh, yeah. OK.

I was surprised that Chryse didn't sympathize with Donna's jealousy, on which she had just commented. However, what I think happened was that Chryse—ever-sensitive to nuances in exchanges between females—saw Donna's behavior as separate from any consideration of David. She interpreted the scene by calling on the notions of "nice" and "snobby." In this exchange, Holly is the "nice" one and this is greeted with "bitchiness" from Donna. Chryse felt that Donna had transgressed on those rules of conduct between females, rather than attributing Donna's bitchiness to poor acting that was supposed to telegraph her anxiety and jealousy. This reaction was taken up by the other girls, who discussed the protocol of when the introduction should have taken place and who was to blame. Ultimately, they agreed that the situation was David's fault—"he just didn't introduce her."

From this point on, both David and Holly gradually slid out of the community, and the subplot lost interest for the viewers. Much of this seemed to be due to the consistently sentimental writing for Holly, a tone that David's lines begin to echo. The sentimentality made the girls uncomfortable and out of tune with the script, even though, to the end, there seemed to be moments when Holly's subjectivity could have been reopened. For example, in the next scene, David visits Holly backstage before a recital and speaks playfully to her hands, telling them to play well:

David and Holly in dressing room. Holly: "I wouldn't want you sneakin' up on me."
ALL: Whoo hoo!
David: "I'm really looking forward to this."
STACEY: Is she a famous pianist?
MARY: I don't know.
David: "You're going to be brilliant."
KAITLIN: Oh, brilliant.
David takes her hands.
ALL: Yup. Here we go. Music, music.
David starts talking to Holly's hands, telling them to play well.
MARY: Oh, God, this is painful to watch.
ALL: Gagging sounds.
David: "That goes for you too, lefty."

MARY: Oh, David.
Holly: "I'm glad you're here."
KAITLIN: Oh, God.
ALL: Laughing.

Even at this point, there seemed to be a moment when Holly could have been reinstated as credible and interesting ("Is she a famous pianist?"). But this possibility was stopped by the mawkish exchange between Holly and David, which is "painful to watch." Mary couldn't believe that David would sink to that level: "Oh, David." Both Holly and David stepped out of the bounds of the community.

The final scene of this subplot crystallized this "read." David takes Holly to the Peach Pit. During their conversation there, Holly suggests to David that he is only infatuated with her, and that he really loves Donna. This bit of perceptiveness was not commented on by the girls, who could only hear her "hoaky" manner of speaking, aggravated by her odd enunciation, and who found more interest in the background music than in the dialog. They concluded by visiting these criticisms on David, reconstructing him as unattractive.

Holly: (about the pie) "Smells like a slice of heaven."
MARY: Oh, I really don't like her.
STACEY: I don't like her teeth. Her teeth are really bothering me.
MARY: I just don't like her, she's hoaky.
CHRYSE: She has to be the sentimental, romantic blind girl, though.
MARY: (referring to her pet) Oh, God, this dog will not go away.
STACEY: And they're playing really bad music.
MARY: I thought you liked that.
STACEY: Oh, yeah. (singing) "'Cause I can't (inaudible) the spirit any more."
MARY: Yeah.
STACEY: It's REO Speedwagon.
ALL: Laughing.
David: "Your hands are so beautiful."
ALL: (mocking) Oohh!!
CHRYSE: There's a Journey song in the background.
STACEY: No, it's REO Speedwagon.
ALL: Laughing, chanting song words.
Holly: "Music can be a pretty heady experience."
KAITLIN: Pretty what?
MARY: Heavy.
KAITLIN: Oh.
David: "No, it's more than just that."
KAITLIN: Wow, that's not really—

David: "I just want to make your life easier."
ALL: (Snort.)
Holly: "I'm not a fairy-tale princess . . ."
KAITLIN: Why does she remind me of [Lisa Smith]?
STACEY: Because she talks slow.
Holly: "An artist has to know his own heart."
ALL: (snorting)
CHRYSE: She's just full of—
KAITLIN: She is.
Holly: "Then maybe you should save the sweet talk for her."
STACEY: He has an ugly chin.
CHRYSE: He does have a really ugly chin. I never noticed that.

The exchange started with renewed criticisms of Holly's appearance, and there was another reference to her enunciation ("she talks slow"). The viewers tuned in and out of the subplot, but—perhaps because they had predicted this breakup from the beginning—they weren't too interested in seeing it play out. Holly has been essentialized as "hoaky," "the sentimental, romantic blind girl"; seen in this light, her wisdom about Donna lost credibility ("she's just full of—[shit]"). Even David has lost sympathy as he evokes and attends to this sentimental talk. Chryse followed her criticism of his appearance (crucially linked with whether or not he was likeable) with the words, "I never noticed that." He was always ugly; why did I ever feel sympathy for him?

Expertise, community, narrative conventions—all worked to insulate viewers from any real exploration of an alternate female identity. David returns to Donna, and viewers greeted the return to narrative equilibrium with cheerful acceptance—thereby pleasurably instantiating and perpetuating the status quo.

Summary

One of the important pleasures of the show was guessing what was going to happen. This process involved considerable expertise, as viewers blended knowledge of the genre with intertextual information such as print and televised interviews with actors, televised previews, and *TV Guide* summaries. However, the expert voice hid the way this process worked, as viewers discursively positioned themselves as authors of their intuitions. Viewers never suggested that the previews might deliberately mislead, for example; instead, they shouldered the blame for wrong guesses and took full credit for right ones. They discursively concealed the way the television industry framed their expectations.

And in so doing, they concealed ways in which this expertise of necessity perpetuated the values of the cultural narratives available in the text. And these patriarchal and consumerist narratives then effortlessly and invisibly blended with self-narratives. As viewers discursively "authored" their predictions, concealing the role played by the show, the previews, and *TV Guide* in their guesses, they pleasurably reproduced and sustained the status quo. In fact, they became connoisseurs of it.

The "Blind Spot" episode's treatment of Holly, and the young viewers' comments about her, exemplify the ways in which a polysemic show can serve as a resource for multiple layers of meaning, and how guessing can work hegemonically to close off some of them. The text does leave room for Holly to have an identity as an independent, talented, sensitive, and even attractive woman despite her handicap. However, the text also constructs certain aspects of Holly's identity more negatively: She is given unusual speech patterns, and the text leaves space for the viewer to extrapolate from that characteristic Holly's essential unattractiveness, foregrounding her identity as both blind and unappealing.

The girls seized on these clues as they guessed about what was going to happen. On first constructing an identity for Holly, the young viewers gave her an identity that emphasized her potential to relate to a man ("the beautiful woman piano teacher"); on discerning her blindness, they predicted she would be incapable of rising above her handicap, permanently "other." And they glibly (and expertly) drew the moral of the show in the code words of the PC '90s—"accepting people," not truly walking in their shoes. There was virtually no exploration of the potentials of Holly's identity. Instead, she was almost immediately closed off in a superficial and stereotyped way. Despite her talents and abilities, and her plucky acceptance of her blindness, Holly ultimately is defined by her relationship—or lack thereof—with man. In the end, the viewers' consent to this disadvantaging status quo was won without resistance. For all their educational training and privileged backgrounds, these girls were not using the text as resource to explore alternate subjectivities.

All viewers enjoyed reifying notions of identity with which they already were comfortable. And the guessing process intersected pleasurably with gaps in the text to close down narrative possibilities, re-establish equilibrium, and hegemonically to win consent to dominant notions of female identity.

Chapter 12
Conclusion: Swimming with the Tide

In listening to the voices of 36 girls and young women as they laughed, cringed, guessed, and criticized in an excited, vital community built around *Beverly Hills, 90210*, I arrived at some dismaying conclusions. Gathering and analyzing empirical evidence of the ways the microprocesses of hegemony play out in talk about the show have led me to conclude that such talk is implicated—for better or worse—in the reproduction of dominant notions of female identity.

I have encapsulated this finding in the metaphor of swimming with the tide: Viewers were active and engaged, but instead of fighting the current they were moving with it. They were not just enjoying its power to carry them along, but they were also enthusiastically stroking and kicking to accelerate their progress. Even learning one's own culture can be hard work; these viewers actively grappled with the subtleties involved in being female in the late twentieth century. And their strategy is completely understandable in a world that encourages our young people to learn our culture and find their places in it. But it is disturbing when they cheerfully absorb the disadvantaging aspects of Western culture along with the liberating ones.

Discourse analysis helps uncover this process, which goes on powerfully but invisibly (like movement of the tide)—probably in many aspects of the transmission of culture but quite evidently in the case of impressionable young viewers of *90210*. A media text offers an identity (sometimes along with an alternative). But it is in the discussion, the amateur punditry, the lighthearted talk of a support group of viewers that the identity (or a variation of it) is reified. In discourse, viewers reinstantiate the idea, take ownership of it, even feel as if they are its authors. And the identities I heard *90210* fans latch onto and perpetuate in discourse were that a woman should be pretty and nice and defined by a male.

Although I saw behavior similar to that documented by other cultural studies researchers, who celebrated viewers' activity and resistance to cultural norms, I interpret my data differently. Unlike some of my colleagues, I have suggested that talk about this television show played an important role as viewers actively constructed, reified, and perpetuated dominant notions of female identity that were not necessarily in their best interests.

For example, the endlessly fascinated discussions of female appearance seemed empirically to confirm Fiske's (1987) theory of a polysemic text with which empowered viewers make multiple meanings. This talk also generated the pleasurable community seen by, for example, Ang (1985) and Brown (1994), support groups that these researchers said empowered the viewers. However, I suggest that resonating under this lively variety of communal responses ran a single meaning—the ominous pedal point of a narrow and restrictive female identity. Moreover, the way this talk reified and perpetuated that identity was concealed by the ubiquitous authorial voice, the "expert" viewer who positioned herself as the source of her meanings. This voice delightedly concealed the role of the television text in offering the identities that viewers eagerly and actively appropriated for themselves.

Similarly, talk about characterizations and plots could be seen to confirm other researchers' findings that viewers were active and resistant, although, using the tools of discourse analysis, I interpret these data another way. As Fiske (1987) suggested, the young viewers did not look like passive dupes of the text; rather, they made multiple meanings—Donna is smart or stupid; Lucinda is admirably strong or too forward, "a piece of work"; the '60s episode was simply an anomaly, or it signaled that Donna and David will have sex. I can comfortably echo Morley's (1980) analysis that the viewer, not wholly the text, determined the reading.

At the same time, however, I argue that this talk worked to construct a community with the characters that inevitably, and hegemonically, intertwined with ways viewers attended to their own lives. Viewers created a community with Kelly, Brenda, Donna, and Andrea (and sometimes Steve, David, Brandon, and Dylan) and pleasurably linked the fictional narratives with their own self-narratives. Even as they attended to the show in the context of their own lives, they also attended to their own lives on the show's terms—terms largely dictated by the less-than-altruistic constraints of prime-time network television.

Like Hobson's (1980) viewers of *Crossroads*, fans of *90210* took cultural possession of the program; like Ang's (1985) viewers of *Dallas*, they "recognized" their own emotional realities in the show. But I would argue, in Althusserian fashion, that this process constituted a "misrecognition" of themselves in the idealized capitalist and patriarchal subject that irresistibly hailed them. Their sense of ownership of the program concealed ways in which their talk pleasurably blended fictional and self-narratives that privileged certain meanings and silenced others. For example, viewers took sides, depending on their own values, over whether Lucinda's sexual forwardness signaled an admirable independence ("she knows what she wants") or a predatory selfishness ("she's on the loose"). But the television narrative also offered a structure in which those values gained additional meaning: In these animated discussions, Lucinda's primary identity was tied, not to her academic achievements or independent lifestyle, but rather to the ways in which she relates to men.

Moreover, the way the young viewers "played pundit" when it came to plots could provide insights for those in the field of media literacy. Viewers memorized, regurgitated, and analyzed plots and relationships, often displaying an encyclopedic knowledge of the show's and actors' history. In so doing, they granted ultimate authority to the fictional narratives to set the terms of the discussion—even as the speakers presented themselves as authors of the meanings they derived.

Like Radway's (1982) romance readers, *90210* fans set aside time for their media encounters, which they guarded jealously. At the same time, however, they presented themselves as authors of their viewing experiences, often reciting a diluted version of limited effects mass media theory to claim that television did not "really" affect them. This use of the "expert" voice concealed ways in which their very viewing rituals shaped the structure and value of their lives—participated in and guided their lively self-enculturation.

Although the young viewers sometimes spoke about moral issues in a variety of justice and care voices, as documented by Gilligan (1982, 1989, 1992), such talk did not typify their conversations about *90210*. Rather, it seemed to be an artifact of the interview situation. When left to themselves, the viewers emphasized their community with the characters to create an overwhelming "us-them" morality that superseded other ethics. My findings also confirmed Morley's (1980) observation that the way a viewer experienced a televised issue depended to a great extent on whether or not she had experienced it in real life. This process strongly limited "reception" of moral "messages" so touted by producers.

The microprocesses of hegemony were perhaps most evident in as viewers talked about dating relationships and guessed what would happen next. Certainly active and sometimes resistant, these viewers nevertheless ultimately reinstantiated dominant notions of female identity. For example, viewers wrestled with issues of relationality and autonomy —issues that, as Gilligan (1982) pointed out, are especially contested for women because of the patriarchal devaluing of our relational voice. But because the show framed such discussions, these viewers continually articulated the problem in patriarchal terms—they could be cocky and aggressive *or* pretty and nice, but there was no stage on which these themes could be played in counterpoint. A woman who says what she means and does what she wants will end up without a man—and, the show says, this last is all-defining.

The process was uneven and contested; in places, the voices leaked out of the hegemonic accord. Like the women Ang (1985), Press (1991), and Brown (1994) interviewed, viewers took great pleasure in mocking the show, calling it "politically correct" and criticizing the "happy endings." As Condit (1994) put it, the hegemonic concord underlying the text spoke with multiple voices. The talk I listened to did open alternate female identities—including the idea that a woman could be independent, strong, nonconformist in appearance, in charge of her own sexuality—but then closed them again in favor of dominant reads. Marginalized positions were offered but then "clawed back" into mainstream meanings, as Fiske and Hartley, 1978, would have it. Viewers were "inoculated" against divergent subjectivities, in Barthes's word (cf. Fiske, 1987). For example, as quoted in Chapter 10, Joan explored a non-dominant female identity when she said, "I was cheering actually. [Brenda] like told [Stuart] and his father off." But ultimately the hegemonic status quo, the narrative equilibrium, reasserted itself, as epitomized in Joan's passionate reiteration, "I really want [Brenda] to be with Dylan. It's like God, I just feel like those two belong." Relationships occupy center stage, and ultimately Brenda must be pretty and nice enough to keep a man.

While these cultural mandates—to be pretty and nice, to avoid conflict, and to settle down with a man—might not seem so terribly oppressive, the often unattainable standards these expectations inflict do in fact disadvantage women in important ways. For example, an impossible definition of "pretty" sets the stage for a painful loss of self-esteem that often is extended to destructive eating disorders, not to mention cancer-causing breast implants. A recent cover of *People* magazine suggested that "media images of celebrities teach kids to hate their bodies" (Schneider et al. 1996). The Beverly Hills definition of beauty paves the way for actual physical harm, in an era only beginning to understand, for example, the extent of anorexia and bulimia in young females. A women's magazine recently reported that a study of 3,000 adolescents found the majority of boys trying to gain weight and appear more like men, but two-thirds of the girls from age 13 to 18 trying to lose weight (Stacey 1995). Women are three times as likely as men to have negative thoughts about their bodies (Schneider et al. 1996).

Moreover, the impossible "nice" standard, as Brown and Gilligan (1992) pointed out, silences girls' and women's voices and ensures their needs are not heard:

For girls in adolescence to say what they are feeling and thinking often means to risk, in the words of many girls, losing their relationships and finding themselves powerless and all alone. . . . Honesty in relationships began to seem "stupid" — it was called "selfish" or "rude" or "mean." . . . And girls enacted this discon- nection through various forms of dissociation: separating themselves or their psyches from their bodies so as not to know what they were feeling, dissociating their voice from their feelings and thoughts so that others would not know what they were experiencing, taking themselves out of relationships so they could better approximate what others want or desire, or look more like some ideal image of what a woman or what a person should be. (pp. 217–18)

And feminists for decades have objected to defining women referen- tially, rather than on our own terms. Reilly (1996b) has pointed the way our culture measures a woman's worth by whether or not she is mar- ried. "Ever-single women are the flip side of femininity, hampered by some terrible fault that makes them unmarriageable," she maintained (p. 105). That expectation can crucially undercut the way we value our- selves:

Sociologists and psychologists say that such a pervasive stigma is a subtle drain on self-esteem. Even when women consciously reject the offending images, they are hard-pressed to ignore the underlying message: If I'm unmarried, there must be something wrong with me. (p. 105)

In other words, my data faithfully reflected the behavior that led to the cultural studies debate over agency: The active viewers mocked and criticized the text; they made multiple and sometimes idiosyncratic meanings of it; they used it to form a pleasurable community. But social construction theory and discourse analytic techniques allowed me to choose a new path at this crossroad — to argue that this very activity con- tributed to perpetuating an impossible and disadvantaging standard for female identity.

One of the important contributions I hope this book makes is to unpack some of the mechanisms of hegemony, the microprocesses of winning consent and naturalizing this identity as "common sense." As viewers created a discursive community with characters, they blended fictional and cultural narratives with their own self-narratives, pleasur- ably succumbing to the beautiful characters, intriguing plot twists, and wealthy, carefree lifestyles. And who can blame them? After all, this is "only" television. Once the show is over, the seductive images seem left behind as viewers returned to their work-a-day worlds. But as they did so, viewers cheerfully accepted the show's subtle invitation to attend to self in certain ways and not others—ways that pleasurably won consent to dominant notions of female identity. And the expert voice concealed this operation, positioning the speaker as author of that ideology. Viewers said it was *they* who wanted to be pretty and nice like Kelly. Almost never did they suggest that it was the television text—and the patriarchal and capitalist culture behind it—that won their consent to these definitions of femininity and sparked their desire to emulate them.

Poststructuralist theory urges us to scrutinize this authorial and autonomous voice, which is inextricably intertwined with the roots of our individualistic culture. It urges us to abandon the Enlightenment straw figure that teaches us it is *we* who think, not our culture and language that gives us the forum to think about anything—including whether such an activity as thought is even possible. Until we have a way to understand our innermost thoughts, desires, and beliefs as woven with materials provided by language and culture, we will be unable to move beyond arguments over whether television can "make" us do anything, the argument that has hamstrung, for example, cultivation analysis. As social construction shows, the enemy here is the fiction of the autonomous self: I am the unique source of my thoughts; culture and language play no role in the meanings I make.

I am personally convinced that interrogating the authorial voice can tear down roadblocks that have brought to a halt conversations about, for example, bigotry of all kinds. But I also understand that the poststructuralist approach can seem a jackhammer, shaking the very foundations of our existence. As Giddens (1979/90) has shown in his theory of structuration, culture enables as well as constrains. We cannot live day to day without unexamined assumptions; we could not have this conversation without culture to provide the stadium and position the players. On one level, these viewers were right to work to understand the way our culture operates, for culture empowers as well as disadvantages: The girls and young women in my study, as well as I myself, enjoy many privileges born of both capitalism and patriarchy. Moreover, women have many advantages today we didn't have 20 years ago—from more inclusive language in books and increasing career opportunities to greater freedom from the pinch in the elevator. In my objections to patriarchy and capitalism, I do not mean to imply that capitalism and patriarchy are simple and categorical evils.

What worries me are the ways in which these aspects of our culture are presented as common sense, naturalized, unexamined. For instance, on one level I am deeply sympathetic to the young women who celebrated the cocky, aggressive female. Certainly, shouting is better than being silenced. What I object to is women's definition of the problem in patriarchal terms, greedily appropriating what the culture used to reserve for men, without examining underlying values. It seems to me that the cultural shift towards the cocky, aggressive female has unpleasantly manifested itself in giving many women free rein to disrespect men publicly in ways that, 20 years ago, we hated and objected to when it was done to us. The positive aspects of "pretty" and "nice" must be preserved even while we insist that our identities not be determined by arbitrary and constraining standards of beauty or by demeaning expectations of self-effacing passivity. This study does not make a case for "ugly" and "mean." Being pretty and nice can often be useful and appropriate for both genders.

Indeed, in no way do I mean to imply that women's battles are unique, or to minimize the ways our culture constrains and hampers other people, even the much-maligned white male. His community around sports, I suspect, can function in the same way as the *90210* community: The assumption of the "expert" voice, and the blending of sports narratives and self-narratives, co-construct a discourse of masculinity that perpetuates a capitalist status quo and locks men into a hierarchical identity that can be disadvantaging.

Further, one could argue that the culture must be learned before it can be changed. As Shotter (1991) pointed out, we all face the task of making what we do relevant in order to avoid being marginalized. The viewers I listened to worked hard to assimilate and understand what teenagers do in our culture, what their concerns and constraints should be. And there is a way in which this behavior was adaptive and appropriate. Even when you're swimming with the tide, you must work to keep your head above water. And as Willis (1978) and McRobbie (1980) saw, swimming in the other direction, upstream, doesn't change the tide; it simply exhausts the swimmer.

This study can only begin to untangle these complex issues. What I hope it accomplishes is to show that the cultural tide washes over us, or bears us up, largely on the discursive level—and that television, for better or for worse, plays an important role in the discursive enculturation process. This study offers intimate glimpses of ways in which watching and talking about a television show can work to transmit culture, and what that can mean in terms of perpetuating or interrogating existing power relations. My perhaps too-sanguine hope is that this book can give readers a provocative way to think about their own viewing experiences. We all delightedly participate in our own enculturation, but our current discourse conceals this process. A discourse that denaturalizes the enculturation process is necessary if we want to start thinking about breaking down the sea walls, diverting the conduits, and reconstructing the banks that channel the tide as it hegemonically transmits our culture.

Appendix: Data Collection and Subjects

Data were collected following ethnographic and cultural studies techniques for conducting qualitative interviews. Subjects were chosen via the "snowball" method.

Data Collection

A top priority was given to preserving to the greatest extent possible the naturalness of the viewing and discussion settings (Marshall and Rossman 1989). With one unhappy exception of an interview that took place in my office, as explained below, interviews took place in the homes or dormitories of participants (Liebes and Katz 1989/91). When possible, the typical viewing situation was used, ranging from a small-group or family setting to a crowded campus lounge (on campuses, the Wednesday airings sometimes became "events" as large groups convened to watch vociferously). Two individual interviews also were conducted (Radway 1984/91).

Because the girls and young women already discussed the show with a small group of friends, I sought out pre-existing groups (Frazer, 1987; Brown, 1994), ranging in size from two to four. I culled interview subjects through a variety of friends living in a mix of neighborhoods as well as through four distinct milieus to which I have access (Rider University, a mid-sized private New Jersey college where I teach; Princeton University, an Ivy League school in the town where I live; a mid-sized Protestant church on the New Jersey Shore attended by a mix of classes, where I work as music director; and a newsroom of educated writers and editors, where I work part time as a copy editor). I expanded each resource using the "snowball" method. Age was generally consistent within groups, although the configurations of pre-existing groups of watchers was maintained regardless of age, so that in one group I had a ninth-grader, tenth-grader, and eleventh-grader, and in two groups I had two junior-high-aged friends joined by a sister in high school.

Eleven of the interviews (61 percent) included watching an episode with the subjects (Liebes and Katz, 1989/91). The number of times I could do this was constrained by the number of Wednesdays that occurred during two months of data-gathering, although in four cases the subjects agreed to delay their viewing of the episode and watch a video-taped version with me later in the week. I was frustratingly hampered by heavy snowfalls that inevitably occurred on Wednesday nights that February and March, causing three Wednesdays of last-minute cancellations by viewers. Moreover, I found there was a drawback to real-time viewing, which was that most viewers went on to watch *Melrose Place*, so my time to talk after the show was limited. Nevertheless, the data I collected are overwhelming in their richness and provide a more than ample base for analysis.

Apart from viewing, in-depth interviewing techniques were used (Mc-Cracken 1988). I also drew on my many years of experience working with girls and young women in attempting to handle the interviews with care and sensitivity. Individual interviews and small group discussions generated talk about events, actors, and characters on the show as well as about events and identity issues in the viewers' lives (Radway 1984/91; Press 1991). Discussion was generated using (1) a prepared list of questions dealing with the show and with the girls' and young women's experience of themselves (see Figure A) and (2) several clips identified by me as potentially provocative. Because these clips generated talk that was in large measure redundant, I chose as representative talk about a scene identified by viewers as interesting in the first viewing session, and then excerpted by me for future use in interviews: a confrontation over drug addiction in which the user's stepsister and girlfriend move out. Interviews were audiotaped (Marshall and Rossman, 1989). Some talk about another scene memorable because of a bright red hat Donna is wearing also is explored in Chapter 5. For maximum clarity, an individual lapel microphone was given to each viewer, and the signals were fed through a mixer. The tapes were transcribed, with these transcriptions serving as the primary data for analysis (Radway 1984/91; Press 1991).

As was mentioned in the introduction, I was not concerned with "getting to know" the girls or penetrating their inner psychological structures. Rather, I was concerned with the ways they discursively constructed identities for me and for each other. I wanted to collect as many different types of talk as possible within time and resource constraints. Therefore, some of the subjects were girls who know me as the music director of their church and students in my college classes (with

Figure A. Interview questions.

The interviews were guided by, but not limited to, the following:

1. What attracted you to the show? How did you get started watching it?
2. How long have you been watching it?
3. How hard do you try not to miss an episode? Would you stop watching if a friend called? A boy called? You had too much homework? What other activities might take precedence? Do you ever forget to watch it?
4. When you talk about it with others, what kinds of things do you talk about?
5. Do you have a favorite character? Who? Why?
6. If that character were a real person, would you be friends with him/her? Why or why not?
7. Do you like/dislike the other characters? Why? Are there characters that you like for some qualities and dislike for others?
8. Do you see any similarities between any of the characters and yourself?
9. How are the characters different from you?
10. Are there ways you wish you were more like the characters?
11. When you talk about the show with your friends, what kinds of things do you talk about?
12. Do you ever think about the show when you're not watching it or talking about it with others? What kinds of things make you think about the show? Where are you? Whom are you with? About how often does that happen?
13. Do you look forward to watching it? How does that feel? How do you feel when the show ends?
14. How do your parents/other family members feel about the show? If they put it down, does that bother you?
15. Do you have other "90210"-related materials, like books, cards, etc.? Where do you keep them? How often do you look at them? What do you think about when you look at them?
16. What was your favorite episode? What was the most memorable thing that happened on the show? What was the stupidest thing?
17. How has the show changed since you've been watching it?
18. Do you think you've changed since you've been watching the show?
19. If the characters were real, what would they be doing at age 25?
20. What do you think YOU will be doing at age 25?
21. Do you think television affects you? Do your parents think it does? In what ways?

whatever baggage that entails, including for some the necessity of a continuing relationship in which I was in a position of authority, and/or was in contact with their parents), while others were people with whom I had no previous relationship (with whatever constraints that imposes, including perhaps less trust, openness, and shared context). My object was to obtain as many different kinds of voices as possible, and my data reveal that I did achieve that goal to my satisfaction.

The episodes themselves were videotaped, and most of the analysis of the show draws on these tapes. I did obtain a script of one episode, "Blind Spot," which is analyzed in the chapters on issues and dating.

Subjects

Subjects were sought among girls and young women in junior high school, high school, and college, who described themselves as fans of *Beverly Hills, 90210*. Viewers were chosen on the basis of their history with the show, with the requirement that they had watched the show for at least a year, and with preference given to those who had been watching since the first season (Radway, 1984/91).

In determining the number of subjects, I aimed to strike a balance among various qualitative studies of women and media, in which sample size has varied widely. Hobson (1989/91) interviewed six women; Radway (1984/91), 16; Seiter, Borchers, Kreutzner, and Warth (1989/91), 26; Press (1991), 45. My study struck a balance toward the high end, interviewing 36 girls and young women between the ages of 11 and 25. Of these, 16, or 45 percent, were college age, because these young women tended to be most "addicted" to the show and had watched it the longest. The remaining 20 viewers were split evenly between junior-high and high school students, 10 of each. I conducted a total of 18 interviews, 5 of which (28 percent) were repeat visits to talk with the same viewers.

The show primarily features white people, and my original intention was to confine myself to white viewers. I expected that my data would be complex and overwhelming without the complicated issue of racial consciousness. Of the 36 viewers I talked to, 33 were Caucasian. Serendipitously included in my sample as friends of my contact people were three girls of Asian descent who had been raised in this country. Despite this potentially complicating factor, I held to my original intent of including issues of class and age in my analysis, while treating ethnic issues (which, incidentally, never were addressed in talk) as outside of the study's scope.

Socio-economic class is a complicated issue, especially with regard to females who are still in school. Press (1991) has offered a discussion of ways in which class has been defined, outlining sociological classifications based on occupation and education as well as ways in which feminists have challenged this approach, particularly when talking about girls. In her study, Press used a combination of education and occupation to determine socio-economic class.

I tried to follow these guidelines in choosing viewers to interview, paying particular attention to the education and occupation of the parents, the type of education the individual was receiving, and her own identification with groups and people, especially her peer group. My goal was to arrange subjects along a range of backgrounds so that as wide a variety of voices as possible could be heard.

All interviewees (and, if they were underage, a parent) signed a consent form, in accordance with Rutgers University requirements for research involving human subjects. Interviewees' names have been changed in the analysis in order to keep their identities confidential.

The individuals I interviewed are listed below. A few biographical details are given, but it is important to keep in mind that I am not making claims about the predictive nature of background on viewer talk. These details are provided more to indicate the variety of voices I heard and the nature of my relationship with the different viewers.

1. Katey and Jane, Wednesday, Feb. 2, 1994. Both of these girls were in seventh grade in a Bucks County, Pennsylvania, public school system. Katey's mother babysits neighborhood children, and I made contact with her through a friend whose child had been cared for there. Jane was Katey's friend and previously unknown to me. Both girls had working-class parents who did not attend college; both said they wanted to attend college but discussed the difficulty of getting grades good enough to go on to higher education. We watched an episode in Katey's living room as it aired.

2. I did a follow-up interview with Katey and Jane on Saturday, Feb. 5, 1994.

3. Marissa and Melanie, Saturday, Feb. 12, 1994. These twins were both in eighth grade in a wealthy suburban New Jersey school district. Their names were given me by one of their classmates, who was the daughter of a colleague professor at Rider. Their father, who was deceased, had been a carpenter and did not attend college; their mother, who worked for the State of New Jersey, had attended college. They struck me as highly verbal and sophisticated for their age. We had a delayed viewing session in their living room, watching the episode that aired the previous Wednesday, Feb. 9, 1994, which snow had prevented me from watching as it aired with viewers. In the subsequent tape, their voices were so much alike that I could not distinguish them; thus they are referred to in the text simply as "M."

4. Courtney and Ruth, Tuesday, Feb. 15, 1995. Both were students

at Princeton University in the pre-med program. Courtney's father was a doctor, and Ruth's an attorney; both had mothers who were homemakers and had attended college. As mentioned above, my interview the previous Wednesday, Feb. 9, had been snowed out, so I went that Wednesday to a dorm television room at the Ivy League school and asked for volunteers. These two young women agreed to be interviewed. The next week, I picked them up and brought them to my house so that we could use my VCR.

5. Jeannette and Kristen, Sunday, Feb. 20, 1994. I had worked with both of these girls at my church, although I was closer to Jeannette. Both were students at a regional high school near the Jersey Shore, Jeannette in tenth grade and Kristen in eleventh. Both of Jeannette's parents had attended college; neither of Kristen's had. Kristen's family lived in Florida; she had chosen to live with her grandmother in order to stay in the school system. Both were focused achievers. Frustratingly, I had been snowed out of viewing the previous Wednesday, Feb. 16, but they had seen the episode. After church, we sat and talked on the floor of Kristen's cluttered bedroom in her grandparents' house.

6. Casey, Alison, and Erika, Sunday, Feb. 20, 1994. That same day I went to Rider to interview these three students in Casey's dorm room. I had taught them all; currently only Casey was in one of my classes. Her mother had gone to college; Alison's father had gone to college; neither of Erika's parents had gone to college. We watched the episode from Feb. 16 on video tape.

7. Joan and Meetra, Saturday, Feb. 26, 1994. Once again I was snowed out on Wednesday, Feb. 23! On Saturday, I went to Joan's mother's New Jersey home, where she lived. Her parents were divorced; neither had attended college. She was a student at Rider and was in a class right after one that I taught, so she heard me asking for viewers and volunteered. Her friend Meetra, of Asian descent brought up in this country, did not go to college; neither did her parents. We talked in Joan's mother's living room.

8. Sandy, Colleen, Maddy, Sunday, Feb. 27, 1994. Ninth-grader Sandy and sixth-grader Colleen were sisters living in row house in Philadelphia and attending parochial schools. A relative worked on the copy desk at the newspaper mentioned earlier, and he gave me their names. Their mother currently was attending college; their father had not attended college. Especially Sandy expressed very mixed feelings about going to college, acknowledging the necessity but saying she hated to study. Colleen's friend and neighbor Maddy was also in sixth grade; her father had gone to college. We talked in Sandy and Colleen's living room.

9. Nicky, Sherry, Penni, and Gracey, Wednesday, March 2, 1994. Nicky was in one of my classes at Rider, and we watched the episode in her

sorority bedroom with a large group of young women. There was the predictable snow storm, but this was one session that profited from the weather, because Nicky's night class was canceled. Both Nicky and Sherry's mother had gone to college; both of Penni's parents had gone to college; neither of Gracey's parents had gone to college. We watched an episode as it aired.

10. Marion and Karey, Saturday, March 5, 1994. Marion was in one of my college classes. She had taken a year off from college, then returned, so she was a year behind her friend Karey, who had graduated the previous year from a state school and worked as a sales representative at the time of the study. Both of Marion's parents had gone to college; Karey's father had gone to college. Because they lived in disparate Jersey locations, they came to my house for the interview. They had agreed to postpone their viewing from the previous Wednesday so we could watch the episode on videotape in my living room.

11. Pam and Pat, Sunday, March 6, 1994. Both were seventh-graders in a New Jersey Shore school system. Due to a combination of circumstances, the interview took place in my office at the church, not a comfortable venue for these girls. We watched the videotaped episode from the previous Wednesday. Neither of Pam's parents had gone to college; both of Pat's had.

12. Joan and Meetra, Wednesday, March 9, 1994. During this second interview with these two, we watched an episode as it aired in Joan's living room.

13. Jackie and Esther, Sunday, March 13, 1994. Both were ninth-graders in a Jersey Shore school system. Jackie had participated in choirs at the church for five years at the time of the study; she was half Asian and half Caucasian. Both of her parents had gone to college. Esther was her friend from school. Of Asian descent, she had been raised in this country. Her parents were divorced and she lived with an aunt. For the first part of the interview, which we did in Jackie's living room, she was alone; Esther joined us later.

14. Jeannette, Kristen, Jackie, Wednesday, March 16, 1994. This regrouping of three members of my church watched an episode as it aired in Kristen's bedroom.

15. Danielle, Amanda, Susie, Wednesday, March 23, 1994. Seventh-grader Danielle was a friend of Jean's (interviewed Feb. 2); sixth-grader Amanda was her neighbor; eleventh-grader Susie was her older sister. They attended Bucks County public schools. Danielle's and Susie's mother had gone to college; both of Amanda's parents had gone to college. We watched an episode as it aired in Danielle's and Susie's living room.

16. Kyle, Sunday, March 27, 1994. A student at Princeton, Kyle was

interviewed in her dorm room. Her father was an orthopedic surgeon and her mother an English teacher with an advanced degree; she was studying to be a chemical engineer. She was referred to me through a complicated network of people I knew slightly.

17. Kyle, Terry, Rebeccah, Wednesday, March 30, 1994. Kyle and her two roommates, all of whose parents had advanced degrees, watched an episode as it aired in their dorm room.

18. Mary, Chryse, Kaitlin, Susie, Wednesday, April 4, 1994. These eleventh-graders commuted to a prestigious Bucks County, Pennsylvania prep school. We watched an episode as it aired in Mary's bedroom. Her family were neighbors of a friend. All of their parents had gone to college; most had advanced degrees.

Glossary

Cross-references to other entries appear in boldface.

Agency This study uses the feminist definition of agency as a challenge of the status quo, specifically a discursive challenge of the patriarchy.

Defined by Webster's New World Dictionary, Third College Edition, as "that by which something is done; means; instrumentality," agency has come to be a somewhat embattled term in postmodern and post-structural theory. As discussed in the entry under **subject**, those of us raised in Western post-Enlightenment society are used to talking and thinking about ourselves as the origin of our motives and desires (for a much more sophisticated discussion, cf., for example, Deetz 1992). In common parlance, then, we think of ourselves as agents when we initiate an activity. However, feminist writers in particular have pointed out that we are not necessarily the authors of our motives and desires; our choice to go on a diet, for example, or to get a haircut is organically linked with our culture's norms for what is attractive and appropriate for females. While it may seem to us that we have a choice of haircuts or body weights, in reality our options are circumscribed and given meaning by what is available and/or acceptable in our culture. And options are important; numerous authors have emphasized that agency only has meaning in the context of choices. As Giddens (1979/90) put it, "It is a necessary feature of action that, at any point in time, the agent 'could have acted otherwise'" (p. 56). And, he added, "The sense of 'could have done otherwise' is obviously a difficult and complex one" (p. 56).

Agency, then, is seen "not an attribute or trait inhering in the will of autonomous individual subjects, but as a discursive effect" (Benhabib, 1992, p. 221); it has been called "an instituted practice in a field of enabling constraints." (Haraway, 1991, p. 135). As described in Chapter 4, Weeden (1987) called this process gaining access to multiple subject positions, or ways of being in the world—i.e., having a choice in the matter, for example, of what counts as attractive or important for females:

"Knowledge of more than one discourse and the recognition that meaning is plural allows for a measure of choice on the part of the individual" (p. 106).

In these terms, an active working to **reinstantiate** and perpetuate a disadvantageous female identity does not count as agency. Rather, feminist authors suggest that the recognition that gender identity, for example, is socially and discursively constructed must precede any agency in changing the meaning of that identity.

Cultural studies This school of media and cultural research, formalized in England in the 1950s, emphasized using qualitative methods to study media users in the busy, messy environments in which they live.

Cultural studies is now the topic of numerous books and articles. Most definitions strive to retain a relatively amorphous and free-floating identity for this school. As Nelson, Treichler, and Grossberg (1992) put it, "cultural studies is not merely interdisciplinary; it is often, as others have written, actively and aggressively anti-disciplinary—a characteristic that more or less ensures a permanently uncomfortable relation to academic disciplines" (p. 2). However, most authors agree, in During's (1993) words, that cultural studies is united by its "study of culture in relation to individual lives, breaking with social scientific positivism or 'objectivism'" and its understanding that "societies are structured unequally, that individuals are not born with the same access to education, money, health-care, etc." Most authors emphasize cultural studies' commitment to working "in the interests of those who have fewest resources" (During 1993, pp. 1–2). The school trail-blazed a move to audience-based, rather than text-based, media research, studying television viewers, for example, in the real-life contexts of their viewing experiences, rather than bringing them solemnly into a laboratory. In the process, cultural studies researchers sometimes ended up glorifying the power of the audiences to make their own meanings in ways this study has questioned; however, that move was at least in part a crucial counterbalance to the power granted to the text by, for example, literary criticism.

Discourse analysis This study uses discourse analysis to focus, not on what is said per se, on the conditions and unspoken assumptions that give statements meaning.

Discourse has numerous common and academic meanings, but it was importantly inflected by Foucault (1972), although his theories are too complex and sophisticated to be summarized here. I would simply emphasize that discourse theory and analysis seeks to determine not, for example, what a speaker meant by a statement (something the speaker herself might define differently in different contexts); rather, it asks what conditions legitimized the statement as meaningful or relevant. As Dillon (1994) put it: "discourse theory . . . distinguishes itself sharply from philosophical concerns with the truth of statements and the validity of arguments, substituting a concern for conditions under which one can be judged to have made a serious, sound, true, important, authoritative statement" (p. 211).

For example, discourses make possible and/or legitimate certain identities, certain ways of being or subject positions (see the entry under **subject**, below) while suppressing others. The terms "woman," "mother," "bitch," "pretty," "nice," etc. automatically invoke discourses that offer us certain choices and not others. As Deetz (1992) put it, discourses do not "represent a meaning or culture behind or beneath them; rather, they perform the production of subject and world" (p. 261). And these identities, these subject positions, are value-laden and enmeshed in power relations that are often so taken for granted as to be invisible.

What Foucault's theories help us see is the ways in which the discourses that structure our lives get **naturalized** (see entry below), so that, for example, the definitions of "bitch" and "nice" appear commonsensical to us rather than socially constructed. In this way, alternate ways of structuring the world get concealed. And because the socially constructed nature of these terms is hidden, choices also are obscured and sometimes unnecessarily constrained—one can be bitchy or nice, but there is no way to combine a strong sense of self with caring for others (cf. Brown and Gilligan, 1992) because the two terms are naturalized as mutually exclusive. Deetz (1992) illustrated the situation:

> For example, a woman with a young child and a position in a corporation is subject to both family discourses and corporate ones. To the extent that these offer conflicting images and behavioral scripts, she will experience considerable tension, a tension that can productively display each image and script as a construction and hence offer her a choice. But more often that tension remains to be suppressed by various means of "articulating" (or joining) the discourses, as in the "have-it-all" script. (p. 263)

Discursive identity This study focuses on female identity as produced, **reified**, and maintained in conversation, suggesting that our culture offers us a range of ways of being female that we adopt, take ownership of, and reproduce as "our" identity.

Feminists have drawn on **social construction** theory to suggest that gender identity is produced and maintained in large part through language. Although in our Western culture we are accustomed to think of identity as something we possess and that is uniquely ours, these writers point out that much of this identity is culled from options offered us by our culture, often codified in language. Our inner life, while hidden from others, is less unique than we usually believe because it is in large measure selected from options made culturally available. As Gergen (1991) put it (as cited in Chapter 4), "To write or speak is not, then, to express an interior world, but to borrow from the available things people write and say and to reproduce them for another audience" (p. 105).

The ways in which talk about television participates in this cycle of discursive identity construction is the central topic of this book.

Essentialize In Western culture, we are accustomed to speak as if certain meanings inhere in objects or people, rather than being socially constructed—that they belong *essentially* to the thing or individual— although social constructionists have challenged this notion.

This concept is important to this book because of the way our culture essentializes so-called female traits. While feminists are in disagreement about whether women are *essentially* more emotional, less logical, more family-oriented, etc., than men, **poststructuralism** allows feminists to ask how these notions came about, and who is benefitted by them. One may believe that women's relationality, for example, is a product of genetic, primal, essential differences between men and women; or one may believe that "female" traits are fostered by differential treatment of the genders, with women typically expected to give first priority to relationships while men are encouraged—even goaded—to move beyond it. Poststructuralism points out that essentializing "female" traits is a value-laden process that invokes a set of hierarchical assumptions that have very real implications that range, for example, from spouse abuse to the glass ceiling. Weedon (1987) suggested that essentializing "female" traits closes off possibilities for constructive change. Looking at women as "socially constituted as different and subject to social relations and processes in different ways to men" (p. 10), she argued, allows us to challenge the status quo in productive ways. In contrast to theories that essentialize "female" traits, poststructuralist feminism (the approach taken by this book) offers "a useful, productive framework for understanding the mechanisms of power in our society and the possibilities of change" (p. 10).

Hegemony theory As summarized in Chapter 3, hegemony theory describes the process by which consent is won to conditions that are not necessarily advantageous to the subject.

In part, this process operates through **naturalizing** the status quo, so that fundamental changes seem unthinkable. As McGuigan (1992) put it:

The concept of hegemony refers to how the dominant class bloc in society constructs and sustains its *leadership* over subordinate groupings. The crucial point is that hegemony does not rely most effectively on coercion (although that is always a possibility) but instead on a complex process of winning *consent* to the prevailing order. As Raymond Williams (1973) put it, hegemony "saturates society," legitimated by intellectual strata but flowing through ordinary practices and meanings on common sense reasoning and everyday representations, working as a kind of social "cement." However, it never sets solid: hegemonic leadership is never accomplished once and for all. There is a constant battle in which the ruling bloc has to struggle for leadership against various resistances and oppositions. Sometimes the ruling bloc makes concessions to subordinate forces and, at other times, hard-won rights and opportunities are withdrawn. The particular hegemonic configuration at any one time depends on economic conditions and the current balance of power between contending forces. Hegemony is, then, endless struggle. (p. 64)

This book particularly focuses on the ways women's consent is won to a status quo that defines her as inferior and other, that constrains her to certain ideals of appearance and behavior, and that positions the genders in a hierarchical duality that curtails life choices.

Identity, discursive See **discursive identity**.

Intertextuality This book draws on Fiske's (1987) suggestion that no television text is read in isolation; rather, the meanings of characters, plots, appearances, etc. are enhanced, transformed, and structured in relation to other texts, including advertisements, articles in the press, televised and personal appearances by actors and actresses, other movies and/or television shows in which an actor or actress has starred, etc.

"Intertextual knowledges pre-orient the reader to exploit television's polysemy by activating the text in certain ways, that is, by making some meanings rather than others" (p. 108), he maintained. Fiske offered a thorough and subtle discussion of the cyclic relationship among television shows, other texts, and culture:

Secondary texts play a significant role in influencing which of television's meanings may be activated in any one reading. Television's pervasiveness in our culture is not due simply to the fact that so much of it is broadcast and that watching it is our most popular leisure activity, but because it pervades so much of the rest of our cultural life—newspapers, magazines, advertisements, conversations, radio, or style of dress, of make-up, of dance steps. All of these enter intertextual relations with television. It is important to talk about their relations with television, and not to describe them as spin-offs from it, for the influence is two-way. Their meanings are read back into television, just as productively as television determines theirs. (p. 118)

This theory helped generate the premise of this study, which is that talk about television shows represents an important aspect of the way the media intersect with our lives.

Metanarrative Our metanarratives are the underlying assumptions that structure our realities; they are generally so **naturalized** that we don't even realize we have them.

For example, as explained in Chapter 4, Bellah et al. (1985) identified four metanarratives common in our culture: (1) the approach that emphasizes the importance of the community "as members of the same body" (p. 28); (2) the idea that individualism is all-important, focusing on "equal and exact justice to all men" (p. 31); (3) the notion that, in the United States, individuals have the opportunity (and responsibility) of getting ahead on their own initiative; and (4) the Romantic notion that one should live "a life of strong feeling" (p. 34). Perhaps our own metanarratives can be made less naturalized if we try to imagine the opposite—for me, that might be an underlying belief that hard work will not pay off or that all of my actions have been preordained.

Naturalize This word refers to the process by which a meaning comes to appear commonsensical, as if it inheres in an object, for example, rather than being discursively and socially constructed. As Deetz (1992) put it, naturalization is "the treatment of the socially produced as given in nature":

> In a naturalizing discourse, the social historical processes (whether in the actual production of objects and institutions or in the production of the subject and structures of experience) are removed from view. . . . In naturalization, one view of the subject matter is frozen as the way the thing is. In this process, the constitution process is closed to inspection and discussion. . . . Naturalization frequently stops discussion—at the determination of what is—at precisely the place where it should be started—how is it that. (p. 191)

Deetz pointed out that a naturalized **discourse**—in the thesis of this book, the discourse of gender identity—is always value-laden, advantaging some members of society and disadvantaging others. Feminists have argued that naturalizing certain aspects of gender identity, such as the notion that women's most important role is as wife and mother, can be limiting, even oppressive. The poststructuralist feminist argument on which this book is based seeks to foreground the socially constructed nature of gender identity. As Weedon (1987) pointed out, "the meanings of femininity and masculinity vary from culture to culture and language to language" (p. 22). Her project is to reproblematize naturalized gender roles.

Polysemic This book draws on Fiske's (1987) description of television texts as containing multiple meanings, a "semiotic excess" that allows them to be read in many different ways.

This notion was important especially as it flew in the face of certain theories of textual analysis that posited the existence of a "right" interpretation for any given text. Fiske argued that producers could never control all meanings audiences would make of a television text.

Poststructuralism Growing out of the French structuralists, who theorized unchanging structures underlying the creation of meaning, poststructuralist theory is useful to this book because of its notion that language plays a key role in constructing and maintaining subjectivity, social organization and power. As Weedon (1987) put it,

[Poststructuralism's] founding insight, taken from the structuralist linguistics of Ferdinand de Saussure, is that language, far from reflecting an already given social reality, constitutes social reality for us. Neither social reality nor the "natural" world has fixed intrinsic meanings which language reflects or expresses. . . . All forms of poststructuralism assume that meaning is constituted within language and is not guaranteed by the subject which speaks it. (p. 22)

This emphasis on language as constructing the individual, rather than the other way around, has been called the decentering of the **subject** (the subject is not primary source of the meanings she makes).

The boundaries between postmodernism and poststructuralism can seem difficult to distinguish, and this glossary is not the forum to enter into a detailed history of the ways these complex terms have been used. Best and Kellner (1991) maintained that postmodernism broadened poststructuralist ideas:

Poststructuralism forms part of the matrix of postmodern theory, and while the theoretical breaks described as postmodern are directly related to poststructuralist critiques, we shall interpret poststructuralism as a subset of a broader range of theoretical, cultural, and social tendencies which constitute postmodern discourses. Thus, in our view, postmodern theory is a more inclusive phenomenon than poststructuralism which we interpret as a critique of modern theory and a production of new models of thought, writing, and subjectivity, some of which are later taken up by postmodern theory. Indeed, postmodern theory appropriates the poststructuralist critique of modern theory, radicalizes it, and extends it to new theoretical fields. . . . The discourse of the postmodern also encompasses a socio-historical theory of postmodernity and analysis of new postmodern cultural forms and experiences. The cultural analysis is influenced by poststructuralist discussions of modernism and the avant-garde by Barthes, Kristeva, Sollers, and others associated with the *Tel Quel* group, but the later postmodern socio-historical discourses develop more comprehensive perspectives on society, politics, and history. (pp. 25–26)

Read This term is used in this book to mean the way viewers interpret a text such as a television show.

Usually this interpretation seems "natural" or obvious to the viewer, as if it inheres in the text, although poststructuralists argue that readers themselves intersect importantly with the meanings they make. A seminal thinker in this argument was Hall (1980), who identified three possible "reads" of a media text: dominant, oppositional, and negotiated. As Fiske (1987) explained Hall's theory:

Briefly, he argued that viewers whose social situation, particularly their class, aligned them comfortably with the dominant ideology would produce dominant readings of a text; that is, they would accept its preferred meanings and their close fit with the dominant ideology. Other viewers, whose social situation placed them in opposition to the dominant ideology, would oppose its meanings in the text and would produce oppositional readings. The majority of viewers, however, are probably situated not in positions of conformity or opposition to the dominant ideology, but in ones that conform to it in some ways, but not others; they accept the dominant ideology in general, but modify or inflect it to meet the needs of their specific situation. These viewers would, Hall argued, produce negotiated readings of the text; these are readings that inflect the meanings preferred by the dominant ideology, to take into account the social differences of different viewers. (p. 64)

Reify This word is used here to refer to the way in which meanings are **naturalized**, "thing-ified," treated as if they are given in nature rather than socially constructed.

Reinstantiate I have used "reinstantiate" to mean the process of concretizing or **reifying** already existing meanings through repeated examples of those meanings.

Social construction To explain the way the term is used in this book, I will draw on Gergen's (1985) definition of social constructionist inquiry as "principally concerned with explicating the processes by which people come to describe, explain, or otherwise account for the world (including themselves) in which they live" (p. 266).

This study draws on the social constructionist writings of Gergen, Shotter, and Edwards and Potter, although (as indicated in Chapter 4), the ideas underpinning these theories are shared by numerous authors and schools of thought. This school developed in opposition to the traditional psychological theories that valued empirical observation and quantitative tests. Instead, Gergen suggested, social constructionist research should take the following guidelines into account:

1. What we take to be experience of the world does not in itself dictate the terms by which the world is understood. . . . How can theoretical categories be induced or derived from observation, it is asked, if the process of identifying observational attributes itself relies on one's possessing categories? . . .
2. The terms in which the world is understood are social artifacts, products of historically situated interchanges among people. From the constructionist position the process of understanding is not automatically driven by the forces of nature, but is the result of an active, cooperative enterprise of persons in relationship. . . .
3. The degree to which a given form of understanding prevails or is sustained across time is not fundamentally dependent on the empirical validity of the perspective in question, but on the vicissitudes of social processes (e.g., com-

munication, negotiation, conflict, rhetoric). . . . Observation of persons, then, is questionable as a corrective or guide to descriptions of persons. Rather, the rules for "what counts as what" are inherently ambiguous, continuously evolving, and free to vary with the predilections of those who use them. (pp. 266–68)

This book has attempted to harness the social constructionist perspective on social science inquiry to study the role talk about a television show plays in the social construction of the female gender, particularly is it **reinstantiates** and perpetuates a status quo that may be disadvantaging.

Subject Poststructuralist theory is based on a conceptualization of the individual subject as "de-centered"—as not the sole author of the meanings she makes or of her identity per se.

As might be expected, these theories place a heavy emphasis on the way that language and discourse provide certain possibilities for subject positions but not others. As Weedon (1987) put it, "Language is not the expression of unique individuality; it constructs the individual's subjectivity in ways which are socially specific" (p. 21). And, as she points out, as soon as a person speaks, she constructs for herself a subject position that makes certain possibilities available and closes down or conceals others. As Weedon, Tolson, and Mort (1980) put it:

The symbolic order is the realm of conscious human thought, laws and culture, and its structures are embodied in the very structures of language itself, which designate positions from which one may speak. Language exists prior to any individual speaking subject, and it is through language acquisition—that is, by taking up the position of speaking subject within language—that the human individual acquires gendered, conscious subjectivity. (p. 202)

This concept of the speaking subject becomes interesting when it is considered in relation to our common Western discourse that positions the speaker as the author of the meanings she makes. This consideration led theorists like Weedon (1987) to suggest that, when we enter into a **discourse** that offers us a subject position (wife, mother, bitch, nice girl) we enter into an "imaginary" relationship with that subject:

[I]n taking on a subject position, the individual assumes that she is the author of the ideology or discourse in which she is speaking. She speaks or thinks as if she were in control of meaning. She "imagines" that she is indeed the type of subject which humanism proposes—rational, unified, the source rather than the effect of language. It is the imaginary quality of the individual's identification with a subject position which gives it so much psychological and emotional force. (p. 31)

For **hegemony** theorists, this imaginary "authoring" of a subject position becomes one of the ways our consent is won to the dominant ideology. As Deetz (1992) put it:

The specific relationship between the subject in a particular world and the individual is *imaginary*. That is, the "subject" is always an image or constructed self rather than an individual in a full set of relations to the world. A "real" form of domination or control is unnecessary to the extent that the individual takes the imaginary construction as if it is real. (p. 135)

Central to poststructuralist feminism is the notion that, in Weedon's (1987) words, "subjectivity is neither unified nor fixed. Unlike humanism, which implies a conscious, knowing unified, rational subject, poststructuralism theorizes subjectivity as a site of disunity and conflict, central to the process of political change and to preserving the status quo" (p. 21). The decentered, destabilized subject opens the possibility of changing the status quo, of gaining access to new subject positions, and of suggesting alternative subjectivities that might advantage women more than those currently available in patriarchy. As cited in Chapter 4, Weedon called both for fiction that pushes the bounds of patriarchy:

Women need access to the different subject positions offered in imaginative alternatives to the present, in humorous critiques and even by positive heroines. . . . Feminist poststructuralist criticism can show how power is exercised through discourse, including fictive discourse, how oppession works and where and how resistance might be possible. (p. 172)

Text For the purposes of this study, "television text" refers to the combination of visuals, dialog, and music that make up the episodes that were analyzed.

Bibliography

Altheide, D.L. (1974). *Creating reality: How TV news distorts events*. Beverly Hills, CA: Sage.

Altheide, D.L., and R.P. Snow (1987). Toward a theory of mediation. *Communication Yearbook* 11, 194–223.

Althusser, L. (1971). *Lenin and philosophy, and other essays*. B. Brewster (trans.). London: Monthly Review Press.

Ang, I. (1985). *Watching Dallas: Soap opera and the melodramatic imagination*. D. Couling (trans.). New York: Methuen.

Barthes, R. (1957/72). *Mythologies*. A. Lavers (trans.). New York: Hill and Wang.

——— (1967/85). *The fashion system*. M. Wang and R. Howard (trans.). London: Jonathan Cape.

——— (1977). Introduction to the structural analysis of narratives. In *Image, music, text*, S. Heath (trans.). New York: Hill and Wang.

Bellah, R.N., R. Madsen, W.M. Sullivan, A. Swidler, and S.M. Tipton (1985). *Habits of the heart: Individualism and commitment in American life*. New York: Harper & Row.

Benhabib, S. (1992). *Situating the self: Gender, community, and postmodernism in contemporary ethics*. New York: Routledge.

Bennett, W.L. (1983). *News: The politics of illusion*. New York: Longman.

Berger, P., and T. Luckmann (1967). *The social construction of reality*. New York: Doubleday.

Best, S., and D. Kellner (1991). *Postmodern theory: Critical interrogations*. New York: Guildford.

Bordwell, D. (1985). *Narration in the fiction film*. Madison: University of Wisconsin Press.

Brannigan, E. (1992). *Narrative comprehension and film*. London: Routledge.

Brown, M.E. (1994). *Soap opera and women's talk: The pleasure of resistance*. Newbury Park, CA: Sage.

——— (ed.) (1990). *Television and women's culture: The politics of the popular*. London: Sage.

Brown, L.M., and C. Gilligan (1992). *Meeting at the crossroads: Women's psychology and girls' development*. Cambridge, MA: Harvard University Press.

Burman, E., and I. Parker (1993). *Discourse analytic research*. London: Routledge.

Butler, J. (1990). *Gender trouble: Feminism and the subversion of identity*. London: Routledge.

Butler, M., and W. Paisley (1980). *Women and the mass media: Sourcebook for action and research*. New York: Human Sciences Press.

Carter, A. (1995). Made in the shade. *Entertainment Weekly*, July 28, p. 22.

Cary, A. (1992). Big fans on campus: If you want to know what'll be hot on TV tomorrow, look at what college kids are watching today—it's what the networks do! *TV Guide*, April 18, pp. 26–31.

Chodorow, N. (1978). *The reproduction of mothering: Psychoanalysis and the sociology of gender.* Berkeley: University of California Press.

Condit, C.M. (1994). Hegemony in a mass-mediated society: Concordance about reproductive technologies. *Critical Studies in Mass Communication* 11 (3), 205–30.

Cunningham, K. (1994). Auld Lang signs? *People Weekly*, October 10, p. 124.

Dayan, D., and E. Katz (1992). *Media events: The live broadcasting of history.* Cambridge, MA: Harvard University Press.

Deetz, S.A. (1992). *Democracy in an age of corporate colonization: SUNY series in speech communication.* Albany: State University of New York Press.

Dillon, G.L. (1994). Discourse theory. In M. Groden and M. Kreiswirth (eds.), *The Johns Hopkins guide to literary theory and criticism.* Baltimore: Johns Hopkins University Press.

During, S. (ed.) (1993). *The cultural studies reader.* Newbury Park, CA: Sage.

Edwards, D., and J. Potter (1992). *Discursive psychology.* Newbury Park, CA: Sage.

Efron, E. (1971). *The news twisters.* Los Angeles: Nash.

Farhi, P. (1994). On TV, Madison Ave. sets the dial for youth. *Washington Post*, September 16, pp. A1, A21.

Feuer, J. (1987). Genre study and television. In R.C. Allen (ed.), *Channels of discourse, reassembled: Television and contemporary criticism.* 2nd ed. Chapel Hill: University of North Carolina Press.

Fink, M. (1994). The Shannen syndrome. *People Weekly*, January 10, p. 35.

Fiske, J. (1987). *Television culture.* London: Routledge.

Fiske, J., and J. Hartley (1978/90). *Reading television.* London: Routledge.

Fitzgerald, K. (1992). TV's hottest number? Teen fans plus *90210* add up to 60 licensing deals. *Advertising Age*, June 1, p. 30.

——— (1993). *90210* promo ZIP: marketers hitch a ride as show goes worldwide. *Advertising Age*, September 6, p. 14.

Foucault, M. (1965). *Madness and civilization: A history of insanity in the age of reason.* R. Howard (trans.). London: Tavistock.

——— (1972). *The archaeology of knowledge.* A.M.S. Smith (trans.). New York: Pantheon.

Frazer, E. (1987). Teenage girls reading "Jackie." *Media, Culture, and Society* 9, 407–25.

Gerbner, G. et al. (1980). The mainstreaming of America. *Journal of Communication* 30 (3), 10–29.

Gergen, K.J. (1985). The social constructionist movement in modern psychology. *American Psychologist* 40 (3), 266–75.

——— (1991). *The saturated self: Dilemmas of identity in contemporary life.* New York: HarperCollins.

——— (1992). Warranting voice and the elaboration of the self. In J. Shotter and K.J. Gergen (eds.), *Texts of identity.* Newbury Park, CA: Sage.

Gerosa, M. (1992). She'll take Manhattan. *Entertainment Weekly*, October 30, p. 16.

Giddens, A. (1979/90). *Central problems in social theory.* Berkeley: University of California Press.

——— (1991). *Modernity and self-identity: Self and society in the late modern age.* Stanford, CA: Stanford University Press.

Gilligan, C. (1982). *In a different voice: Psychological theory and women's development.* Cambridge, MA: Harvard University Press.

Gilligan, C., N.P. Lyons, and T.J. Hanmer (1990). *Making connections.* Cambridge, MA: Harvard University Press.

Gitlin, T. (1978). Media sociology: The dominant paradigm. *Theory and Society* 6 (1), 205–54.

———— (1979). Prime-time ideology: The hegemonic process in television entertainment. *Social Problems* 26 (3), 251–66.

———— (1980). *The whole world is watching: Mass media in the making and unmaking of the New Left.* Berkeley: University of California Press.

———— (1983). *Inside prime time.* New York: Pantheon.

Gledhill, C. (1992). Recent developments in feminist criticism. In G. Mast, M. Cohen, and L. Braudy (eds.), *Film theory and criticism.* 6th ed. New York: Oxford.

Gliatto, T., C. Tomashoff, and B. Sandler (1992). Nobody's pussycat. *People,* October 9, pp. 78–84.

Goodman, M. (1994). A breakout for Tiffani. *People Weekly,* September 12, p. 71.

Gramsci, A. (1971). *Selections from the prison notebooks.* Q. Hoare and G. Nowell-Smith (eds. and trans.). London: Lawrence and Wishart.

Grossberg, L. (1993). Cultural studies and/in new worlds. *Critical Studies in Mass Communication* 10, 1–22.

Grossberg, L., C. Nelson, and P.a. Treichler (eds.) (1992). *Cultural studies.* New York: Routledge.

Hall, S. (1980). "Encoding, decoding." In S. Hall, D. Hobson, A. Lowe, and P. Willis (eds.), *Culture, media, language: Working papers in cultural studies, 1972–79.* London: Unwin.

———— (1988). The rediscovery of "ideology": Return of the repressed in media studies. In M. Gurevitch, T. Bennett, J. Curran, and J. Woollacott (eds.), *Culture, society, and the media.* London: Routledge.

Hall, S. and T. Jefferson (eds.) (1976). *Resistance through rituals: Youth subcultures in post-war Britain.* London: Hutchinson.

Haraway, D.J. (1991). *Simians, cyborgs, and women: The reinvention of nature.* London: Routledge.

Harre, R. (1992). Language games and the texts of identity. In J. Shotter and K.J. Gergen (eds.), *Texts of identity.* Newbury Park, CA: Sage.

Harre, R., and G. Gillett (1994). *The discursive mind.* Thousand Oaks, CA: Sage.

Hawkins, R.P., and S. Pingree (1990). Divergent psychological processes in constructing social reality from mass media content. In N. Signorielli and M. Morgan (eds.), *Cultivation analysis: New directions in media effects research.* Newbury Park, CA: Sage.

Hebdige, D. (1979). *Subculture: The meaning of style.* London: Methuen.

Hobson, D. (1982). *Crossroads: The drama of a soap opera.* London: Methuen.

———— (1989/91). Soap operas at work. In E. Seiter, H. Borchers, G. Kreutzner, and E. Warth (eds.), *Remote control: Television, audiences, and cultural power.* London: Routledge.

Hot property! (1994). *People Weekly,* February 21, p. 63.

James, C. (1991). *90210* goes to the head of the class. *New York Times,* August 4, p. 29.

Jenkins, H. III. (1988). *Star Trek* rerun, reread, rewritten: Fan writing as textual poaching. *Critical Studies in Mass Communication* 5, 2: 85–107.

Jensen, E. (1994). Still kicking: A year ago, the networks seemed headed for extinction. No longer. *Wall Street Journal*, September 9, p. R1.

Jhally, S. (1994). Intersections of discourse: MTV, sexual politics, and *Dreamworlds*. In J. Cruz and J. Lewis (eds.), *Viewing, reading, listening: Audiences and cultural reception*. Boulder, CO: Westview.

Jhally, S., and J. Lewis (1992). *Enlightened racism: The Cosby Show, audiences, and the myth of the American Dream*. Boulder, CO: Westview.

Kanner, B. (1992). Licensed to thrill. *New York*, January 27, p. 20.

Katz, E., J.G. Blumler, and M. Gurevitch (1974). Utilization of mass communication by the individual. In J.G. Blumler and E. Katz (eds.), *The uses of mass communications: Current perspectives on gratifications research*. Beverly Hills, CA: Sage.

Katz, E., and P. Lazarsfeld (1955). *Personal influence: The part played by people in the flow of mass communications*. Glencoe, IL: Free Press.

Katz, E., and T. Liebes (1986). Decoding *Dallas*: Notes from a cross-cultural study. In G. Gumpert and R. Cathcart (eds.), *Inter/media: Interpersonal connection in a media world*. New York: Oxford.

Kohlberg, L., and E. Turiel (1971). Moral development and moral education. In G.S. Lesser (ed.), *Psychology and educational practice*. Glenview, IL: Scott, Foresman.

Kohlberg, L. (1981). *The philosophy of moral development*. San Francisco: Harper and Row.

Kozloff, S.R. (1987). Narrative theory and television. In R.C. Allen (ed.), *Channels of Discourse, reassembled: Television and contemporary criticism*. Chapel Hill: University of North Carolina Press.

Landler, M. (1992). They want their MTV. They don't want ABC, NBC, CBS . . ." *Business Week*, December 14, p. 82.

Leeds-Hurwitz, W. (1993). *Semiotics and communication: Signs, codes, cultures*. Hillsdale, NJ: Lawrence Erlbaum.

Liebes, T., and E. Katz (1989/91). On the critical abilities of television users. In E. Seiter, H. Borchers, G. Kreutzner, and E. Warth (eds.), *Remote control: Television, audiences, and cultural power*. London: Routledge.

Lipton, M. (1994). Gaby's *90210* ode to joy: Gabrielle Carteris delivers a 7-pound spinoff. *People Weekly*, July 4, p. 88.

Littlejohn, S.W. (1989). *Theories of human communication*. 3rd ed. Belmont, CA: Wadsworth.

Luke Perry: Cool hand with killer sideburns, TV's teen turn-on is *90210's* hottest number. (1991). *People Weekly*, December 30, p. 42.

Marshall, C., and G.B. Rossman (1989). *Designing qualitative research*. Newbury Park, CA: Sage.

McCracken, G. (1988). *The long interview*. Beverly Hills, CA: Sage.

McGuigan, J. (1992). *Cultural populism*. New York: Routledge.

McKinley, E.G. (1995). Negotiating media female identity: Girls and young women talk about Donna and Lucinda from *Beverly Hills, 90210*. Paper presented at the 18th Annual Conference of the Organization for the Study of Communication, Language, and Gender, Minneapolis, Minn.

——— (1996). Discursive construction of female identity as girls and young women talk about *90210* and *Friends*. In M. Pomerantz and J. Sakeris (eds.), *Pictures of a generation on hold*. Toronto: Media Studies Working Group.

McRobbie, A. (1978). *Working class girls and the culture of femininity*. Birmingham: Center for Contemporary Cultural Studies.

——— (1980). Settling accounts with subcultures: A feminist critique. *Screen Education* 34, 37–49.

——— (1981). Just like a "Jackie" story. In A. McRobbie and T. McCabe (eds.), *Feminism for girls*. London: Routledge.

——— (1984). Dance and social fantasy. In A. McRobbie and M. Nava (eds.), *Gender and generation*. London: Macmillan.

Moores, S. (1993). *Interpreting audiences: The ethnography of media consumption*. Thousand Oaks, CA: Sage.

Morgan, M., and N. Signorielli (1990). Cultivation analysis: Conceptualization and methodology. In N. Signorielli and M. Morgan (eds.), *Cultivation analysis: New directions in media effects research*. Newbury Park, CA: Sage.

Morley, D. (1980). *The nationwide audience*. London: British Film Institute.

——— (1986). *Family television: Cultural power and domestic leisure*. London: Comedia.

——— (1992). *Television, audiences, and cultural studies*. New York: Routledge.

Mother blames a deadly fire on an MTV cartoon. (1993). *New York Times*, October 10, p. A14.

Mumby, D.K. (1993). *Narrative and social control: Critical perspectives*. Newbury Park, CA: Sage.

Murphy, M. and D. Bailey (1991). Shannen Doherty of *Beverly Hills, 90210* is feeling the pressure of being a teen role model. *TV Guide*, August 24, p. 8.

No defendas of Brenda: Hollywood's nastiest newsletter rips into Shannen Doherty, the many-enemied star of *90210*. (1993). *People Weekly*, February 22, p. 92.

O'Sullivan, T., J. Hartley, D. Saunders, and J. Fiske (1983). *Key concepts in communication*. London: Methuen.

Palmgreen, P., and J.D. Rayburn II (1985). An expectancy-value approach to media gratifications. In K.E. Rosengren, L.A. Wenner, and P. Palmgreen (eds.), *Media gratifications research: Current perspectives*. Beverly Hills, CA: Sage.

Parenti, M. (1986). *Inventing reality: The politics of the mass media*. New York: St. Martin's.

Pecora, V.P. (1994). The Frankfurt School. In M. Groden and M. Kreiswirth (eds.), *The Johns Hopkins guide to literary theory and criticism*. Baltimore: Johns Hopkins University Press.

People's choice: Week 28 according to Nielsen ratings. (1995). *Broadcasting & Cable*, April 10, p. 56.

Poster, M. (1994). Foucault. In M. Groden and M. Kreiswirth (eds.), *The Johns Hopkins guide to literary theory and criticism*. Baltimore: Johns Hopkins University Press.

Press, A.L. (1991). *Women watching television: Gender, class, and generation in the American television experience*. Philadelphia: University of Pennsylvania Press.

Press, A.L., and E. Cole (1994). Women like us: Working class women respond to television representations of abortion. In J. Cruz and J. Lewis (eds.), *Viewing, reading, listening: Audiences and cultural reception*. Boulder, CO: Westview.

Prince, G. (1994). Narratology. In M. Groden and M. Kreiswirth (eds.), *The Johns Hopkins guide to literary theory and criticism*. Baltimore: Johns Hopkins University Press.

Propp, V.I. (1928/68). *Morphology of the folktale*. L.A. Wagner (ed.), L. Scott (trans.). Austin: University of Texas Press.

Radway, J.A. (1984/91). *Reading the romance: Women, patriarchy, and popular literature*. Chapel Hill: University of North Carolina Press.

—— (1994). Romance and the work of fantasy: Struggles over feminine sexuality and subjectivity at century's end. In J. Cruz and J. Lewis (eds.), *Viewing, reading, listening: Audiences and cultural reception.* Boulder, CO: Westview.

Ratings roundup. (1991). *Broadcasting*, March 18, p. 26.

Reilly, L. (1996a). *Women living single.* Boston: Faber and Faber.

—— (1996b). The power of one. *Self*, August, pp. 1043–111.

Richardson, E. (1995). The age of rage. *Elle*, April, pp. 107–10.

Robichaux, M. (1994). Slicing it thin: A look at the audience share for cable channels shows how fragmented the market is. *Wall Street Journal*, September 9, p. R8.

Robins, J. (1994). *90210* extends European reach. *Variety*, October 17, p. 185.

Rosengren, K.E., L.A. Wenner, and P. Palmgreen (eds.) (1985). *Media gratifications research: Current perspectives.* Beverly Hills, CA: Sage.

Rosengren, K.E., and S. Windahl (1989). *Media matter: TV use in childhood and adolescence.* Norwood, NJ: Ablex.

Rouse, J. (1994). Power/knowledge. In G. Gutting (ed.), *The Cambridge companion to Foucault.* Cambridge: Cambridge University Press.

Ruben, B.D. (1988). *Communication and human behavior.* New York: Macmillan.

Russell, G. (1992). Can *90210* keep its zip? *Variety*, April 27, p. 30.

Sampson, E.E. (1992). The deconstruction of the self. In J. Shotter and K.J. Gergen (eds.), *Texts of identity.* Newbury Park, CA: Sage.

Sampson, E.E. (1993). *Celebrating the other: A dialogic account of human nature.* Boulder, CO: Westview.

Schleifer, R. (1994). Saussure. In M. Groden and M. Kreiswirth (eds.), *The Johns Hopkins guide to literary theory and criticism.* Baltimore: Johns Hopkins University Press.

Schneider, K.S., S. Levitt, D. Morton, P. Yoo, S. Skolnik, A. Brooks, R. Jones, R. Arias, L. McNeil, J. Sugden, D. Sider, M. Salcines, B. Sandler, and M. Nelson (1996). Mission impossible. *People Weekly*, June 3, p. 65.

Schramm, W. (1954). How communication works. In W. Schramm (ed.), *The process and effects of mass communication.* Urbana: University of Illinois Press.

Schwarzbaum, L. (1994a). The mommy track. *Entertainment Weekly*, March 11, pp. 12, 15.

—— (1994b). Luke before he leaps. *Entertainment Weekly*, March 11, pp. 16–21.

Seiter, E. (1987). Semiotics and television. In R.C. Allen (ed.), *Channels of discourse: Television and contemporary criticism.* Chapel Hill: University of North Carolina Press.

Seiter, E., H. Borchers, G. Kreutzner, and E. Warth (1989/91). "Don't treat us like we're so stupid and naive": Towards an ethnography of soap opera viewers. In E. Seiter, H. Borchers, G. Kreutzner, and E. Warth (eds.), *Remote control: Television, audiences, and cultural power.* London: Routledge.

Seller, A. (1995). Best bet for stardom: Dina Meyer. *USA Today*, May 26, p. D1.

Sessums, K. (1992). Wild about Perry. *Vanity Fair*, July, p. 94.

Shannon, C.E., and W. Weaver (1949). *The mathematical theory of communication.* Urbana: University of Illinois Press.

Shannen Doherty. (1993). *People Weekly*, December 27, p. 56.

Shannen Doherty may return to "Beverly Hills, 90210." (1994). *Entertainment Weekly*, May 6, p. 11.

Shaw, J. (1994a). Dis-tressing. *Entertainment Weekly*, June 17, p. 10.

——— (1994b). Combing for trends in Beverly Hills. *Entertainment Weekly*, October 21, p. 14.

Shotter, J. (1993). *Conversational realities: Constructing life through language*. Thousand Oaks, CA: Sage.

Simonetti, M. (1994). Teenage truths and tribulations across cultures: *Delgrassi Junior High* and *Beverly Hills 90210*. *Journal of Popular Film and Television* 22 (1), pp. 38–42.

Slack, J.D., and M. Allor (1983). The political and epistemological constituents of critical communication research. *Journal of Communication* 33 (3), 208–18.

Sloane, A. (1994). Brenda bashing: Is 90210's Shannen Doherty getting what she deserves . . . or a bum rap? *Soap Opera Digest*, February 1, pp. 34–37.

Smith, L. (1994). Shannen Doherty: "I'm not a wild girl." *TV Guide*, November, pp. 12–16.

Spence, J., and L. Sawin (1985). Images of masculinity and feminity: A reconceptualization. In V. O'Leary et al. (eds.), *Women, gender, and social psychology*. Hillsdale, N.J.: Erlbaum.

Stacey, M. (1995). The real waif look. *Elle*, April, pp. 114–15.

Stout, J. (1988). *Ethics after Babel*. Boston: Beacon.

Teenage crush: TV's Luke Perry sets 10,000 hearts aflutter. (1991). *People Weekly*, August 26, p. 38.

Teitell, B. (1991). God cometh to the Galleria. *Boston Magazine*, December, p. 27.

Tracy, K. (1991). Discourse. In B.M. Montgomery and S. Duck (eds.), *Studying interpersonal interaction*. New York: Guilford.

Tuchman, G. (1978). *Making news: A study in the construction of reality*. New York: Free Press.

Turow, J. (1992). *Media systems in society: Understanding industries, strategies, and power*. New York: Longman.

van Zoonen, L. (1994). *Feminist media studies*. Newbury Park, CA: Sage.

Wayne, G. (1992). The greatest Tori ever told. *Vanity Fair*, December, p. 184.

Weedon, C., A. Tolson, and F. Mort (1980). Theories of language and subjectivity. In S. Hall, D. Hobson, A. Lowe, and P. Willis (eds.), *Culture, media, language: Working papers in cultural studies, 1972–79*. London: Unwin Hyman.

Weedon, C. (1987). *Feminist practice and poststructuralist theory*. Cambridge: Blackwell.

Weedon, C., A. Tolson, and F. Mort (1980). Theories of language and subjectivity. In S. Hall (ed.), *Culture, media, language*. London: Unwin Hyman.

Weintraub, B. (1991). One of television's shapers is distressed by the outcome. *New York Times*, October 14, pp. D1, D6.

West, D. and J. Flint (1994). The wonder's still in wireless. *Broadcasting & Cable*, January 24, pp. 20–26.

Williams, C.T. (1992). *"It's time for my story": Soap opera sources, structure, and responses*. Westport, CT: Greenwood.

Willis, P.E. (1977/81). *Learning to labour—How working-class kids get working-class jobs*. Aldershot: Gower.

Wimmer, R.D., and J.R. Dominick (1983). *Mass media research: An introduction*. Belmont, CA: Wadsworth.

Zinn, L. (1992). Move over, boomers: The busters are here—and they're angry. *Business Week*, December 14, pp. 74–82.

Zoglin, R. (1991). Cute and preppy in Beverly Hills. *Time*, July 22, p. 56.

——— (1993). Fox's growing pains: Can the fourth network expand its young core audience without losing its brand-name identity? *Time*, August 23, p. 66.

Index

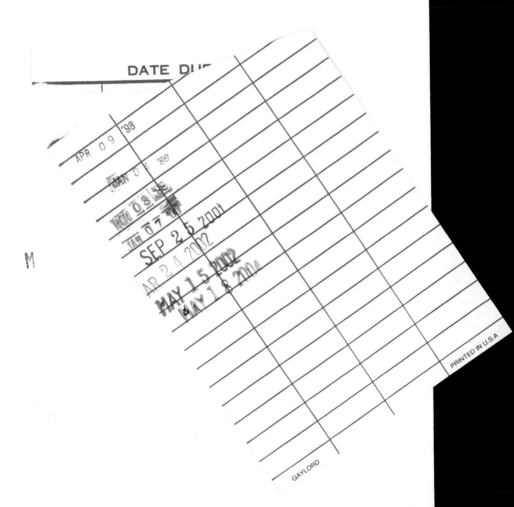